T0255346

Lecture Notes
in Business Information Processing   **206**

More information about this series at http://www.springer.com/series/7911

Malu Castellanos · Umeshwar Dayal
Torben Bach Pedersen · Nesime Tatbul (Eds.)

Enabling Real-Time Business Intelligence

International Workshops, BIRTE 2013
Riva del Garda, Italy, August 26, 2013,
and BIRTE 2014
Hangzhou, China, September 1, 2014
Revised Selected Papers

 Springer

Editors
Malu Castellanos
Hewlett-Packard
Palo Alto
USA

Umeshwar Dayal
Hitachi Laboratories
Santa Clara, CA
USA

Torben Bach Pedersen
Aalborg University
Aalborg
Denmark

Nesime Tatbul
Intel Labs and MIT
Cambridge, MA
USA

ISSN 1865-1348   ISSN 1865-1356 (electronic)
Lecture Notes in Business Information Processing
ISBN 978-3-662-46838-8   ISBN 978-3-662-46839-5 (eBook)
DOI 10.1007/978-3-662-46839-5

Library of Congress Control Number: 2015938085

Springer Heidelberg New York Dordrecht London

Printed on acid-free paper

Springer-Verlag GmbH Berlin Heidelberg is part of Springer Science+Business Media
(www.springer.com)

Preface

In today's competitive and highly dynamic environment, analyzing data to understand how the business is performing, and to predict outcomes and trends have become critical. The traditional approach to reporting is no longer adequate. Instead users now demand easy-to-use intelligent platforms and applications capable of analyzing real-time data to provide insight and actionable information at the right time. The end goal is to support better and timelier decision making, enabled by the availability of up-to-date, high-quality information. Although there has been progress in this direction and many companies are introducing products toward meeting this goal, there is still a long way to go. In particular, the whole lifecycle of business intelligence requires innovative techniques and methodologies capable of dealing with the requirements imposed by these new generation BI applications. From the capture of real-time business data to the transformation and delivery of actionable information, all the stages of the Business Intelligence (BI) cycle call for new algorithms and paradigms to support value-added functionalities. These functionalities include dynamic integration of real-time data feeds from operational sources, optimization and evolution of ETL transformations and analytical models, and dynamic generation of adaptive real-time dashboards, just to name a few. In addition, the need to handle the 3 V's of Big Data, in particular "Velocity" of fast dynamic data streams, has boosted research efforts both in academia and in industry, leading to the emergence of new technologies and platforms for big data; and the expectation is that this trend will continue.

The BIRTE (Business Intelligence for the Real-Time Enterprise, which later became simply Real-Time Business Intelligence) workshop series aims at providing a forum for presentation of the latest research results, new technology developments, and new applications in the areas of business intelligence and real-time enterprise. Building on the success of its previous six editions, BIRTE continued the tradition of being colocated with the VLDB Conference. BIRTE 2013 was held in Riva del Garda, Italy on August 26, 2013 and BIRTE 2014 was held in Hangzhou, China on September 1, 2014.

Both workshops featured exciting technical programs including a total of three keynote speeches, three invited industrial talks, a panel, plus a number of peer-reviewed papers from different countries in USA, Europe, Africa, and Asia. Each submission received three reviews from the members of the distinguished Program Committee consisting of leading researchers in the field from academia and industry. From these submissions, a total of six full research papers and one short position paper, along with two demo papers, were selected for presentation. Based on the feedback of the reviewers and the feedback received during the workshops, the authors prepared revised versions of their papers. We are happy to present these contributions in this joint post-proceedings volume.

Both BIRTE 2013 and BIRTE 2014 were extremely well attended: the former with a peak audience of over 70 people, making it by far the most attended of the VLDB workshops held on August 26, 2013; and the latter breaking an attendance record in the history of the BIRTE workshop series with about 80 participants during the keynote session. In what follows, we provide an overview of each workshop.

BIRTE 2013

After the welcome by the chairs, the program started with a highly interesting keynote by Michael J. Carey from UC Irvine, entitled "AsterixDB: A New Platform for Real-Time Big Data BI." In this keynote, Prof. Carey explained the key ideas and principles behind the AsterixDB BDMS (Big Data Management System). AsterixDB has a number of features that sets it apart from other systems for managing Big Data. First, it has a unique flexible, semi-structured data model (Asterix Data Model) based on JSON. Second, it has a high-level declarative query language (AQL – Asterix Query Language) that can express a wide range of BI-like queries. Third, it has a highly scalable parallel runtime engine, Hyracks, which has been tested up to thousands of cores. Fourth, it supports new data intake very efficiently through its partitioned LSM-based data storage and indexing. Fifth, it has support for externally stored data (e.g., in HDFS) as well as natively managed data. Sixth, it features a rich set of primitive types, including spatial, temporal, and textual data types. Seventh, it has a range of secondary indexing options, including B+ tree, R tree, and inverted files. Eighth, it has support for fuzzy, spatial, and temporal queries as well as for parametric queries. Ninth, the notion of "data feeds" supports continuous ingestion from relevant data sources. Finally, it has basic transactional capabilities like those of a NoSQL data store. Asterix is a system where "one size fits a bunch."

The next session featured two full research papers and a position paper. The paper "LinkViews: An Integration Framework for Relational and Stream Systems" by Yannis Sotiropoulos and Damianos Chatziantoniou from Athens University of Economics and Business, addresses the current lack of a unified framework for querying (persistent) relational and stream data. Concretely, the authors proposed a view layer defined over standard relational systems to handle the mismatch between relational and stream systems. Here, database administrators define a special type of views (called Link-Views) which combine relational data and stream aggregates. The authors showed how this could achieve transparent integration of relations and streams and how queries could be optimized. Next, the paper "OLAP for Multidimensional Semantic Web Databases" by Adriana Matei, Kuo-Ming Chao, and Nick Godwin from Coventry University, proposed a new framework for doing OLAP over Semantic Web data. The framework has multiple layers including additional vocabulary, extended OLAP operators, and the SPARSQL query language, allowing the modeling of heterogeneous semantic web data, the unification of multidimensional structures, and enabling interoperability between different semantic web multidimensional databases. Finally, the paper "A Multiple Query Optimization Scheme for Change Point Detection on Stream Processing System" by Masahiro Oke and Hideyuki Kawashima from University of Tsukuba, showed how to apply multiple query optimization, well known from relational database technology, to change point detection (CPD) queries. The authors propose a two-stage learning approach based on autoregressive model and divide CPD into four operators.

To accelerate multiple CPD executions—needed for parameter tuning—they use multi-query optimization (MQO). The authors showed how MQO enables sharing a large part of the CPD processing, leading to significantly improved performance.

After lunch, the program continued with the second very interesting keynote, by Prof. Johann-Christoph Freytag from Humboldt-Universität zu Berlin. This keynote was entitled "Query Adaptation and Privacy for Real-Time Business Intelligence" and aimed at taking a holistic view of the challenges and issues that relate to real-time business intelligence systems, by discussing both technical and non-technical aspects. First, the keynote introduced a number of real-world applications and used these to derive technical and non-technical requirements for real-time business intelligence. Based on these requirements and the experience of Prof. Freytag in co-developing the Stratosphere database management system with other Berlin research groups, the talk described techniques for query adaptation and histogram building that will be built into Stratosphere to support real-time business intelligence. The second part of the keynote discussed important aspects of privacy when dealing with personal data. It then out-lined the necessary requirements for implementing real-time business intelligence systems to protect privacy, and discussed the trade-off between the level of privacy and the utility expected by those who perform real-time business analytics.

After the keynote, the two demo papers were presented. First, the demo paper "Big Scale Text Analytics and Smart Content Navigation" by Karsten Schmidt, Philipp Scholl, and Sebastian Bächle from SAP AG, and Georg Nold from Springer Science +Business Media, showed how to use the SAP Hana platform for flexible text analysis, ad-hoc calculations and data linkage. The goal is to enhance the experience of users navigating and exploring publications, and thus to support intelligent guided research in big text collections. Case data from the major scientific publisher Springer SBM was used. Second, the demo paper "Dynamic Generation of Adaptive Real-time Dash-boards for Continuous Data Stream Processing" by Timo Michelsen, Marco Graw-under, Dennis Geesen, and H.-Jürgen Appelrath from University of Oldenburg presented a novel dashboard concept for visualizing the results from continuous stream queries, based on several individually configurable dashboard parts, each connected to a (user defined) continuous query, the results of which are received and visualized in real time.

Next, Dr. Morten Middelfart from TARGIT gave an inspiring invited industrial talk on "The Inverted Data Warehouse based on TARGIT Xbone - How the biggest of data can be mined by the "little guy." The talk presented TARGIT's Xbone memory-based analytics server and defined the concept of an Inverted Data Warehouse (IDW), a DW storing query results rather than raw data. The concept and system were exemplified with a large-scale solution in which TARGIT Xbone and IDW were applied on Google search data with the aim of Search Engine Optimization (SEO).

The workshop ended with a panel on "Real Time Analytics on Big Data" moderated by Meichun Hsu from HP Labs. The panel featured six distinguished panelists: Alejandro Buchmann from TU Darmstadt, Shel Finkelstein from SAP, Johann-Christoph Freytag from Humboldt University of Berlin, C. Mohan from IBM, Ippokratis Pandis from IBM, and Torben Bach Pedersen from Aalborg University. Each panelist gave a short pre-sentation on his perspective on the general topic and his responses to four questions posed by the moderator: What does real-time analytics on big data really mean? What are the compelling applications that motivated such capabilities? What is the status of the technology stack that delivers this capability and what are the gaps and challenges? Relative to the technology attributes often used to characterize big data such as extreme scale-out, NoSQL, and open source, and the emerging technologies such as SQL-on-Hadoop and in-memory stores, how do we see real-time analytics relate? After the presentations a lively (and somewhat controversial) debate ensued between the panelists and the highly active audience.

BIRTE 2014

The workshop opened with a session of accepted papers after a short introduction welcoming the participants. This session consisted of a position paper of co-authors from TU Dresden in Germany and the SAP Labs in USA, and a research paper of co-authors from University at Buffalo, SUNY, and the Oracle Corporation in USA. First, Michael Rudolf presented a flexible approach for multi-dimensional graph data analysis in their paper entitled "SynopSys: Foundations for Multidimensional Graph Analytics." The key feature that distinguishes SynopSys from existing technologies, which require upfront modeling of analytical scenarios and are difficult to adapt to changes, is the ability to express ad-hoc analytical queries over graph data. The second paper, entitled "Detecting the Temporal Context of Queries" and presented by Ying Yang, focuses on the concept of contextual dependency – a term used by the authors to explain and attribute mistaken assumptions made by end users of BI applications. A formal definition for contextual dependence is given, followed by several strategies to efficiently detect and quantify the effects of contextual dependence on query outputs.

The next session was dedicated to the invited industrial talks. Inviting industrial speakers to present their perspective on real-world BI problems, solutions, and applications has been a tradition of BIRTE since its inception in 2006. This year's workshop featured two industrial talks. First, in his talk entitled "Building Analytics Engines for the Big Data Age," Dr. Badrish Chandramouli of Microsoft Research presented the challenges of a temporal streaming engine called Trill. Trill has been architected as a library to support embedded execution within cloud applications and distributed fabrics. Second, Dr. Qiming Chen of HP Labs gave a talk about "Optimistic Failure Recovery in Distributed Stream Processing." More specifically, he presented the backtrack-based and the window-oriented recovery mechanisms in the Fontainebleau distributed stream analytics system built on top of the Storm platform. Both of these talks covered industry-scale stream processing applications and solutions, and demonstrated the importance of stream processing technology for real-time business intelligence and other big-velocity applications.

After lunch, the program continued with the keynote speech. This year's keynote speaker was Dr. C. Mohan from the IBM Almaden Research Center. Dr. Mohan has been a well-known pioneer in database systems and has made numerous contributions to relational database research and technology in various different roles at IBM for more than 30 years. In his talk "Big Data: Hype and Reality," he presented a concrete and detailed picture of the current landscape of big data systems. According to Mohan, as users and developers gain a deeper understanding of the needs of real use cases (including real-time BI applications), the initial hype around big data systems (including noSQL, newSQL, and others) has been fading away. It is now becoming clearer that most of the so-called distinctive features of big data systems have in fact been well-known principles of relational database systems for decades. Mohan's comprehensive and critical survey of this popular field attracted much attention from a big audience and was very well received.

Finally, the last session of the workshop consisted of two paper presentations: an application paper jointly written by co-authors from Aalborg University in Denmark and Universite Libre de Bruxelles in Belgium, and a research paper from University of Southern Denmark. First, Dilshod Ibragimov explained during his talk, entitled "Towards Exploratory OLAP over Linked Open Data - A Case Study", how to integrate real-time data from web sources described in RDF into the analysis process in BI environments. To achieve this, a system that uses a multi-dimensional schema of the OLAP cube expressed in RDF vocabularies is proposed. The second presentation of this session was on "Efficient Pattern Detection over a Distributed Framework" by Ahmed Khan Leghari. In this talk, Leghari described an event stream partitioning scheme that partitions streams over time windows without considering any key attributes.

Overall, BIRTE 2014 was a great success. We have once again witnessed that real-time business intelligence continues to be a critical topic for both database researchers and practitioners. Talks covered a diverse set of real-world BI use cases, and indicated strong collaborations between academic and industrial community in this field. This year, we have observed that big data analytics has been a common theme for all BIRTE presentations, with a striking emphasis on the analysis of streaming and graph-structured data.

The BIRTE 2013 and BIRTE 2014 chairs would like to thank all the authors of submitted papers for their interest in the workshop and the high quality of their papers, and the distinguished PC members for their conscientious work, both during the reviewing and the discussion phases. Our workshop would not have been as successful as it was without the talks given by our invited speakers Prof. Michael J. Carey, Prof. Johann-Christoph Freytag, Dr. Morten Middelfart, Dr. C. Mohan, Dr. Badrish Chandramouli, and Dr. Qiming Chen, to whom we are deeply grateful. We would like to also express our gratitude to the Organizing Committees of VLDB 2013 and VLDB 2014, especially the General Chairs and the Workshop Chairs, for their support to BIRTE. Thanks also go to our Proceedings Chairs, Katja Hose (2013) and Jennie Duggan (2014), for their excellent job in putting this combined proceedings together, as well as to our webmaster, Emmanouil Valsomatzis (2013), for efficiently managing the workshop web site. Last but not least, we are grateful to the BIRTE 2014 session chairs, Prof. Damianos Chatziantoniou and Dr. Qiming Chen for their great support during the workshop in Hangzhou.

February 2015

Malu Castellanos
Umeshwar Dayal
Torben Bach Pedersen
Nesime Tatbul

Organization

The BIRTE 2013 and 2014 workshops were organized in the context of the 39th and 40th International Conference on Very Large Data Bases (VLDB) in Riva Del Garda and Hangzhou, respectively.

Organizing Committee

General Chair

Umeshwar Dayal   Hitachi Labs, USA

Program Committee Chairs

Malu Castellanos	Hewlett-Packard, USA
Torben Bach Pedersen	Aalborg University, Denmark
Nesime Tatbul	Intel Labs and MIT, USA

Program Committee

Christof Bornhövd	SAP Labs, USA
Badrish Chandramouli	Microsoft Research, USA
Ben Chin Ooi	National University of Singapore, Singapore
Hakan Hacigumus	NEC Labs, USA
Howard Ho	IBM Almaden Research Center, USA
Meichun Hsu	HP Labs, USA
Alfons Kemper	Technische Universität München, Germany
Wolfgang Lehner	Dresden University of Technology, Germany
Alexander Loeser	Technische Universität Berlin, Germany
Jose Norberto Mazon	University of Alicante, Spain
Renee Miller	University of Toronto, Canada
Fatma Ozcan	IBM Almaden Research Center, USA
Torben Bach Pedersen	Aalborg University, Denmark
Karthik Ramasamy	Twitter, USA
Elke Rundensteiner	Worcester Polytechnic Institute, USA
Amit Rustagi	Intuit, USA
Donovan Schneider	SalesForce, USA
Eric Simon	SAO-BO, France
Nesime Tatbul	Intel Labs and MIT, USA
Christian Thomsen	Aalborg University, Denmark
Hans Zeller	Hewlett-Packard, USA

Proceedings Chair

Jennie Duggan	MIT, USA
Katja Hose	Aalborg University, Denmark

Web Chair

Emmanouil Valsomatzis   Aalborg University, Denmark

Keynotes

AsterixDB:
A New Platform for Real-Time Big Data BI

(Extended Abstract)

Michael J. Carey

Computer Science Department
University of California, Irvine
Irvine, CA 92697 USA
mjcarey@ics.uci.edu

Abstract. This invited keynote presentation will provide a technical overview of AsterixDB, a new open source Big Data management system from UC Irvine and UC Riverside. The emphasis of the talk will be on the architectural and user-level features of AsterixDB that are particularly relevant to Big Data use cases involving real-time BI.

Keywords: Big Data · Business intelligence · Data warehouse · Scalability · Real time · Semi-structured data

1 The AsterixDB BDMS

AsterixDB is a full-function Big Data Management System (BDMS) that has a uniquely rich feature set that sets it apart from the other Big Data platforms that are available in today's open source Big Data ecosystem. We believe that its feature set makes it ideally-suited to modern needs such as web data warehousing, social data storage and analysis, and other real-time business intelligence (BI) use cases related to what we now commonly refer to as "Big Data". In brief, AsterixDB has:

- A flexible, semistructured NoSQL style data model (ADM) based on JSON.
- A declarative query language (AQL) that can be used to express a wide range of BI queries.
- A parallel runtime engine (Hyracks) that has been scale-tested out to 1000's of cores.
- Partitioned LSM-based data storage and indexing to support efficient data intake as well as queries.
- Support for externally stored data (e.g., in HDFS or local files) as well as for natively stored and indexed data.
- A rich set of primitive types, including support for spatial, temporal, and textual data types, to cover modern Web and social data use cases.
- B+ tree, R tree, and inverted keyword (both exact and similarity-based) secondary index options.
- Support for fuzzy, spatial, and temporal queries as well as for the usual range of parametric queries.

- A notion of data feeds to support Big Data use cases involving continuous data ingestion from external data sources.
- Basic transactional capabilities akin to those of a modern NoSQL store.

This talk will provide a technical overview of AsterixDB as well as covering a bit of the history and technical context that led us to start of the project in 2009. The talk will touch briefly on all aspects of the system, but the main emphasis of the talk will be on the architectural and user-level features of AsterixDB that are most relevant to serving use cases involving real-time BI over Big Data. Figure 1 shows a high-level view of the system's shared-nothing architecture.

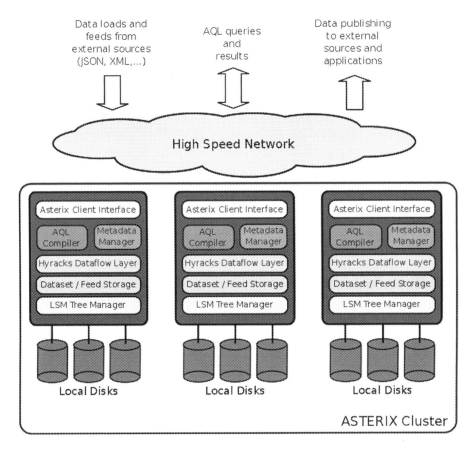

Fig. 1. AsterixDB Architectural Overview

The first Beta release of AsterixDB made its public debut in early June of 2013. More information about the overall AsterixDB Big Data Management System can be found in [1, 2, 4, 5], and additional details about its underlying runtime platform can be found in [3]. The AsterixDB system is available for download at [6].

Acknowledgments. The AsterixDB project has been supported by a UC Discovery grant, by NSF IIS awards 0910989, 0910859, 0910820, and 0844574, and by NSF CNS awards 1305430, 1059436, and 1305253. The project has also benefitted from generous industrial support from Amazon, eBay, Facebook, Google, HTC, Microsoft, Oracle Labs, and Yahoo! Labs.

References

1. Alsubaiee, S., Behm, A., Grover, R., Vernica, R., Borkar, V., Carey, M., Li, C.: ASTERIX: scalable warehouse-style web data integration. In: Proceedings of the Ninth International Workshop on Information Integration on the Web (IIWeb 2012). ACM, New York (2012)
2. Behm, A., Borkar, V.R., Carey, M.J., Grover, R., Li, C., Onose, N., Vernica, R., Deutsch, A., Papakonstantinou, Y., Tsotras, V.J.: ASTERIX: towards a scalable, semistructured data platform for evolving-world models. Distrib. Parallel Databases **29**(3), 185–216 (2011)
3. Borkar, V., Carey, M., Grover, R., Onose, R., Vernica, R.: Hyracks: a flexible and extensible foundation for data-intensive computing. In: Proceedings of the 2011 IEEE 27th International Conference on Data Engineering (ICDE 2011), pp. 1151–1162. IEEE Computer Society, Washington, DC (2011)
4. Borkar, V., Carey, M.J., Li, C.: Inside "big data management": ogres, onions, or parfaits? In: Rundensteiner, E., Markl, V., Manolescu, I., Amer-Yahia, S., Naumann, F., Ari, I. (eds.) Proceedings of the 15th International Conference on Extending Database Technology (EDBT 2012), pp. 3–14. ACM, New York (2012)
5. Borkar, V., Carey, M., Li, C.: Big data platforms: What's next? XRDS **19**(1), 44–49 (2012)
6. AsterixDB. http://asterixdb.ics.uci.edu/

Query Adaptation and Privacy
for Real-Time Business Intelligence

(Abstract)

Johann-Christoph Freytag, Rico Bergmann, Lukas Dölle

Humboldt-Universität zu Berlin
Unter den Linden 6, 10099 Berlin, Germany
{freytag,bergmann,doelle}@informatik.hu-berlin.de
http://www.dbis.informatik.hu-berlin.de

Abstract. This paper discusses several technical challenges and issues that need special attention when dealing with real-time business intelligence (RTBI) systems. While most contributions of previous BIRTE Workshops focused on (database) technology this extended abstract will take a more holistic view by covering technical and non-technical aspects. First, we introduce and discuss two real-world applications to derive technical and non-technical requirements that are quite diverse in the context of real-time business intelligence. Based on those requirements and based on our experience in developing the Stratosphere database management system [1] we outline our already existing and future approaches to query adaptation and of statistics building that are about to be implemented into Stratosphere to support RTBI.

In the second part of the extended abstract we discuss important aspects of privacy when dealing with personal data, and outline necessary requirements for implementing real-time business intelligence systems to protect people's privacy (to some extent). It will become apparent that often there exists a trade-off between the level of privacy and the utility expected by those who perform real-time busines analytics.

Contents

Query Adaptation and Privacy for Real-Time Business Intelligence

Extended Abstract

Johann-Christoph Freytag$^{(\boxtimes)}$, Rico Bergmann$^{(\boxtimes)}$, and Lukas Dölle$^{(\boxtimes)}$

Humboldt-Universität zu Berlin, Unter den Linden 6, 10099 Berlin, Germany
{freytag,bergmann,doelle}@informatik.hu-berlin.de
http://www.dbis.informatik.hu-berlin.de

Abstract. This paper (extended abstract) discusses several technical challenges and issues that need special attention when dealing with real-time business intelligence (RTBI) systems. While most contributions of previous BIRTE Workshops focused on (database) technology this extended abstract will take a more holistic view by covering technical and non-technical aspects. First, we introduce and discuss two real-world applications to derive technical and non-technical requirements that are quite diverse in the context of real-time business intelligence. Based on those requirements and based on our experience in developing the Stratosphere database management system [1] we outline our already existing and future approaches to query adaptation and of statistics building that are about to be implemented into Stratosphere to support RTBI.

In the second part of the extended abstract we discuss important aspects of privacy when dealing with personal data, and outline necessary requirements for implementing real-time business intelligence systems to protect people's privacy (to some extent). It will become apparent that often there exists a trade-off between the level of privacy and the utility expected by those who perform real-time business analytics.

Keywords: Real-time business intelligence · Big data · Map Reduce paradigm · Query optimization · Privacy · k-anonymity · Adversary knowledge

1 Looking at the Real World

During the last decade, the challenges in RTBI systems have been on extending existing database technology to fit better the needs of this area. However, now we are at the brink that this technology is used more and more thus penetrating everyone's lives. For example, a new startup in Berlin named Tazaldoo/Tame [2] uses twitter feeds to perform sentiment analysis for journalists to provide them with leads for the next big stories (before anyone else is aware of them) and for politicians to make them aware of existing positive or negative popularity trends in

© Springer-Verlag Berlin Heidelberg 2015
M. Castellanos et al. (Eds.): BIRTE 2013 and 2014, LNBIP 206, pp. 1–8, 2015.
DOI: 10.1007/978-3-662-46839-5_1

their realm. Tazaldoo/Tame provides this analysis incrementally in (almost) real time. The same techniques carry over to discover economic trends and changes early enough that companies are able to react appropriately as early as possible.

A second example indicates the trade-offs of RTBI-technology when it infringes on people's privacy. In the Square Mile of London, the company Renew London [4] installed garbage bins which include screens on all four sides of the bin being able to show in HD quality any kind of visual information, see Fig. 1. By connecting to people's (unprotected) phones and by gathering enough information about those people passing by the company provides personal advertisement on the spot.

Fig. 1. Stalking bins in London

Their solution uses the technology developed by the Tech-Company PresenceOrb [5]. The company claims that its technology allows "for rich analytical insight and immediate on site reactions ...". Such massive intrusion of privacy caused general protests that caused the removal of the *stalking bins*.

Both examples show the new abilities and consequences RBTI technology may have, at the same time they motivate the two topics that we shall discuss in the rest of this paper. The next section outlines how to improve MapReduce-style execution environments such as Hadoop [3] or Stratosphere [1] for RBTI by gathering and storing statistical information about the data sources accessed. Such information will be the basis to adapt query execution "on the fly" (which is not part of this extended abstract). The following section then outlines how to model the knowledge an adversary gathers when asking a sequence of queries to a database that returns anonymized answers. We do not provide a detailed presentation of these two topics, as they are work in progress by Ph.D. students of the DBIS research group at Humboldt-Universität zu Berlin.

2   Gathering Statistics in a MapReduce Environment

Over the last years, the MapReduce paradigm has gained momentum as a model and a programming paradigm for data intensive applications that should take advantage of parallelism in a compute cluster environment. Hadoop is probably the most prominent system implementing the MapReduce paradigm [11]. Stratosphere developed by several research groups in Berlin (TU Berlin, HU Berlin, HPI Potsdam) is an alternative system that extends the MapReduce paradigm with additional second order functions at the same time using database oriented concepts for its implementation, including the ability of query optimization [1,6]. As the execution of a MapReduce program may take minutes, hours or even days it might be advantageous to check if the current execution plan is the best possible. That is, the system could execute an alternative plan that

could execute faster and/or with fewer resources than the current one. As this
is a classical query optimization problem, we explore adaptive optimization in
the context of MapReduce systems as a promising addition to the query execution environment. There have been several approaches for traditional object-
relational DBMS as reported in [7,8]. In our context, we see four major steps to
develop an integrated approach for adaptive query optimization in Stratosphere
as shown in Fig. 2:

1. Measure, i.e. understand the current status of executed query;
2. Analyze if the current status should/must be adapted;
3. Re-optimize by generating alternative (partial) query execution plans;
4. Deploy alternative (partial) plans into the currently executing query.

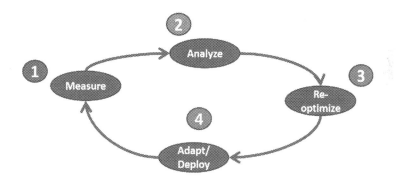

Fig. 2. Cycle for query adaptation

Rather than starting query execution from scratch the underlying idea is to
smoothly integrate changes of the execution plan into the currently executing
plan without changing the outcome of the query (such as generating duplicate
results). For the purpose of this paper, we focus on Step 1 of this cyclic adaptation process, i.e. how to measure the current state by gathering statistics about
the data sources accessed. We see such statistics as the basis of making decision
about alternative execution plans as in traditional DBMS. The goal of our work
is to provide an environment for building histograms incrementally and adapt-
able with minimal overhead for the running query. Furthermore, we envisage
that the plan generator automatically adds statistical operators to an execution
plan rather than a programmer or an administrator. That is, we gather statistics
about the results of partial plans that could lead the current (and future) execution of queries in a more informed manner most likely improving response time
for RTBI. To implement our vision we currently design a Statistics Store that
incrementally stores gathered statistics in such a way that future queries could
benefit from past executions of similar queries. Additionally, we design algorithms how to detect the needs for new statistics, how to find similar statistics
in the statistics store, and how to determine which statistics to collect by adding

operators to an (existing) execution plan (operator injection) thus combining statistics collection with regular query execution (piggybacking). The general steps for injecting statistical operators into an execution plan are the following:

1. The Query Optimizer requests specific statistics from the Cost Estimator component;
2. The cost Estimator component in turn asks Statistics Store if such statistics exists. If so, the Statistics Store returns requested statistics;
3. If the requested statistics is not found, a request for collecting statistics is generated;
4. Whenever the Optimizer component has generated an execution plan the Injector component checks if there exist statistics requests that could be generated by the current query;
5. If possible, the Injector components selects the corresponding statistic request(s) and generates appropriate statistics operators that are integrated into the current query execution plan;
6. During query execution, the injected statistics operators emit statistical data that are transmitted to and written into the (distributed) statistics store for further use.

Based on these steps we currently design and implement Statistics Store that we shall integrate into the Stratosphere system. Such Statistics store is one of the necessary steps to make Stratosphere more amenable for RTBI queries. R. Bergmann will publish results in his Ph.D. thesis in more details [13].

3   Modeling the Adversary's Knowledge for Detecting Privacy Breaches

Privacy has been an active research field for over ten years. The work by Samarati and Sweeny [9] on k-anonymity as well as the work by Dwork [10] on differential privacy spawned an increasing amount of research work and results both of which are not the focus of this paper. Rather we focus on an often-neglected aspect of privacy, i.e. how to model and how to represent the adversary's knowledge that (s)he gains with results generated by (a sequence of) queries. Such an explicit representation of his/her knowledge could provide the basis for deciding how many queries to answer before rejecting further answers to queries. In the following, we present first steps on how to represent the increasing knowledge of an adversary by bi-partite graphs before outlining challenges and some initial algorithms on how to determine when to stop answering queries. We use the notion of k-anonymity to outline our approach. We assume that the reader is familiar with the k-anonymity approach: if we want to publish a table with personal (sensitive) data, we transform a given table into its anonymized equivalent as follows: the identifying attributes are removed; the values of the quasi-identifying attributes are anonymized. We show such a scenario in Fig. 3 with Name being the identifying attribute, Zipcode, Age, and Sex being quasi-identifiers, and Disease being the sensitive attribute.

Name	Zipcode	Age	Sex	Disease
Alison	10000	18	F	Asthma
Ben	11000	19	M	Bronchitis
Clark	12000	20	M	Cold
Debra	12000	21	F	Diabetes
Elaine	12000	22	F	Earache
Fiona	12000	23	F	Flu
Gary	14000	24	M	Earache

Microdata table *T*

Zipcode	Age	Sex	Disease
10–12000	18–20	*	Asthma
10–12000	18–20	*	Bronchitis
10–12000	18–20	*	Cold
12–14000	21–24	*	Diabetes
12–14000	21–24	*	Earache
12–14000	21–24	*	Flu
12–14000	21–24	*	Earache

3-anonymous release table *T**

Fig. 3. k-anonymity example

If we know a person's Zipcode, Age, and Sex we cannot determine the exact disease that (s)he has when accessing the anonymized release table. However, when considering the example of Fig. 4 we recognize that we can derive that Clark has a Cold based on answers R_1 and R_2. Similarly we also derive that Gary must have Earache based on the answers for queries Q_2 and Q_3.

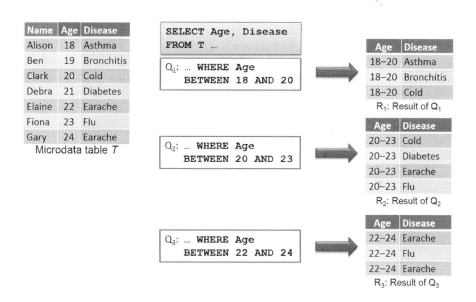

Fig. 4. Sequence of queries with privacy breach

These privacy breaches are not immediately obvious and not always easy to detect. Therefore, it becomes necessary to develop a systematic approach to determine when a privacy breach occurs. Our approach uses bi-partite graphs to model the set of existing identifiers and the set of existing sensitive values. Figure 5 shows edges between identifier vertices and vertices for sensitive values to indicate possible value assignments between both. In general, there must exist at least k edges between identifier vertices and vertices for sensitive values to

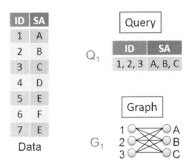

Fig. 5. Bipartite graph modeling relationships between identifiers and sensitive values

satisfy k-anonymity. Such a graph is the basis for computing different *perfect matchings* between identifiers and sensitive values, i.e. matchings where each identifier vertex is connected to exactly one vertex for a sensitive value and vice versa. The light red edges in the six different graphs of Fig. 6 indicate the six possible alternative matchings between identifiers and sensitive values. However, for a sequence of query results the underlying vertex structure might change due to additional constraints (i.e. increase of knowledge) resulting from additional answers to new queries as shown for the example in Fig. 7.

Here we realize that G_1 changed due to the query answer modeled by G_2: ID Vertex 3 now has only one edge relating it to Vertex C since sensitive value C is the only one present in both graphs for making a consistent value assignment for ID Vertex 3 that is possible in both of them. Thus, only one matching is at most possible between ID Vertex 3 and Vertex C representing the corresponding sensitive value.

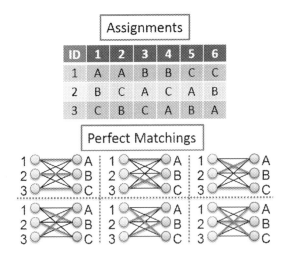

Fig. 6. Perfect matchings between identifiers and sensitive values

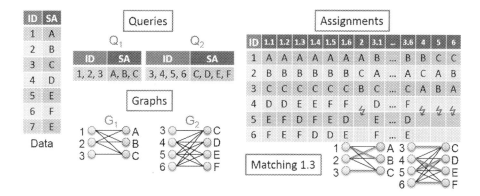

Fig. 7. Two query answers with corresponding graph and perfect matchings

Using this approach to model the (increasing) knowledge of the adversary with an increasing number of queries, we developed a series of polynomial approximation algorithms – the general problem is NP-complete – to detect privacy violations before returning an answer to a submitted query. These polynomial algorithms are necessary to decide in real-time whether to answer a query or not. Only then, we can guarantee that such an approach is usable and feasible in an RBTI query execution environment. More detailed results are to be published soon in the Ph.D. thesis by Lukas Dölle [12].

4   Summary

This paper discusses two important challenges for implementing RTBI. The first challenge is to provide an adequate basis for long running analytical queries by gathering statistical information about the data sources accessed. Our approach is to integrate statistical operators into user queries automatically and to store the statistical results in a statistics store for future use. Second, we focus on supporting privacy protection better by modeling the adversary's knowledge by (a set of) bi-partite graphs that allow us to perform inferences about the knowledge gained by each query. Lukas Dölle and Rico Bergman currently develop both approaches as part of their Ph.D. thesis at the DBIS research group at Humboldt-Universität zu Berlin.

References

1. Stratosphere. http://www.stratosphere.eu. Accessed Dec 2013
2. Tazaldoo/tame. http://www.tame.it. Accessed Dec 2013
3. Hadoop. http://hadoop.apache.org/. Accessed Dec 2013
4. Renew London. http://renewlondon.com. Accessed Dec 2013
5. PresenceOrb. http://www.presenceorb.com/. Accessed Dec 2013

6. Hueske, F., Peters, M., Sax, M., Rheinländer, A., Bergmann, R., Krettek, A., Tzoumas, K.: Opening the black boxes in data flow optimization. PVLDB **5**(11), 1256–1267 (2012)
7. Deshpande, A., Ives, Z.G., Raman, V.: Adaptive query processing. Found. Trends Databases **1**(1), 1–140 (2007)
8. Rundensteiner, E.A., Ding, L., Sutherland, T.M., Zhu, Y., Pielech, B., Mehta, N.: CAPE: continuous query engine with heterogeneous-grained adaptivity. In: VLDB Proceedings of the Thirteenth International Conference on Very Large Data Bases, Toronto, Canada, pp. 1353–1356 (2004)
9. Samarati, P., Sweeney, L.: Generalizing data to provide anonymity when disclosing information (abstract). In: PODS 1988, p. 188 (1998)
10. Dwork, C.: Differential privacy. In: Bugliesi, M., Preneel, B., Sassone, V., Wegener, I. (eds.) ICALP 2006. LNCS, vol. 4052, pp. 1–12. Springer, Heidelberg (2006)
11. Dean, J., Ghemawat, S.: MapReduce: simplified data processing on large clusters. In: OSDI 2004, pp. 137–150 (2004)
12. Dölle, L.: Detecting privacy breaches when answering a sequence of queries, Ph.D. thesis (in German), Humboldt-Universität zu, Berlin (2014)
13. Bergmann, R.: Gathering statistics for query adaptation. Ph.D. thesis (in German). Humboldt-Universität zu, Berlin (2014)

The Inverted Data Warehouse Based on TARGIT Xbone

How the Biggest of Data Can Be Mined by "The Little Guy"

Morten Middelfart[(✉)]

TARGIT, Tampa, FL, USA
morton@targit.com

Abstract. We present TARGIT's Xbone memory-based analytics server and define the concept of an Inverted Data Warehouse (IDW). We demonstrate the high-performance analytics properties of this particular design, as well as its resistance to failures. Additionally, we present a large scale solution in which TARGIT Xbone and IDW are implemented incorporating Google search data. The solution is used for so-called Search Engine Optimization (SEO) and can reveal interesting information about Google's algorithmic behavior on specific searches. Finally, we demonstrate the combined TARGIT Xbone and IDW to be very cost-effective and thus available to small enterprises that would normally not benefit from Big Data analytics.

1 Introduction

Publicly available data, such as social data and open data, play a big part of business decision-making, and the solutions within an organization have to be ready to accommodate that. In this context, it is notable that there are different growth paces for the internal and the external data available. In other words, the data we have in a company will likely grow at a pace close to the growth rate of the company itself. From a numbers perspective, very few companies have growth above 100 % for long; a big company will be considered successful with yearly growth rates of 20–30 %.

According to IDC's most recent estimate (2011) [3], there are 1.8 zettabytes of digital data in the world, projected to grow to 7.9 zettabytes by 2015. (A zettabyte is 10^{21} or 1,000,000,000,000,000,000,000 bytes, 1 trillion gigabytes, or 1 quadrillion megabytes.) The pace of this growth is driven chiefly by external data, rather than internal data. Therefore, we are steadily approaching a tipping point at which the majority of data relevant for competitive analytics will be coming from outside the organization. Since at this point we will have to compete on data that doesn't "belong" to us, it's a total paradigm shift on the way business decisions are made. Data that's available today may be gone or made unavailable by its owner tomorrow, and there may never be full knowledge

M. Castellanos et al. (Eds.): BIRTE 2013 and 2014, LNBIP 206, pp. 9–22, 2015.
DOI: 10.1007/978-3-662-46839-5_2

of data quality. But it's still pertinent to the decision to be made now, and it's critical to analyze that data to uncover the useful bits of information that can make that decision more informed.

It is important to note that very few companies will have the ability to download all the external data they need for competitive analytics; this ability will only be available to very few companies with massive resources. In other words, most companies (those below the Fortune 500 level, perhaps) will have to sample the relevant external data and accept the fact that these data represent an incomplete, imperfect, yet relevant slice of information. Despite the imperfection, this data can offer an understanding of trends and early indicators that a business may want to analyze deeper. During such a sampling process, the ability to flexibly add, remove, and analyze data sets is crucial.

Another part of this sampling process is that it allows for an intelligent distinction of useful and non-useful data. For example, a user can identify irrelevant data as early in the process as possible, and thereby drastically reduce the amount of data to be processed. Or instead, focus on pushing as much of the workflow toward the source of the sample before the sample is extracted in order to reduce the workload further.

The inverted data warehouse (IDW) is structured differently from the traditional data warehouse in that:

1. It is physically distributed to multiple machines close to the end-users for optimal analytical performance, and
2. It is deliberately designed for continuous sampling of a big data source.

In a traditional data warehouse all data are stored on a centralized server system where the analytics processing is also done. In the IDW we push all data and analytics processing to the clients, thus we refer to this architecture as *inverted* compared to the traditional.

The TARGIT Xbone server technology [12] is designed to analyze a data set on-the-fly without the traditional Extract Transform Load (ETL) process. In other words, it is optimized for working with sampled data in a very efficient way, as it requires very little effort to assess and sample. Additionally, its in-memory architecture allows it to deliver a very responsive user experience.

The remainder of this paper is structured as follows: in the following section we discuss related work. In Sect. 3, we present the general principles of the Inverted Data Warehouse, along with a case based on Google search data. In Sect. 4, we present the TARGIT Xbone architecture as well as the architecture of TARGIT Decision Suite in general. In Sect. 5, we present an assessment of the data volumes analyzed, as well as an experimental evaluation of the performance of our IDW case from Sect. 3. Finally, in Sect. 6, we conclude and present future work.

2   Related Work

The building of a "classic" data warehouse with an Extract-Transform-Load (ETL) process has been very well documented in [4]. This work describes the continuous learning process from data acquisition to presentation as a cycle of improvement.

In [5,6], a decision-centric cycle is described, in which a user travels through Observation Orientation Decision Action (OODA) with as few interactions as possible. This work primarily deals with user interaction with data in a data warehouse, and furthermore, how to render a user capable of making very fast fact based decisions.

In traditional Business Intelligence software, users perform two tasks to create the report desired. First, the user defines a query to examine a subset of data stored within the organization's data warehouse. And second, the user defines a graphical representation of the data that was retrieved. Typically, the presentation means are selected from a report generator or "chart wizard", from which default layout properties (or user-specified layout properties) are identified before making the presentation.

Conventional Business Intelligence software requires users to adhere closely to formal syntax, as the underlying databases require syntactically correct queries to properly retrieve information. Conventional Business Intelligence solutions are frequently configured with user interfaces that guide a user directly to a presentation of retrieved data, often through a wizard. In addition, a user is expected to understand the correct principles off this utilizing the data found [1].

Close conformance to formal syntax places a burden on the user to know the rules of database syntax and to be able to work quickly within them to retrieve the data desired. US Patents 7,783,628 [8] and 7,779,018 [7] identify two methods for making a presentations of data using so-called meta-morphing. The technology allows users to enter a business question through the user interface:

1. I would like to see 'cost' grouped by 'time, month'
2. I would like to see 'revenue' grouped by 'time, month', 'customer, group' and 'product, name'
3. I would like to see 'revenue'
4. I would like to see 'country'

Example: A user submits the question "I would like to see customers".

Step 1: parses all words in the sentence representing the questions (Fig. 1(b)), and these words are subsequently matched against the meta-data of the data warehouse (Fig. 1(a)). If a word in the sentence is not matched in the meta-data it is simply thrown away. The output from Step 1 is a set of dimensions and/or measures; and if the set is empty, the meta-morphing process is simply terminated. In our example, the only word that will remain from this parsing is "customers".

Step 2: compensates for the problem of the user's question containing only measures or dimensions. In a traditional system, asking incomplete questions like "I would like to see customers" or "Show me revenue" would at best return a list of customers (the members of the customer dimension) or the sum of revenue for all data in the data warehouse. By creating an association between

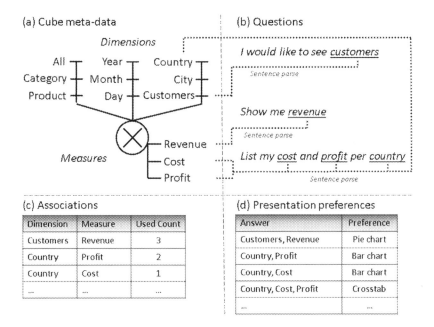

Fig. 1. The meta-morphing model

measures and dimensions (Fig. 1(c)), the system will learn the *individual* user's behavior based on what he clicks, e.g., if he clicks to select revenue and customers at the same time, then an association between revenue and customers will be created. Therefore, the answer to both questions will be a list of customers with their respective revenue. Associations are also created while the user loads any analysis, meaning that he does not need to actively pose a question including the association. This means that the user will simply feel that he is receiving information in the way he is used to. In the event that a user has never seen or asked for a given relationship, the meta-morphing process will look into which dimension or measure the user most often uses, and then create an association that is used most often, i.e., the measure or dimension from the association with the highest Used Count (see Fig. 1(c)). The output of Step 2 is a combination of measures and dimensions.

Step 3: is, given Step 2 output, a trivial query in the data warehouse retrieving "revenue" for each member on the "customers" dimension. The output of this step is a dataset as well as the dimensions and measures used to provide it.

Step 4: preferences are created for each user given the way they would normally see an answer given its dimension/measure combination, e.g., customer/revenue is usually displayed as a pie-chart (see Fig. 1(d)), profit per country is usually displayed as a bar-chart, etc. Given the "experience" with the user's preferences that are collected whenever the user sees or formats a piece of information, the dataset received from Step 3 is formatted and displayed to the user. In the event that no preferences have been collected for the user, an expert system will inspect the dataset and make a call for the best presentation object (pie, bar, geographic map, table, etc.), this expert system is based on input from a TARGIT BI domain expert. In our example, the returned revenue for each customer will be presented as a pie chart based on the data in Fig. 1(d).

Although providing some degree of user freedom, the options provided in US Patents 7,783,628 [8] and 7,779,018 [7] in above example are limited to possible combinations of measures, dimensions and criteria (where "I would like to see" was part of a rigid syntax).

US Patent 8,468,444 [9] introduces so-called Hyper Related OLAP which leverages the meta-morphing functionality, and thus allows a user to apply meta-morphing in one interaction (typically mouse click) on any report or dashboard in a Business Intelligence implementation. The visualizations In this case are aligned with best practices [1]. This functionality adds a lot of analytical freedom to a decision process since it essentially moves the user from the observation to the orientation phase in one interaction. However, the freedom is not complete since the analytics is limited to the dashboard or reporting context from which the Hyper Relation was initiated.

The idea to disregard the vast majority of results in a streaming set of Big Data has been presented by European Organization for Nuclear Research (CERN) in relation to their experiments with their Large Hadron Collider (LHC). In [2], it is stated that they "throw away" 99 percent of what is recorded by the sensors in the LHC.

The novel contribution of this paper is to apply the same principles as CERN to a Big Data source (Google) in a way such that it is achievable for a small or medium-sized enterprise. In this context, we break with the traditional ETL principles in data warehousing by running data sample queries continuously while at the same time, synchronizing the resulting data set with multiple analytics client nodes.

We benefit from the same user-friendliness achieved through US patents [7–9], however, we operate on a metadata layer that is dynamically created based on reading the raw data is synchronized using TARGIT Xbone server.

3   The Inverted Data Warehouse IDW

3.1   Architecture

As shown in Fig. 2 the architecture of the Inverted Data Warehouse (IDW) is significantly different from a traditional data warehouse. In the traditional data warehouse, there are a number of data sources that are queried with a certain frequency (this is known as the extraction part of ETL). From this point, the data are transformed in a staging area before being loaded into cubes. The entire ETL process runs end-to-end and its three steps are synchronized. In addition, a traditional data warehouse would normally not be operational in the event that the ETL process fails, since users typically query the cubes loaded on a centralized server.

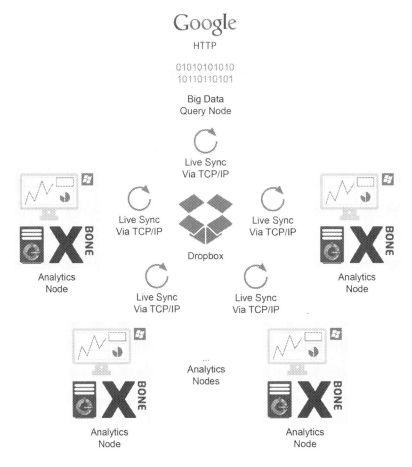

Fig. 2. An Inverted Data Warehouse with four analytics nodes

In an IDW, we run continuous queries as close to the data source as possible, since we intend to push as much of the workload to the source as possible. In this case meaning that we run a query on Google and only concentrate on reading the result of this query. In addition we attempt to ignore all undesired data as early as possible; ideally at the source. It is important to note that the work done on the node interacting with the data source (Google in this case) is not synchronized with any of the nodes analyzing the output. Synchronization of data with the analytics nodes is done using a separate process (in our example in Sect. 5 we use the cloud-based service Dropbox www.dropbox.com). As we will see in Sect. 5, the number of relevant records from a business perspective is eight orders of magnitude smaller than the records processed on Google, and thus the volume needed to be synchronized between the nodes is completely manageable for this type of architecture.

Since all the data selected for analysis are mirrored to all analytics nodes, the IDW has no single point of failure in regards to users being able to analyze data. In the event that the node with the continuous query fails, all users will simply experience that data does not continuously update until the node is back online. In the IDW architecture it is of course possible to compensate for this single point of failure by adding more nodes to query the data source. However, given the fact that end-users are unaffected from a business standpoint in our example (Sect. 5), we have not explored this variant further in this article.

The IDW in this article dynamically works with the following formats: NoSQL records on source (Google internal storage), HTML documents as output from Google queries, flat-file structured .txt files with selected data from HTML, and column-store format data on TARGIT Xbone that are presented in dimensions and measures to the analyst user in TARGIT Decision Suite.

Example: we test the query "analytics dynamics ax" on Google to see if certain named vendors appear in the first 100 results and in which order.

Query Node

Step 1: the query is sent from the query node to Google as a http request: www. google.com/search?hl=en&lr=&q=analytics+dynamics+ax&btnG=Search This step repeats until the first 10 pages are read since we are interested in the first 100 Google results in this as our sample.

Step 2: the relevant links in the resulting document from Step 1 are identified by the tag $<$ h3 class="r"$>$. Furthermore, the links are matched against patterns where one or more identifies the link as belonging to a certain vendor, e.g., the pattern `targit.com` identifies TARGIT as the vendor associated with the link www.targit.com/en.

Step 3: only the links that belong to vendors of interest, defined by the patterns in Step 2, are stored by appending a semicolon separated text file in a Dropbox folder with the following format: `day;vendor;page;search;rank`

Analytics Node

Step 4: upon each update of the text file from Step 3, the TARGIT Xbone server loads the updated dataset into memory and identifies all data items that can be used as measures, dimensions, or both. In addition, TARGIT Xbone will identify hierarchies based on identifying date/time or members that fully include subsets of other members (the latter can be done effectively using the fast distinct count abilities). In this example, only the data item "day" in the dataset from Step 3 has the potential for becoming a hierarchy; all other data items become flat dimensions. In addition, "rank" also becomes a measure (in addition to a dimension). Once a new dataset is fully loaded, any previous version of the dataset is flushed from memory. By doing loads in this order, the analytics user does not feel the update as downtime.

Steps 1–3 are run continuously on the query node in a cycle covering all the queries we want to test. Step 4 is run continuously on the analytics node.

In our experience with running the IDW for a four-month period, we never saw the "query source" node fail, and users experienced close to real-time performance when answering business questions. We therefore note that we had a robust and high performing analytical environment based on commodity hardware and software. The data volumes and the analytical performance are further discussed in Sect. 5. The analytical performance optimizations using in-memory storage, solid-state drives (SSD), and column-store architecture on the individual nodes will be described in the following section.

3.2   Business Perspective

For nearly any company in business, a share of their customers will discover them through search engines on the Internet. Therefore it is highly relevant for a company to understand and optimize its position in search results delivered to potential customers looking for products or services.

It is very likely that a company already has a basic understanding of what their customers are looking for, and therefore it is also very likely that they can guess which sorts of questions a potential customer will pose to a search engine. This leads to the first element of reducing the big data at the source, which we call "the shotgun approach". In the shotgun approach, we simply guess which questions a potential customer would "ask" a search engine. We do this from a very greedy perspective, meaning that we fire off a lot of queries that a user may or may not ask. Our intent is to overshoot the number of queries, such that we are sure that most real end-user queries are a subset.

Philosophically, one could say that we are proposing a hypothesis that a user may ask a certain question, and then we test how relevant our company is in the results delivered by the search engine. We assess the relevancy of the query based on the position in the search results, meaning that the top result is very relevant, whereas position 101 and beyond is completely irrelevant. By capturing the position between 1 and 100 of our company as well as our competitors, we now have a useful tool to improve our own position but also to understand how our competitors are optimizing/communicating.

The shotgun approach allows us a very useful tool for continuously operationally optimizing our "relevancy" in the business space we desire, while at the same time understanding competitors' communication in the space where we expect potential customers. This presents some very interesting strategic information.

The shotgun approach is therefore very useful from a business standpoint, and it is very good at significantly reducing the data volumes we analyze. In Sect. 5, we present metrics for the Big Data size before and after applying "the shotgun".

4   TARGIT Xbone and TARGIT Decision Suite

On each analytics node from Fig. 2, we have installed the TARGIT Decision Suite as well as the TARGIT Xbone server [12]. This means that the node is a self-contained analytics client to which data sets can be synchronized. As seen in Fig. 3, the analytics node has three layers: TARGIT Decision Suite, TARGIT ANTserver, and TARGIT Xbone.

TARGIT Decision Suite is the interface where all analytics "questions" are asked and answered to the user. This user interface is designed in accordance with the Computer Aided Leadership and Management (CALM [5]) philosophy in mind, meaning that we seek to reduce the number of interactions needed for a user to travel a complete observation-orientation-decision-action cycle. In order to allow this, we apply the specific patented technologies [7–9] described in Sect. 2. We note that these technologies support both the OODA cycle and the creation of analytics from scratch.

TARGIT ANTserver is an intermediate layer that handles connections to multiple databases, while at the same time storing metadata in multiple languages. In this particular case, we only focus on the connection to TARGIT Xbone (below), but this server would allow access to more than this if needed.

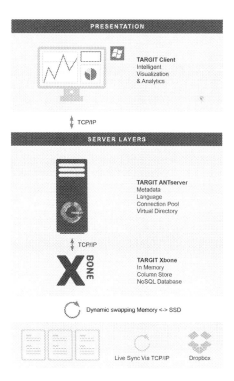

Fig. 3. Analytics Node layer overview

TARGIT Xbone is a high-performance analytics server that does all the computations requested from TARGIT Decision Suite through TARGIT ANTserver. TARGIT Xbone has its name because it is a very lean design "stripped to the bone" to reduce overhead, while incorporating large RAM memory stores as well as fast solid-state drives. TARGIT Xbone can automatically detect the structure of the dataset and therefore requires no configuration to allow the user to analyze it (see Sect. 5). The data sets in TARGIT Xbone are flat files, and the server dynamically swaps these between memory and SSD whenever the data is needed or when memory needs to be freed for the data. Upon loading data from SSD to RAM it is stored in a column store format such that each dimension is compressed to a "column" of unique values under which the references to the original rows are stored. This format is very fast in delivering subset information, especially when one or more measures are presented over one dimension. In addition, we note that this architecture is extremely fast in performing operations like minimum, maximum, and distinct counts since these can be found by reading only one value for a given column (dimension) with no need to access information on a row level. In Sect. 5 we present TARGIT Xbone experiments on real-world data that support the expected performance.

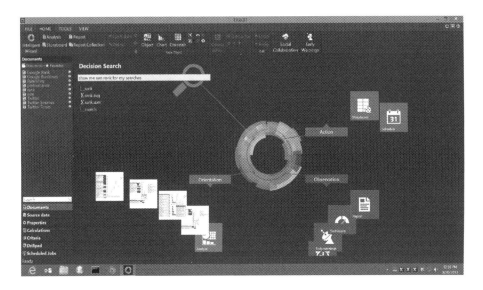

Fig. 4. TARGIT Decision Suite with Intelligent Wizard

It is important to note that the end-user only interacts with the TARGIT Decision Suite, thus the entire underlying setup is completely transparent. The user will be greeted by TARGIT's Intelligent Wizard as shown in Fig. 4, and from there begin asking "questions" in either human language or by interacting with the interface in a more traditional GUI-way. In Fig. 4, we note that the user simply asks "show me SEO rank for my searches" and the system presents him with both existing and analysis as well as options to create something new on-the-fly. The Intelligent Wizard has described in detail in [10], so in this paper the user simply clicks the existing most left analysis and the output is shown in Fig. 7.

In the following section we will see how the IDW architecture combined with the TARGIT software delivers an effective and very intuitive analytics experience.

5   Experiments

In the experiments we perform on the IDW, we use one query node and ten analytics nodes. The analytics nodes reside both within and outside the TARGIT organization. As we note from Figs. 2 and 3, the physical location and number of analytical nodes will have no impact on an individual node's performance. Therefore we limit our tests to one analytics node in this IDW.

The query node is a dual-core AMD Opteron 2 GHz based server with 1 GB RAM, running Windows Server 2008 R2 64 bit, and physically located in Denver, Colorado. The analytics node is a quad-core Intel 3.40 GHz CPU with 12 GB RAM, running Windows 8 64 bit, and physically located in Tampa, Florida. In addition, the analytics node is running TARGIT Decision Suite and TARGIT Xbone.

In Fig. 5, we see the number of records queried and downloaded respectively over a 13-day period. We see that the data found on this server side varies from 24.5 to 32.5 billion records per day, whereas the data actually pushed to the analytics node varies only from 375 to 675 rows per day. In other words, we reduce the data size eight orders of magnitude by limiting the data to a sample relevant to us (in this case top-100). It is important to note that we do not limit ourselves analytically in any way as we still include all pages and competitors;

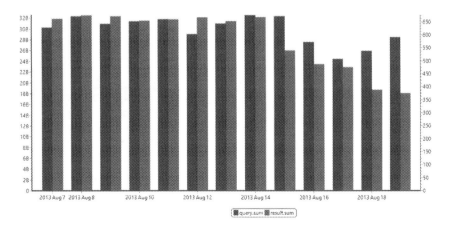

Fig. 5. Number of records queried and rows stored on the Query Node.

rather, we simply eliminate the irrelevant data similarly to [2]. We deliberately use the term records about the format a given website is stored on Google since we assume the source is a NoSQL format, whereas the resulting dataset we produce is a structured flat format with columns and rows.

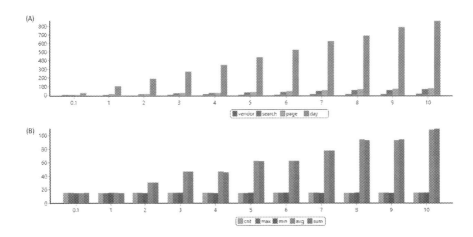

Fig. 6. Performance in milliseconds over millions of rows in TARGIT Xbone

In Fig. 6, we see the performance on the analytics node. Note that the runtimes are in milliseconds and the size of data sets are in the millions of records. The smallest data set (about 0.1 million records) is the real size of the data set, thus in these experiments we scale two orders of magnitude bigger than the actual system. In Fig. 6(A), we note that even at the largest synthetic dataset, we still have response times less than one second. In Fig. 6(B), we notice the distinctly different behavior of a column store [11] compared to a traditional table, since performance of count, minimum, and maximum operations are substantially different from the performance of sum and average operations. This is due to the fact that TARGIT Xbone stores data in columns rather than rows, and therefore counting, minimum and maximum can be directly read without even going to the row-level (see Sect. 4).

Referring back to Fig. 4, we now see the output of the "natural language question" in Fig. 7. As mentioned earlier in Sect. 4, we choose one of the existing visualizations in this case. The intelligent wizard supports "answering" most natural language queries with meaningful visualizations [10], but in this case we stick with a predefined visualization as shown above.

As shown in Fig. 7, we see how well our organization's website (in this case targit.com) ranks on a Google search for "analytics dynamics ax". In other words, a reasonable guess for what a potential customer might ask when searching for analytics software to complement a Microsoft Dynamics AX (ERP) system. On the analytics node, the user is able to explore each guessed query and

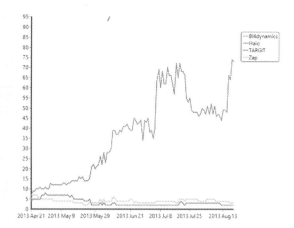

Fig. 7. Example of Intelligent Wizard output on an Analytics Node (Color figure online).

rank his organization as well as competitors. As we can see in Fig. 7, the competitors show distinctively different behavior: one competitor seems to be competing for that position as number one in "analytics dynamics ax" whereas to other competitors are not fighting for this space at all. Therefore, the information that we see does not only show our ability to attract customers; it also shows the priorities of the competition. Information that allows an organization to understand not only its current position, but also competitive strategic intent, is highly valuable to most organizations.

Qualitative Assessment: During the four-month period that this showcased IDW implementation has been operational, the information from the IDW has helped TARGIT to improve its average ranking on Google from 44 to 7 within all search *sentences* deemed strategically important. In addition, TARGIT is ranking number one on specific (confidential) search sentences. We note that the information about search ranking at this "atomic level" is not available on any other tool, e.g., Google Analytics, since the information is too specific for those tools to collect. We therefore conclude that the combined IDW with the "shotgun approach" delivered highly valuable and strategically important information. We also note that commodity hardware in very limited amounts was able to produce these results, even though the daily query results at the server end amounted up to 32 billion records.

6 Conclusion

In this article, we presented a so-called Inverted Data Warehouse (IDW) with analytics nodes running on TARGITs Xbone memory-based analytics server. We demonstrated a real-world implementation, in which strategic information was generated with each query running in less than 0.1 s. In addition, we demonstrated that similar queries could be run on a 2 orders of magnitude larger synthetic volume in less than one second. All of this was done using commodity hardware and in accordance with the principle of pushing the Big Data workload towards the server, and furthermore by eliminating irrelevant data at an early stage.

We demonstrated in concrete examples how the entire solution is highly relevant for an organization's ability to navigate in a competitive market. In addition, we showed how this specific implementation of IDW can be used for Search Engine Optimization (SEO). In summary, we have demonstrated how an organization with very little financial ability can conduct highly valuable data mining and visualization on a Big Data source.

Acknowledgments. This work was supported by TARGIT and Center for Data-Intensive Systems (Daisy) at Aalborg University.

References

1. Few, S.: Show Me the Numbers: Designing Tables and Graphs to Enlighten. Analytics Press, US (2012)
2. Cern,N.H.,: Where the Big Bang meets big data. TechRepublic. www.techrepublic.com/blog/european-technology/cern-where-the-big-bang-meets-big-data/, as of 14 Aug 2013
3. Roe, C.: IDC summary. The Growth of Unstructured Data: What To Do with All Those Zettabytes? Dataversity. www.dataversity.net/the-growth-of-unstructured-data-what-are-we-going-to-do-with-all-those-zettabytes/, 12 Aug 2013
4. Kimball, R.: The Data Warehouse Lifecycle Toolkit: Expert Methods for Designing, Developing, and Deploying Data Warehouses. Wiley, New York (1998)
5. Middelfart, M.: CALM: Computer Aided Leadership and Management. iUniverse (2005)
6. Middelfart, M.: Improving business intelligence speed and quality through the OODA concept. In: Proceeding of DOLAP, pp. 97–98 (2007)
7. Middelfart, M.: Presentation of data using meta-morphing. US Patent 7,779,018. Issued 17 Aug 2010
8. Middelfart, M.: Method and user interface for making a presentation of data using meta-morphing. US Patent 7,783,628. Issued 24 Aug 2010
9. Middelfart, M.: Hyper related OLAP. US Patent 8,468,444. Issued 18 June 2013
10. Middelfart, M.: Intelligent Wizard for human language interaction in Business Intelligence. To appear in eBISS 2013
11. Wikipedia. Column-oriented DBMS en.wikipedia.org/wiki/Column-oriented_DBMS, 21 Aug 2013
12. TARGIT. TARGIT Xbone - Ad-hoc analytics for everyone www.targit.com/en/experience-targit/products/xbone, 12 Aug 2013

Building Engines and Platforms
for the Big Data Age

Badrish Chandramouli[(⊠)]

Microsoft Research, One Microsoft Way, Redmond, WA 98052, USA
badrishc@microsoft.com

Abstract. Big data analytics involves the collection of real-time operational data into large clusters, followed by the execution of analytics queries to derive insights from the data. The results of these insights are periodically deployed into the real-time pipeline, in order to perform business actions or raise alerts. We are currently witnessing a move towards *fast data analytics*, where some of the offline activities may be performed in memory, directly over the real-time input streams, in order to reduce the time taken to derive and exploit insights from the data. Further, there is an increasing emphasis on enabling data scientists to derive quick approximate insights from large volumes of offline data interactively and at low cost, i.e., without having to process the entire dataset each time. Such hybrid and interconnected workflows across offline and real-time data, stored and processed across multiple machines, and with varying latency needs and complex application logic, requires a rethinking of both data and query processing models and software artifacts that realize such models. This paper surveys the challenges and requirements created by such workflows, and summarizes our research efforts on addressing these problems.

Keywords: Big data · Streaming · Fast data · Analytics · Performance · Latency · Programming languages · Query processing · Iterative · Incremental

1 Introduction

Traditional big data analytics involves the monitoring and archiving of real-time operational data into large cluster storage such as HDFS, Azure Blobs, and SCOPE/Cosmos [16]. This is followed by the execution of offline analytics queries to derive insights from the massive data. The results of these insights are then deployed into the real-time pipeline in order to control and perform business actions or raise alerts, thereby deriving value from the collected data.

Cloud applications that follow this data-centric business model include Web advertising, recommender systems, financial risk analysis, online gaming, and call-center

---

B. Chandramouli—This paper is based on joint work with Jonathan Goldstein, Mike Barnett, Rob DeLine, Danyel Fisher, John C. Platt, James F. Terwilliger, John Wernsing, Justin Levandoski, Suman Nath, Ivo Santos, Songyun Duan, Wenchao Zhou, Abdul Quamar, and several other collaborators.

M. Castellanos et al. (Eds.): BIRTE 2013 and 2014, LNBIP 206, pp. 23–37, 2015.
DOI: 10.1007/978-3-662-46839-5_3

analytics. We describe two such applications next, recommender systems and behavior targeted advertising.

Recommender Systems [2, 17]. Platforms such as NetFlix, Reddit, Google News, and Microsoft Xbox need to recommend movies, news items, blog posts etc. to customers. They monitor and archive user ratings of items (e.g., movie ratings or news "likes"). They analyze the collected data by building similarity models (e.g., between users and items) using platforms such as Hadoop. The similarity models feed periodically into a real-time scoring platform (e.g., Storm) that provides recommendations to users by applying the model to that user's current ratings and preferences.

Behavior Targeted Advertising [20, 24]. Advertising platforms such as Google Doubleclick and Bing Ads show targeted ads to users based on their historical behavior. They collect and archive user behavior in the form of ad (advertisement) impression and ad click logs, search history, and URLs visited. They analyze the data to eliminate automated bots, remove spurious clicks, reduce dimensionality, and build machine learning models for users. Finally, during live operations, they track recent per-user behavior in real time and, given an opportunity to show an ad, score the user in real-time and display the most relevant ad.

1.1   New Application Requirements

With increasing quantities of acquired data and the value of timely analytics over the data, Cloud applications such as those outlined above are seeing new requirements that need to be supported by modern data processing engines and platforms. We outline some of these requirements below.

1.1.1   Fast Analytics Over Varied Data Sources

We have recently been witnessing a shift towards *fast data analytics*, where all the activities including data acquisition, analytics or model building, and scoring are performed directly over the real-time streams. This approach dramatically reduces the responsiveness and time to insight of the business, thereby deriving better value from new data as it is collected. For instance, a real-time recommender system can suggest news articles or blog posts within seconds, in time for them to be relevant. An advertising platform can use rapidly changing trends (e.g., flash sales or unexpected events) to target users. The data sources may also be diverse ranging from Cloud-and browser-generated data to device data (e.g., GPS and accelerometer readings) from smartphones, cars, and game consoles. Thus, there is a need to provide users with a powerful language for expressing their complex activities, and a low-overhead runtime that can execute their activities at low latency and directly over real-time streams, potentially distributing the computation across the Cloud and devices.

1.1.2   Unification of Real-Time and Offline

Apart from pushing more processing work to real-time, there is also a strong need to unify the expression and execution of analytics across real-time and offline data sources. We provide several examples of the need for such a unification below:

(1) We may wish to correlate real-time data with events that occurred seven days back in our historical log, in order to detect and report anomalies, defined as significant deviations from expected behavior.

(2) We may wish to "back-test" real-time queries over historical logs. For example, we may have a real-time query deployed in production, and would like to test or execute over offline data, perhaps with different parameter settings, without having to rewrite the query logic. Efficiency of execution is particularly critical during offline execution, due to the large quantities of data being analyzed.

(3) We may wish to take the results of our offline analysis and operationalize them (i.e., deploy them in real-time) without having to change the query logic.

All of these activities need an expressive query model and platforms that can execute that query model efficiently over real-time and/or offline datasets.

1.1.3 Interactive Exploration

The data acquired in real time is usually stored in large clusters for offline analysis by data scientists. Analytics over the large volumes of collected data can be very expensive. The pay-as-you-go paradigm of the Cloud causes computation costs to increase linearly with query execution time, making it possible for a data scientist to easily spend large amounts of money analyzing data. The problem is exacerbated by the interactive and exploratory nature of analytics, where queries are iteratively discovered and refined, including the submission of many off-target and erroneous queries (e.g., bad parameters). In traditional systems, queries must execute to completion before such problems are diagnosed, often after hours of expensive compute time are exhausted.

We define *progressive analytics* as the generation of early results to analytical queries based on partial data, and the progressive refinement of these results as more data is received. Progressive analytics allows users to get early results using significantly fewer resources, and potentially end (and possibly refine) computations early once sufficient accuracy or query incorrectness is observed. We need query models and runtimes that can support workflows that include such progressive analytics over offline datasets, in addition to being able to process time-oriented queries on real-time and/or offline data. The progressive queries themselves should be easy to author by data scientists in an interactive and visual manner, and should be easy to operationalize into a real-time pipe.

1.2 Today's Solutions

Partly as a result of the diverse and inter-connected nature of analytics as outlined above, the big data analytics landscape of today is quite rich in terms of available systems for performing data processing. Database systems such as Vertica [44] and Microsoft SQL Server [39] are used for relational analytics. Map-reduce systems such as Hadoop [6] and its variants [34] are used for partitioned queries over offline data, with front-ends such as Hive to support relational queries. Spark [46] (and Spark SQL) offer high-performance data transformations over offline data that may be cached in main memory. Separate systems such as GraphLab [37] support iterative queries for graph analytics. S-STORE [15] provides a unified engine to handle transaction processing and streaming computation. Systems such as BlinkDB [13] and CONTROL [29, 30] enable approximate early results for analytics queries. Stream processing engines such as STREAM [8], Borealis [1], NiagaraST [38], Nile [28], DataCell [35], and Microsoft StreamInsight [5] are used for running real-time queries. Distributed streaming platforms such as Storm [7], Spark Streaming [47], MillWheel [4], and Naiad [40] are used for distributed stream processing. The Berkeley Data Analytics Stack [11] provides several tools and systems to perform analytical, graph, streaming, and transactional computations.

The data platforms landscape map [26] illustrates the enormous number of platforms and systems that now exist in the big data ecosystem, with disparate tools, data formats, and techniques [36]. Combining these disparate tools with application-specific glue logic in order to execute end-to-end workflows is a tedious and error-prone process, with potentially poor performance and the need for translation at each step. Further, the lack of a unified data model and query semantics precludes reusing the same logic across all the tools, handling cross-platform query processing (e.g., across devices and the Cloud), developing queries on historical data and then deploying them directly to live streams, or back-testing live queries (with possibly different parameters) on historical datasets.

1.3   Towards a Unified Analytics Solution

Over the last several years, we have been working on developing and refining models, methods, and system architectures to help alleviate the range of challenges outlined above. Starting from query and data models all the way to concrete system designs and architectures, we have been rethinking the way we build engines and platforms so that Cloud applications can support the new requirements, without having to suffer the impedance mismatch introduced by simply putting together complex and diverse technologies. Our research work spans the areas of semantics, engines, and platforms:

We have worked on unifying the use of the tempo-relational model and its refinements for big data [9, 20, 21, 23, 33, 38], significantly improving upon semantic clarity, expressiveness, and algorithms in an incremental setting;
We have built temporal streaming engines that realize such models, such as:

- StreamInsight [5], which shipped as part of Microsoft SQL Server;
- Trill [19], a .NET-based engine that provides best-of-breed or better performance across the entire latency spectrum; and
- JStreams [42], a Javascript-based temporal engine for Web browsers and devices.

Our engines are designed with a goal of running seamlessly on different scale-out platforms with varying latency goals. We have demonstrated this layered approach via systems such as:

- TiMR [20], which allows us to embed an unmodified streaming engine within an unmodified map-reduce system for offline temporal analytics;

- Race [18], which enables real-time streaming queries to efficiently execute across *edge devices* (e.g., smartphones) and the Cloud; and
- Now! [23], which enables an unmodified streaming engine to run progressive relational queries in a pipelined map-reduce setting.

The goal of this paper is to summarize our key insights and learnings in the process of providing new and unified data processing solutions for the complex big data analytics landscape. We start in Sect. 2 by describing a unified query model that can support all of the complex workflow requirements outlined earlier. In Sect. 3, we focus on the runtime, and discuss several key system requirements, architectural choices, and solutions that can enable big data applications to execute their workflows seamlessly and efficiently while leveraging and reusing the breadth of platforms available today. We use a case study in Sect. 4 to demonstrate the use of these tools to solve data processing problems in the context of Web search and advertising, and conclude the paper in Sect. 5.

2   Choosing a Query Model for the Big Data Age

We need a query model that can effectively support the range of analytics described above. The standard relational model used in database systems is expressive, but does not handle low-latency real-time queries over changing data. Support for incremental iterative processing is necessary to handle queries over changing graphs. Further, the data in our applications is temporal in nature, i.e., time is a first class citizen. For example, Web advertising queries operate on reports of ad clicks, ad impression, and Web searches by users; each of these activities is associated with a timestamp of occurrence. Given the temporal nature of data, many application activities consist of queries that have a fundamental temporal component to them. For example, the first step of Web advertising usually consists of eliminating the influence of black-listed *bot users*, who are defined as spurious users (usually automated clickers) who, at a given instant of time, have clicked on more than a specified threshold of ads within a short time period. The tempo-relational data and query model, with appropriate extensions for streaming computation, turns out to be a very good fit for handling the entire range of analytics described above, and can serve as the backbone for big data analytics. We describe this model next.

2.1   The Tempo-Relational Data and Query Model

A *streaming engine* enables applications to execute long-running *continuous queries* (*CQs*) over data streams in real-time. Streaming engines are used for efficient real-time processing in applications such as fraud detection, monitoring RFID readings from sensors, and algorithmic stock trading. While streaming engines target real-time data, they are usually based on some variant of the tempo-relational data and query model from early work on temporal databases.

2.1.1   Data Model

Logically, we can view a stream as a *temporal database* (*TDB*) [33] that is presented incrementally, as in CEDR [9], Nile [28], NiagaraST [38], etc. The TDB is a multi-set of logical *events*, each of which consists of a relational tuple p (called the payload) and an associated validity interval denoted by a validity start time V_s and a validity end time V_e which define a half-open interval $[V_s, V_e)$. One can think of V_s as representing the event's timestamp, while the validity interval is the period of time (or *data window*) over which the event is active and contributes to output. In the tempo-relational model, the dataset gets divided into *snapshots*, a sequence of data versions across time, that are formed by the union of unique interval endpoints of all events in the input TDB. In Fig. 1 (left), we show three interval events that divide the timeline into five snapshots.

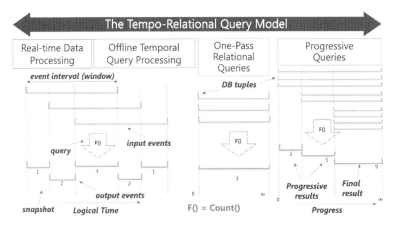

Fig. 1. Expressive power of the tempo-relational query model.

Physically, different streaming engines make different choices with respect to stream contents. For example, STREAM represents events as I-streams and D-streams. In Trill, events may either arrive directly as an *interval*, or get broken up into a separate insert into (called *start-edge*) and delete from (called *end-edge*) the TDB. A special case of interval events is a *point* event $[V_s, V_s + 1)$, which has a lifetime of one *chronon* (the smallest possible unit of time), and represents an instantaneous occurrence of an event. Punctuations [38] are used in systems such as NiagaraST, StreamInsight, and Trill to denote the progress of time in the absence of data. Further, systems such as Trill batch events for higher performance, and therefore use punctuations for the secondary purpose of forcing the flushing of partial batches from the engine.

2.1.2   Query Model

Users can express a query Q over the timestamped data. The query is specified using a language such as StreamSQL [32] or temporal LINQ [43], and is compiled into a graph of streaming operators. Logically, Q maps one TDB instance to another: the query Q is logically executed over every snapshot. A result is present in the output TDB at timestamp T if it is the result of Q applied to data that is "alive at" (whose validity intervals are stabbed by) T. Figure 1 (left) shows a Count query that outputs, for each snapshot, a count of events in that snapshot. Physically, the output TDB is computed and emitted incrementally as input events are presented to operators in the engine, usually in timestamp order.

2.1.3 Temporal Operators

All standard relational operations such as *Filter, Project, Union, Join, Aggregation*, and set difference with *AntiSemiJoin* – also called *WhereNotExists* – have equivalent temporal counterparts. The *SelectMany* operator introduced in LINQ maps each row to zero or more transformed output rows. A *Multicast* operator is used to copy an input stream into more than one output stream. The class of stream operators that incrementally process stream elements and produce per-snapshot output are called snapshot operators (e.g., in-built and user-defined aggregates). Most engines also have the ability to process grouped computations with the *GroupApply* operation [20], which logically executes a sub-query on every sub-stream consisting of events with the same grouping key value. Streaming engines usually also support sequential pattern detection operators to detect complex regular-expression-style sequences of event occurrences [22, 45]. These are useful, for example, to detect complex chart patterns (e.g., the *candlestick* pattern) in algorithmic stock trading.

Further, streaming engines include incremental operators that can manipulate time in safe ways. The *Window* operator sets the lifetime of each event to a specified value, and can be used to window the data, for example, to output a sliding-window aggregate over the last 5 min. The start time of events may also be modified to, for instance, create hopping windows. *Clip* is a special data-dependent windowing operator that takes two input streams. It windows the data on the left stream based on matching future data in the right stream. For example, we can clip a start-session stream with an end-session stream to generate a sequence of session events, each with a start and end time that correspond to session start and end timestamps respectively. In Sect. 5, we will use a case study of Web advertising to show how some of these operators can be used to answer complex questions over temporal data.

2.2 Temporal, Relational, and Iterative Query Support

Since the tempo-relational model is based on application time, query results are a function of the data and query alone, and are not dependent on the wall-clock time of actual execution. This allows us to seamlessly execute real-time queries on historical logs and vice versa. Further, we can meaningfully execute queries that correlate real-time data with historical data using application time.

Further, it is easy to see that this model is a superset of the relational model, as shown in Fig. 1 (center). By setting all events to have the same time interval (say, $[0, \infty)$), we create a single snapshot that represents the execution of a standard relational query. Further, iterative queries (both relational and temporal) can be supported by adding looping support to the query plan, taking additional care to detect and propagate the progress of time in an incremental setting [21].

2.3   Progressive Query Support

We have shown in prior work [23] that one can use the tempo-relational model to also support progressive relational queries. The key idea, shown in Fig. 1 (right), is to re-interpret application time to instead mean query computation progress. Based on a user-specified (or system generated) data sampling strategy, we simply timestamp the data as $[0, \infty), [1, \infty), \ldots$ to denote (usually increasing) subsets of data in a series of snapshots. Executing a query using an unmodified temporal streaming engine, over data annotated in this manner, results in the generation of early results that are refined as more data is processed. For example, Fig. 1 (right) shows the results of a simple relational Count query as early results 3 and 5, that are finally refined to the exact (final) value of 9. This technique provides determinism and repeatability for early results – two runs of a query provide the same sequence of early answers. This greatly enhances our understanding and debuggability of early results.

Sampling strategies are simply encoded as timestamp assignments. For example, with a star-schema, we may set all tuples in the (small) dimension table to have an interval of $[0, \infty)$, while progressively sampling from the fact table as $[1, \infty)$, $[2, \infty), \ldots$, which effectively causes a temporal Join operator to fully "preload" the dimension table before progressively sampling the fact table for meaningful early results.

3   System Designs for the Big Data Age

Based on our query and data model, we now describe key design and architectural choices that need to be made when creating a unified analytics stack that can handle a variety of analytics scenarios. Our proposed approach consists of first building a general-purpose and powerful streaming query engine as a reusable component. Such an engine is then reused in different settings, and embedded within a variety of platforms to handle different user scenarios.

3.1   Design Considerations for a Streaming Engine as a Component

3.1.1   Performance and Overhead

A single streaming engine used for a variety of analytics scenarios outlined in this paper requires very high and best-of-breed performance across the latency spectrum from offline to real-time. High performance also translates to low overhead, which can be critical in monitoring applications, and when stream processing is offloaded to devices. As an example, batching is becoming a standard technique used by engines such as Naiad, Storm (with the Trident API), Spark Streaming, and Trill to gain high performance. In the same vein, systems such as Trill expose a dynamic latency-throughput tradeoff to users in order to provide high performance across the latency spectrum, and adopt several database-style optimizations such as columnar processing to provide even higher performance gains.

3.1.2 Server Versus Library Execution

We find that the traditional server model of databases – where the database "owns" the machine (or set of machines), manages thread scheduling, and uses native memory management with a rigid type system (e.g., SQL types) – is a poor fit for streaming in the big data age, due to several reasons. The Cloud application is usually in control of the end-to-end application, and invokes the engine as part of its data processing. Complex data-types such as machine learning models often need to be supported and streamed through the engine. Further, user-defined extensions and libraries are very common, and are usually written using high-level languages. Such extensions and libraries need to seamlessly integrate at with query processing without loss of performance or a need for fine-grained data transformations. Further, threads are often already managed and owned by scale-out fabrics, and thus do not inter-operate well with engines that try to take on such a role. As a result, many streaming engines offer deep high-level language support (e.g., Naiad, Storm, Spark Streaming, and Trill) or can optionally execute as a library that does not own threads (e.g., Rx [41] and Trill). Finally, the engine also needs to expose operator state checkpointing capabilities that can be leveraged by the surrounding platforms to achieve resiliency to failure.

Fig. 2. Architecture of Cloud-Edge applications.

3.2 Platforms for Big Data Analytics

As discussed earlier, a temporal streaming engine can be embedded within a variety of distribution platforms to handle various scenarios. We overview some of the ways we have enabled specific requirements in the past using this layering approach.

3.2.1 Cloud-Edge Applications Across Real-Time and Offline Data

Figure 2 shows the architecture of a typical Cloud-Edge application. Data generated in the Cloud and by edge devices such as smartphones (such as GPS readings), as well as offline reference data (such as social network graphs) is made available for querying by the Cloud application. For example, a social Foursquare application may wish to notify a user whenever any of her friends checks in or visits a nearby location. Such applications can be expressed as streaming queries, and the corresponding query graph can be partitions to execute on edge devices and in the Cloud. In order to accomplish this, we can leverage a hybrid deployment of streaming engines based on a common temporo-relational model, but targeted towards different platforms. For instance, we could combine Trill running in the Cloud with JStreams – a temporal streaming engine written in Javascript – running on smartphones. Devices may have constraints on capabilities (e.g., CPU, memory, battery usage) as well as data upload (e.g., due to bandwidth costs or privacy settings). Deciding which operators execute at which location is an optimization problem that is hard in general, but needs to be addressed in this hybrid setting; see [18] for some solutions we have proposed in this space. The real-time processing component that executes in the Cloud may itself need to be scaled out, as we discuss next.

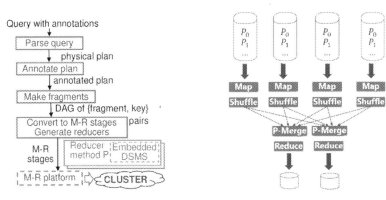

Fig. 3. TiMR design.   Fig. 4. Now! architecture.

3.2.2   Real-Time Scaled-Out Processing in the Cloud

Unlike offline data processing, very high event rates are usually not a requirement for real-time analytics. For example, most internet activity such as searches and tweets consist of fewer than 100 K events per second [31]. However, scale out is still necessary for the scalable ingress of data, and because many real-time processing queries is memory constrained. For example, we may need to track the activity of millions of users in a real-time advertising platform. Orleans [12] is a programming model and fabric that enables low-latency (in milliseconds) distributed streaming computations with units of work called grains. Orleans owns threads and manages the distributed execution of user code, but offers no declarative language or query processing capabilities. Streaming libraries such as Rx or Trill are often embedded within Orleans grains in order to execute real-time queries, thus allowing applications to scale their real-time computation on to multiple machines; [14] describes such an application. Another example of such a fabric that can embed a streaming engine is REEF [25].

3.2.3   Temporal Analytics on Offline Datasets

The acquired real-time data is usually stored in large storage clusters such as HDFS and Cosmos. We may wish to take our real-time queries and execute them on the offline data. Map-reduce (M-R) is a common paradigm for executing queries on large offline datasets. With the streaming engine as a library, one can easily embed the engine within reducers in map-reduce, in order to execute the same temporal queries on the offline data. We built a framework called TiMR (pronounced timer), to process temporal queries over large volumes of offline data [20]. Figure 3 depicts the design of TiMR.

Briefly, TiMR combines an unmodified data stream management system (DSMS) with an unmodified map-reduce distributed computing platform. Users perform analytics using a temporal language (e.g., temporal LINQ or StreamSQL). The query DAG (directed acyclic graph) is converted into map-reduce jobs that run efficiently on large-scale offline temporal data in a map-reduce cluster. Further, the queries are naturally ready to operationalize over real-time data. TiMR leverages the tempo-relational model underlying the DSMS for repeatable behavior across runs.

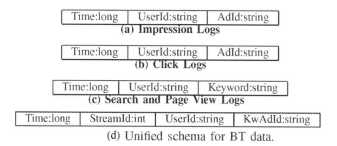

(a) **Impression Logs**

(b) **Click Logs**

(c) **Search and Page View Logs**

(d) Unified schema for BT data.

Fig. 5. Data schema for behavior targeted advertising.

3.2.4 Enabling Progressive Analytics for Data Scientists

Recall that the tempo-relational model can support progressive queries by re-interpreting time to mean computation progress. We built a distributed platform called Now! (see Fig. 4), which improves upon a standard map-reduce framework to include pipelining and support for time (or more accurately, progress) as a first-class citizen within the framework. Consider a large progress-annotated dataset, that is split into a sequence of partitioned *progress batches* P_i, each of which represents a chunk of input data with the same validity interval of $[i, \infty)$. Now! understands that data consists of a sequence of progress batches; therefore, after the map phase, its shuffle operation creates a sequence of progress batches per destination reducer. On the reduce side, the incoming progress batches from multiple mappers are merged in timestamp order (using the P-Merge operator shown in Fig. 4), before being fed to a *progressive reducer* in a pipelined timestamp-ordered fashion. With this architecture, we were able to embed an unmodified streaming engine into the reducer as in TiMR, and execute large-scale queries progressively. More details on Now! can be found in our research paper [23].

From a usability perspective, we built a Web-based front end for issuing progressive queries, called Tempe (formerly Stat!) [10, 27], which allows data scientists to collaboratively author queries with progressive processing and visualization.

4   Case Study: Web Advertising

Behavior targeted advertising operates on data with the (simplified) data format shown in Fig. 5(a–c). Each ad impression (or click) entry has a timestamp, the id of the user to who was shown (or clicked on) the ad, and the id of the ad itself. The keyword search and page view entries are similar, consisting of a timestamp, the id of the user, and the search term or page URL. This data may be acquired in real-time, and stored in large storage clusters such as HDFS and Scope/Cosmos. For simplicity, we assume a single unified schema for the data, as shown in Fig. 5(d). Here, we use StreamId to disambiguate between the various sources. StreamId values of 0, 1, and 2 refer to ad impression, ad click, and keyword (searches and pageviews) data respectively. Based on StreamId, the column KwAdId refers to either a keyword or an AdId. Our queries are written to target the new schema, and thus operate on a single input data source.

4.1   Temporal Query: Bot Elimination

The goal of bot elimination is to get rid of activity corresponding to users that have "unusual" behavior characteristics. We define a bot as a user who either clicks on more than T_1 ads, or searches for more than T_2 keywords within a time window τ. Before feeding data to training models, it is important to detect and eliminate bots quickly, as we receive user activity information; otherwise, the actual correlation between user behavior and ad click activities can be diluted by the spurious behavior of bots.

The CQ shown in Fig. 6 gets rid of bots. We first create a hopping window (implemented using the Window operator) with hop size h = 15 min and window size w = 6 h, over our input unified point event stream S1. This updates the bot list every 15 min using data from a 6 h window. The GroupApply (with grouping key UserId) applies the following sub-query to each UserId sub-stream. From the click and search input streams for that user, we perform the count operation on each stream, filter out counter events with value less than the appropriate threshold (T_1 or T_2), and use Union to get one stream S2 that retains only bot users' data. We finally

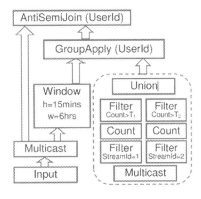

Fig. 6. Bot elimination CQ.

perform an AntiSemiJoin (on UserId) of the original stream S1 with S2, to output only non-bot users' data. Note that UserId can serve as the partitioning key for this CQ's execution in a scaled-out setting.

4.1.1   Real-Time Versus Offline Bot Elimination

The bot elimination CQ can be used directly on real-time streams, for example using Trill with Orleans. It can also be executed over offline data using TiMR running over SCOPE/Cosmos. Note that bot elimination is temporal – on offline data, it does not simply create and use a single list of bot users on the entire dataset. Rather, it computes, reports, and filters the input data based on the *varying* set of bot users over time, allowing for users to enter and exit the bot classification over the lifetime of the log.

4.2   Progressive Query: Top-K Correlated Search Terms

Assume we have collected a large quantity of search logs, and a data scientist wishes to analyze the data for effective user targeting. A query they may wish to execute on the dataset is: reports the top-k search terms that are most correlated with an analyst-provided *search parameter* (e.g., "birthday"), according to a goodness score, in the search dataset. The data scientist knows that taking random samples by UserId will yield good approximate answers for queries of this nature, so they timestamp the data accordingly in the cluster, and materialize it sorted by timestamp in the cluster.

The query can be expressed using two GroupApply operations, and is executed as follows using the Now! framework with Trill running within the progressive reducers. The first stage uses the dataset as input and partitions by UserId. Each reducer tokenizes the data into search terms using SelectMany, and uses GroupApply to compute a (partial) histogram that reports, for each search term in that partition, the number of searches with and without the search parameter, and the total number of searches. The next stage groups by search term, aggregates the partial histograms from the first stage reducers, computes a per-search-term goodness. Finally, we use a top-k aggregate to report the search terms that are most closely correlated to the input search parameter. Using an interactive environment such as Tempe, the data scientist can receive immediate results for such a query.

4.3   Cloud-Edge Query: Location-Aware Advertising

Assume we have built a scoring (machine leaning) model in the Cloud that, given the historical searches and page views of a user, can score any advertisement (or coupon) for its relevance to that user. Further, assume that advertisements are for physical stores, and we wish to target users with smartphones such that they receive advertisements relevant to their search history when they are in close proximity (say, within 1 mile) of the corresponding store location. This query involves a join of user searches (from their browser or search apps), their changing locations (from GPS readings on their device), slow-changing reference data of store locations available at the Cloud, and the scoring model which itself may change over time. In such a Cloud-Edge topology, we may wish to execute parts of the join on the users' smartphones by downloading the model and advertising information streams to the device, instead of constantly uploading their locations to the Cloud. This approach can also allow users to receive relevant ads in the presence of device constraints or privacy settings where they prevent their local searches and/or location information from being sent to or stored in the Cloud.

5   Conclusions

Big data analytics involves the collection of real-time data, followed by the execution of analytics queries to derive insights from the data. The results of these insights are deployed into the real-time pipeline, in order to perform business actions or raise alerts. We are witnessing an increasing need for fast data analytics in order to reduce the time to derive insights from data. Further, there exists remarkable diversity in the types of analytics that need to be performed, including latencies (real-time to offline) and settings (such as temporal, relational, iterative, and progressive). In this paper, we observe that the tempo-relational model can form a strong foundation that cuts across this diversity of analytics and provides a unified view of data and queries. We then overview several design choices and system architectures that leverage the tempo-relational model to build unified engines and platforms for big data analytics. Finally, we use a case study of Web advertising to illustrate the value of these models and system design choices.

References

1. Abadi, D.J., et al.: The design of the borealis stream processing system. In: CIDR (2005)
2. Adomavicius, G., Tuzhilin, A.: Toward the next generation of recommender systems: a survey of the state-of-the-art and possible extensions. TKDE **17**(6), 734–749 (2005)
3. Agarwal, S., et al.: BlinkDB: queries with bounded errors and bounded response times on very large data. In: EuroSys (2013)
4. Akidau, T. et al.: MillWheel: fault-tolerant stream processing at internet scale. In: VLDB (2013)
5. Ali, M. et al.: Microsoft CEP server and online behavioral targeting. In: VLDB (2009)
6. Apache hadoop. http://hadoop.apache.org/
7. Apache storm. http://storm.incubator.apache.org/
8. Babcock, B., et al.: Models and issues in data stream systems. In: PODS (2002)
9. Barga, R.S., et al.: Consistent streaming through time: a vision for event stream processing. In: CIDR, pp. 363–374 (2007)
10. Barnett, M., et al.: Stat! - an interactive analytics environment for big data. In: SIGMOD (2013)
11. Berkeley data analytics stack (BDAS). https://amplab.cs.berkeley.edu/software/
12. Bernstein, P., et al.: Orleans: distributed virtual actors for programmability and scalability. MSR Technical report (MSR-TR-2014-41, 24). http://aka.ms/Ykyqft
13. BlinkDB. http://blinkdb.org/
14. Building real-time services for halo. http://research.microsoft.com/apps/video/?id=198324
15. Cetintemel, U., et al.: S-Store: a streaming new SQL system for big velocity applications. In: VLDB (2014)
16. Chaiken, R., et al.: SCOPE: easy and efficient parallel processing of massive data sets. PVLDB **1**(2), 1265–1276 (2008)
17. Chandramouli, B., Levandoski, J.J., Eldawy, A., Mokbel, M.: StreamRec: a real-time recommender system. In: SIGMOD (2011)
18. Chandramouli, B., Nath, S., Zhou, W.: Supporting distributed feed-following apps over edge devices. PVLDB **6**(13), 1570–1581 (2013)
19. Chandramouli, B., Goldstein, J., Barnett, M., DeLine, R., Fisher, D., Platt, J.C., Terwilliger, J.F., Wernsing, J.: Trill: a high-performance incremental query processor for diverse analytics. In: VLDB (2015, to appear)
20. Chandramouli, B., Goldstein, J., Duan, S.: Temporal analytics on big data for web advertising. In: ICDE (2012)
21. Chandramouli, B., Goldstein, J., Maier, D.: On-the-fly progress detection in iterative stream queries. In: VLDB (2009)

22. Chandramouli, B., Goldstein, J., Maier, D.: High-Performance dynamic pattern matching over disordered streams. In: VLDB (2010)
23. Chandramouli, B., Goldstein, J., Quamar, A.: Scalable progressive analytics on big data in the cloud. PVLDB **6**(14), 1726–1737 (2013)
24. Chen, Y., et al.: Large-scale behavioral targeting. In: KDD (2009)
25. Chun, B., et al.: REEF: retainable evaluator execution framework. PVLDB **6**(12), 1370–1373 (2013)
26. Data platforms landscape map. http://blogs.the451group.com/information_management/2014/11/18/updated-data-platforms-landscape-map/
27. Fisher, D., Chandramouli, B., DeLine, R., Goldstein, J., Aron, A., Barnett, M., Platt, J.C., Terwilliger, J.F., Wernsing, J.: Tempe: an interactive data science environment for exploration of temporal and streaming data. MSR Technical report MSR-TR-2014–148 (2014). http://research.microsoft.com/apps/pubs/?id=232385. Accessed Nov 2014
28. Hammad, M., et al.: NILE: a query processing engine for data streams. In: ICDE (2004)
29. Hellerstein, J.M., Avnur, R.: Informix under control: online query processing. J. Data Min. Knowl. Discov. **12**, 281–314 (2000)
30. Hellerstein, J.M., Haas, P.J., Wang, H.J.: Online aggregation. In: SIGMOD (1997)
31. Internet live stats. http://www.internetlivestats.com/
32. Jain, N., et al.: Towards a streaming SQL standard. In: VLDB (2008)
33. Jensen, C., Snodgrass, R.: Temporal specialization. In: ICDE (1992)
34. Li, B., et al.: A platform for scalable one-pass analytics using MapReduce. In: SIGMOD, pp. 985–996 (2011)
35. Liarou, E., et al.: Enhanced stream processing in a DBMS kernel. In: EDBT (2013)
36. Lim, H., et al.: How to fit when no one size fits. In: CIDR (2013)
37. Low, Y., Gonzalez, J., Kyrola, A., Bickson, D., Guestrin, C., Hellerstein, J.M.: Distributed GraphLab: a framework for machine learning in the cloud. In: VLDB (2012)
38. Maier, D., Li, J., Tucker, P., Tufte, K., Papadimos, V.: Semantics of data streams and operators. In: Eiter, T., Libkin, L. (eds.) ICDT 2005. LNCS, vol. 3363, pp. 37–52. Springer, Heidelberg (2005)
39. Microsoft SQL server. http://www.microsoft.com/en-us/server-cloud/products/sql-server/
40. Murray, D., et al.: Naiad: a timely dataflow system. In: SOSP (2013)
41. Reactive extensions for .NET. http://aka.ms/rx
42. Santos, I., Tilly, M., Chandramouli, B., Goldstein, J.: DiAl: distributed streaming analytics anywhere anytime. In: VLDB (2013)
43. The LINQ project. http://aka.ms/rjhi00
44. Vertica. http://www.vertica.com/
45. Wu, E., Diao, Y., Rizvi, S.: High-performance complex event processing over streams. In: SIGMOD (2006)
46. Zaharia, M., et al.: Resilient distributed datasets: a fault-tolerant abstraction for in-memory cluster computing. In: NSDI (2012)
47. Zaharia, M., et al.: Discretized streams: fault-tolerant streaming computation at scale. In: SOSP (2013)

Backtrack-Based and Window-Oriented Optimistic Failure Recovery in Distributed Stream Processing

Qiming Chen$^{(\boxtimes)}$, Meichun Hsu, and Malu Castellanos

HP Labs, Palo Alto, CA, USA
{qiming.chen,meichun.hsu,Castellanos.malu}@hp.com

Abstract. Support transaction property and fault-tolerance is the key to applying stream processing to industry-scale applications; however the corresponding latency overhead must be minimized for accommodating real-time analytics. This issue has been studied in various contexts. In this work we develop the ***backtrack failure recovery*** mechanism to allow a task to roll forward without waiting for acknowledgement from its downstream target tasks in the failure-free case, but to request its upstream source tasks to resend the missing tuples only during failure recovery which is the rare case thus has limited impact on the overall performance. For further reduced latency we extend our solution in another dimension by applying the notion of ***optimistic checkpointing*** to stream processing, and propose the **Continued** stream processing with ***Window-based Checkpoint and Recovery*** (CWCR) approach, allowing a task to emit results tuple by tuple continuously but checkpoint in batch, and acknowledge, only once per window (e.g. time window). We also tackle the hard problems found in implementing a transactional layer on-top of an existing stream processing platform. We have implemented the proposed mechanisms on *Fontainebleau*, the distributed stream analytics infrastructure we built on top of the open-sourced Storm platform. Our experiment results reveal the novelty of the proposed technologies and the feasibility to support fault-tolerance with minimal latency overhead for real-time stream processing.

Keywords: Stream processing · Failure recovery · Dataflow transaction · Pessimistic checkpointing · Optimistic checkpointing

1 Introduction

To apply stream processing to industry-scale applications, ensuring transaction property and fault-tolerance is the key issue. A stream processing application is modeled as a continued dataflow process - ***streaming process***, where the parallel and distributed tasks are chained in a graph-structure with each task transforming a stream to a new stream. The transaction property guarantees the streaming data, called *tuples*, to be processed in the order of their generation in every dataflow path, with each tuple processed once and only once, under the notion of *eventual consistency* [3, 15, 17, 18].

© Springer-Verlag Berlin Heidelberg 2015
M. Castellanos et al. (Eds.): BIRTE 2013 and 2014, LNBIP 206, pp. 38–64, 2015.
DOI: 10.1007/978-3-662-46839-5_4

1.1 Prior Art

There exist multiple lineages of transactional stream processing. The first thread of work is characterized by applying the database transaction semantics to unbounded data stream with the concept of *snapshot isolation* [2, 4, 6, 7, 10], namely, to split a stream into a sequence of bounded chunks and handle each chunk in a transaction boundary. In this way, processing a sequence of data chunks generates a sequence of state snapshots. However, this mechanism only cares about the *state oriented* transaction boundary without addressing failure recovery.

The second thread is originated from reliable dataflow based on message logging and resending for failure recovery. One current approach, represented by Storm's "transactional topology" [18], treats the whole stream processing topology as a single operation thus suffers from the loss of intermediate results in the occurrence of failures. Another limitation of this approach is the ignorance of the states of data buffered in tasks.

The third thread is based on checkpointing and *forward tracking* where a task, T, checkpoints each output tuple, t, before emitting it, then T waits for the target tasks (recipients) to confirm (by acknowledgement - ACK), the success of processing t, before emitting the next output tuple; if T does not receive the ACK after a timeout (e.g. in case the target task fails, it takes a while to be restored), T will resend t, again and again, until being acknowledged [14, 15, 17]. Although the "once and only once" semantics can be enforced by ignoring duplicate tuples, waiting for ACK and keeping resending on the per tuple basis cause extremely high latency.

The forth thread is the variation of the above approach; it is also based on checkpointing and message resending, but characterized by "*backward tracking*", namely, allowing a task to process tuples continuously without waiting for acknowledgements and without resending tuples in the failure-free case, but to request (with the **ASK** message) the source tasks to resend the missing tuples only when it is restored from a failure which is a rare case thus has limited impact on the overall performance. Our experience shows that compared with *forward tracking*, the *backward tracking* approach can reduce the overall latency of stream processing significantly. However, it still suffers from the overhead of per-tuple checkpointing.

The fifth thread, referred to as *optimistic checkpointing*, also focuses on reducing the latency in failure free case [13, 19]. Unlike per-tuple based *pessimistic checkpointing* [16, 19], optimistic checkpointing allows messages to be checkpointed occasionally in batch. However, in general distributed computing, the use of this mechanism may cause uncontrolled task rollbacks known as the domino effects [19].

1.2 Proposed Approach

In the context of graph-structured, distributed stream processing, the checkpoint based failure recovery approaches discussed so far are in general limited to pessimistic and forward tracking ones. In this work we take the initial step to **combine optimistic checkpointing** and **backward tracking failure recovery**, which allows us to gain the benefits of both for low-latency, real-time stream processing.

With the **backtrack failure recovery** mechanism, a task does not wait for ACK and re-emit output on the per-tuple basis, but requests the missing tuples from its upstream source tasks only in failure recovery which is the rare case thus has limited impact on the overall performance.

For further reduced latency we extend our solution in another dimension – instead of per-tuple based *pessimistic* checkpoint protocol, we adopt the ***optimistic checkpoint protocol*** under the criterion of *eventual consistency* [3, 15], which allows the checkpoints to be made occasionally in batch and asynchronously with tuple processing and emitting. We solve the uncontrollable rollback problem found in the context of instant consistency of global state, by associating checkpoint boundary with the window semantics of stream processing to provide the commonly observable and semantically meaningful synchronization point of task rollbacks. We propose the ***Continued stream processing with Window-based Checkpoint and Recovery*** (**CWCR**) approach, under which the stream processing results are emitted tuple by tuple continuously (thus different from batch processing), but checkpointed once per-window (typically time-window). Since the failure recovery is confined in the commonly observable window boundaries, the so called domino effect in chained rollbacks can be avoided even in the situation of failure in failure.

To implement the proposed transaction layer on-top of an existing stream processing platform we need to deal with the hard problem on how to keep track the input/output messaging channels in order to realize re-messaging during failure recovery. Since common to the modern component-based distributed infrastructures, the data routing between tasks is handled by separate system components inaccessible to individual tasks, making it trivial for tasks to track. Our solution is characterized by tracking physical messaging channels logically, for that we introduce the notions of ***virtual channel***, ***task alias*** and ***messageId-set*** in reasoning, recording and communicating the channel information. We also provide a ***designated messaging hub***, separated from the regular dataflow channel, for signaling ACK/ASK messages and for resending tuples, in order to avoid interrupting the regular order of data flow.

We have implemented the proposed mechanisms on *Fontainebleau*, the distributed stream analytics infrastructure we develop on top of the open-sourced Storm platform. Our experiments reveal the novelty and value of these mechanisms. The combination of optimistic checkpointing and backtrack recovery significantly reduces the latency of transactional stream processing thus making it feasible for real-time applications; and the virtual channel mechanism allows us to handle failure recovery correctly in the elastic stream processing infrastructure.

The rest of this paper is organized as follows: Sect. 2 outlines the concept of graph-structured distributed streaming process and out platform; Sect. 3 describes backtrack failure recovery; Sect. 4 discusses Continued stream processing with Window-based Checkpoint and Recovery (CWCR); Sect. 5 discusses how to track messaging channels intelligently; Sect. 6 illustrates the experiment results; Sect. 7 concludes.

2   Distributed Stream Processing Infrastructure

2.1   Graph Structured Streaming Process

A stream is an unbounded sequence of events, or tuples. Logically a stream processing operation is a continuous operation to apply to the input stream tuple by tuple to derive a new output stream. In a distributed stream processing infrastructure, a logical *operation* may have multiple instances running in parallel, called *tasks*. A graph-structured *streaming process* is a continuous dataflow process constructed with distributed tasks over multiple server nodes. A task runs cycle by cycle; in each cycle it processes an input tuple, updates the execution state and emits the resulting tuples. Tuples transmitted between tasks are carried in messages,

Let us observe a streaming process example for matrix manipulation based event analysis. In this streaming process, the source tuples are streamed out, with second-based timestamps, from "matrix spout" with each contains 3 equal-sized float matrices generated randomly in size and content (the application background is the sensor readings from oil wells). The tuples first flow to the tasks of operation "*tran*" for transformation, then to "*gemm*" (general matrix multiplication) and "*trmm*" (transpose and multiplication) with "fields-grouping" on different hash keys; the outputs of "*gemm*" tasks are distributed to "*ana*" (analysis) tasks with "all-groupuing", and the outputs of "*trmm*" tasks are distributed to "*agg*" (aggregation) tasks with "fields-grouping". The logical operations, links and grouping types are illustrated in Fig. 1 and specified below.

BlueTopologyBuilder builder = **new** BlueTopologyBuilder();
builder.setSpout("matrix_spout", matrix_spout, 1);
builder.setBolt("tran", tran, 4).shuffleGrouping("matrix_spout");
builder.setBolt("gemm", gemm, 2).fieldsGrouping("tran", **new** Fields("site", "seg"));
builder.setBolt("ana", ana, 2).allGrouping("gemm");
builder.setBolt("trmm", trmm, 2).fieldsGrouping("tran", **new** Fields("site"));
builder.setBolt("agg", agg, 2).fieldsGrouping("trmm", **new** Fields("site"));

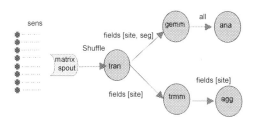

Fig. 1. A logical streaming process

Physically, each operation has more than one task instances. Given a pair of source and target operations, say *trans* and *gemm*, the tuples transmitted between their tasks are grouped with the same criteria defined on the operation level, as illustrated in Fig. 2. The possible input and output channels of a task can be extracted from the streaming process topology statically, but the actual channels used in distributing an emitted tuple are resolved dynamically during execution according to the grouping type, tuple content (e.g. fields hash value) and loading balance.

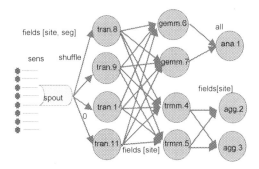

Fig. 2. A physical streaming process where an operation is instantiated as multiple tasks

2.2 Distributed Stream Processing Platform

We have developed a *parallel, distributed* and *elastic* stream analytics platform, with code name **Fontainebleau**, for executing *continuous, real-time* streaming processes. Our platform is built on top of Storm – an open sourced data stream processing system.

Architecturally *Fontainebleau* is characterized by the concept of **open-station**. In stream processing, data flow through *stationed* operators. Although the operators are defined with application logic, many of them have common execution patterns in I/O, blocking, data grouping, etc., as well as common functionalities such as the transactional control to be discussed in this report, which can be considered as their "meta-properties" and categorized for providing unified system support. This treatment allows us to ensure the operational semantics, to optimize the execution, as well as to ease user's effort for dealing with these properties manually which can lead to fragile code, disappointing performance and incorrect results. With the above motivation we introduce the notion of *open-station* as the container of a stream operator, that provides canonical system support but open for plugging in application logic. In the OO programming context, an open-station is provided with the open-executor coded by invoking certain abstract methods to be implemented by users based on their application logic.

We treat transaction enforcement with failure recoverability as a kind of task execution pattern, and provide the corresponding open stations hierarchy for supporting it automatically and systematically. The basic transactional station is defined as an abstract class *BasicCkStation* with several major system methods:

- *prepare* – invoked when the task is initially setup or restored from a failure, therefore the *recovery*() method discussed below is invoked, when necessary, inside the prepare() method.
- *execute* – invoked cycle by cycle for per-tuple processing, checkpointing, acknowledging, emitting, etc.
- *recovery* – invoked for recovery, including rolling back to the last checkpoint, re-emit output to the right target tasks at the downstream, and re-acquire the latest input from the source task at the upstream, etc.
- *outputFields* – used to specify the fields of the output tuples.

These methods invoke certain abstract methods which will be implemented based on application specific semantics (e.g. setup initial state, processing a tuple) and resource specific properties (e.g. the specific checkpoint engine based on files or databases). In order to create a transactional operation (tasks are instances of operations), the user only needs to define a corresponding class that extends the abstract BasicCkStation class, and implement the above abstract methods (and any inherited abstract methods).

With the open station architecture, the checkpointing and failure recovery are completely transparent to users as they only need to care about how to process each tuple for their applications.

2.3   Backtrack Based Failure Recovery

The checkpointing based failure recovery in stream processing is typically character-ized by *forward tracking* or **ACK**-based, i.e. a task cannot emit the next tuple until the successful processing of the last emitted tuple is acknowledged; and if such ACK is not received in timeout the task must resend the last tuple again and again, until being acknowledged. Although the "once and only once" semantics can be enforced by ignoring duplicate tuples, waiting for ACK and re-emitting output on the per tuple basis causes extremely high latency.

For enhanced overall performance, we stick on the *backtrack* or **ASK**-based recovery approach, where a task does not wait for acknowledgement before moving forward; instead, acknowledging is asynchronous to task executing and only used to remove the buffered tuples already processed by the target tasks.

Specifically, a task keeps an emitted tuple in a pool until there is no need to resend it for failure recovery; the task can determine the fan-out of an emitted tuple based on the topology, and detect whether that tuple is fully processed (thus fully acknowledged) by all the target tasks it was distributed to. A fully acknowledged tuple can be removed from the message pool. Since acknowledgement is only used to trigger the removal of the acknowledged tuple and all the tuple prior to that tuple, any ACK is allowed to be lost.

During failure recovery, the reestablished task tells each source task the last tuple it has seen, and **ask**s the source task to resend the next one; and if not received after timeout it would ask again and again. Since failures are rare, such backtrack process has limited impact on the overall performance.

2.4   Separated Message Hub for Recovery

A hard problem in supporting message resending on top of an existing stream pro-cessing platform is how to ensure the order of regular tuple delivery not interrupted by the task recovery process, when there lacks the accessible message re-sorting facility [14, 15, 17]. Because the recovered task with multiple source tasks may receive more than one resent tuples, and besides the one really missing, the others, may have been delivered and queued but not yet taken by the task; in that case, appending the resent tuple to the queue would interrupt the order of the queued tuples. We solve this problem in the following way.

- A second massaging hub, separated from the regular dataflow channel, is provided for a task, for signaling ACK/ASK and resending tuples (Fig. 3).
- When a task T is restored from a failure, it first requests and processes the resent tuples from all input channels, before going to the normal execution loop. In this way, if a resent tuple has been put in the input queue of T previously but not yet taken by T, that tuple can be identified as duplicate one and ignored in the normal execution loop.

For this designated messaging hub each task has a distinguish socket address (SA) and an address-book of its source and target tasks; the SA is carried with its output tuples for the recipient task to ACK/ASK through that messaging hub. Due to the change of SA when a task is restored from a failure (in that case the task may even be launched to another machine node), and due to the unavailability of the SA in the first correspondence, a Home Locator Registry (HLR) service is provided.

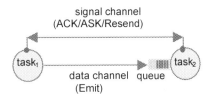

Fig. 3. Secondary messaging hub for ACK/ASK and resend

Checkpoint based failure recovery requires a task to know exactly the messaging channel and record it before emitting a tuple. For now we assume this requirement is satisfied. We will present our channel resolution mechanism later in Sect. 5.

3   Pessimistic Checkpointing with Backtrack Recovery

In stream processing, the typical checkpointing protocol is *pessimistic* where every output message (carrying resulting tuple) of a task is checkpointed before sent. Recovery based on pessimistic checkpointing is relatively simple since for each input channel only one possible missing tuple is concerned.

As mentioned above, for enhanced overall performance, we stick on the *back-tracking* based failure recovery, where a task continuously emits resulting tuples without waiting for ACKs, but requests the missing tuples only after reestablished from a failure (by ASK message) from its source tasks. In this section we discuss pessimistic checkpointing incorporated with the *backtracking* based failure recovery.

Task Execution. A task runs cycle by cycle continuously for processing input tuple by tuple. The tuples transmitted via a dataflow channel are sequenced and identified by the seq#, and guaranteed to be processed in order; a received tuple, t, with seq# earlier than the expected will be ignored; later than the expected ("jumped") will trigger the resending of the missing ones to be processed before *t*. This ensures each tuple to be processed once and only once and in the right order. After the tuple is processed, the resulting state, the input message-id, the output messages (holding tuples), etc., are checkpointed (serialized and persisted to file); the transaction is "committed", acknowledged and the output messages are emitted. The algorithm of *execution()* is outlined in Fig. 4.

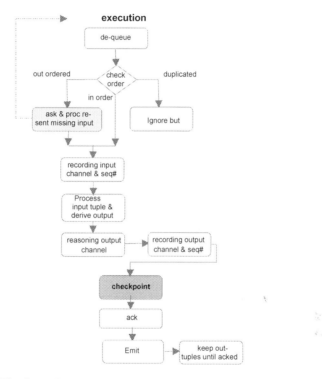

Fig. 4. Task execution with pessimistic checkpointing

Task Recovery. Supported by the underlying Storm platform, a failed task instance is re-initiated on an available machine node by loading the serialized operation class to the node and creating an instance over there.

As shown in Fig. 5, recovery a failed task is a triple-folds problem:

- restore its execution state from checkpoint,
- request the possible missing input, again and again until received
- re-emit the last output tuple; in case that tuple has not been lost, as a duplicate tuple it will be ignored by recipient tasks.

When the recovering task has multiple source tasks, it cannot determine where the missing tuple came from, therefore it has to ask each source task to resend the possible next tuple wrt the latest tuple it received and recorded in its input-map that is a part of

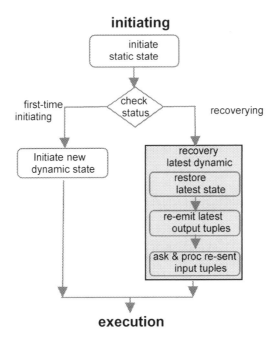

Fig. 5. Task initiate/recovery with pessimistic checkpointing

the checkpoint content. The resent tuples are processed first before the restored task entering the regular data processing loop. If a resent tuple has already transmitted to the input queue, then the queued tuple will be identified as duplicated and ignored.

Due to the disk access overhead of per-tuple checkpointing and the messaging overhead in acknowledging each tuple, the pessimistic protocol is inefficient in the failure-free case; even if incorporated with the backtrack recovery. As a result, it cannot satisfy the latency requirement for real-time stream processing. To make transactional stream processing a feasible and acceptable technique we need to explore another kind of checkpointing protocol – the *optimistic* checkpointing protocol.

4   Optimistic Checkpointing with Backtrack Recovery

4.1   Concept and Problem

In the modern computing environment, failures are infrequent and the overall performance is primarily contributed by the failure-free performance, which has motivated us to investigate the failure recovery mechanism based on *optimistic* checkpointing.

Unlike the pessimistic checkpointing mechanism with which the checkpointing is synchronized with the per-tuple processing, the optimistic checkpointing mechanism is characterized by checkpointing *occasionally* and *asynchronously* with the per-tuple processing. Under this mechanism, a task checkpoints once after processing multiple tuples, while still emits result tuple by tuple continuously. As a result, the failure-free performance can be significantly improved due to reduced disk access, and the real-time feature can be retained since the per-tuple processing is not blocked by checkpointing.

However, when a task is restored from a failure with its state being rolled back to the last checkpoint, the effects of processing multiple tuples would be lost and should be redone; for that the task would request its source tasks to resend multiple tuples emitted since then. These resent tuples are processed in advance, before the restored task goes to the regular per-tuple processing loop, towards the "*eventual consistency*" [3, 11].

It is worth noting the difference between optimistic checkpointing and batch processing. With optimistic checkpointing, although the output tuples of a task is checkpointed in batch, they are emitted tuple by tuple continuously in real-time stream processing.

The notion of optimistic checkpointing was previously studied in the context of general distributed systems where the instant consistency of globally state is of the primary concern [16, 19]. In that case rolling back a task may cause any other task to rollback until a consistent global state has been reached; if without a commonly observable and semantically meaningful synchronization point for "cutting off" rollback propagation, it may eventually lead to the domino effect – an uncontrolled propagation of task rollbacks.

The concept of synchronization point for rollback propagation can be explained by the following example. Assume a pair of source and target tasks T_A and T_B checkpoint their states/messages per 100 input tuples respectively, and out of one input tuple T_A derives 4 output tuples and sends them to T_B. As mentioned before a checkpoint state includes the information about input/output messages and computation results. Considering the following situation after T_A and T_B start running simultaneously:

(a) After T_B processed 100 input tuples received from T_A since T_B's last checkpoint, it persists its state into a new checkpoint p_b. By then, however, T_A only processed 25 input tuples since its last checkpoint, with the result not being checkpointed. In this case, we say that the checkpoint p_b is an **unstable checkpoint** since it is not supported by the checkpoint history of T_A.

(b) Assume that T_B failed after processing some tuples since point (a), it is restored and rolled back to p_b and tends to request T_A to re-send the missing tuples. In case T_A also failed and lost the un-checkpointed history of output tuples since its last checkpoint, T_A cannot identify the tuples requested by T_B.

(c) As a result, both T_A and T_B must further rollback to a possible common synchronized point. Such rollback propagation is uncontrolled; in the worst case, both tasks have to roll back to the very beginning.

It can be seen from the above example that in order to apply optimistic checkpointing to the failure recovery of stream processing, in addition to adopting the notion of "*eventual consistency*" [3, 11], it is necessary to provide a commonly observable and semantically meaningful synchronization point to avoid uncontrolled rollback propagation. We solve this problem by incorporating the concept of synchronization point with the window semantics of stream processing.

4.2   Window Semantics of Stream Processing

Although a data stream is unbounded, very often applications require those infinite data to be analyzed granularly. Particularly, when the stream operation involves the aggregation of multiple events, for semantic reason the input data must be punctuated into bounded chunks. This has motivated us to execute such operation *epoch by epoch* to process the stream data *chunk by chunk*, and this has given us the fitted framework for identify the synchronization points for optimistic checkpointing.

For example, if the stream contains time-series data with timestamps (e.g. per second), and an operation aims to deliver time-window (e.g. per minute) based aggregation, then the execution of this operation on an infinite stream is made in a sequence of *epochs*, one on each stream chunks falling in that time-window. In general, given an operator, O, over an infinite stream of relation tuples S with a criterion ϑ for cutting S into an unbounded sequence of chunks,

$$< S_0, S_1, \ldots, S_i \ldots >$$

where S_i denotes the *i-th* "chunk" of the stream according to the chunking-criterion ϑ. The semantics of applying O to the unbounded stream S lies in

$$O(S) \rightarrow < O(S_0), \ldots O(S_i), \ldots >$$

which continuously generates an unbounded sequence of results, one on each *chunk* of the stream data.

The *paces* of dataflow wrt timestamps can be different at different operators; for instance, an operation for hourly aggregation has a larger pace then the operation for per-minute aggregation.

Punctuating input stream into chunks based on a window-boundary is a template behavior common to many stream operations, thus we consider it as a kind of meta-property of stream operations and support it systematically. To handle window boundary in a task, a base unit, τ (e.g. 1 min or 1 tuple) is required, and the following three variables are defined:

- w_{delta}: the window size by τ, e.g. 1 min, or 100 tuples;
- $w_{current}$: the current window sequence number; e.g. 1 for the window of minute 1, 2 for the window of minute 2, ... etc.;
- $w_{ceiling}$: the starting sequence number of the next window by number of τ; e.g. 2 for the window of minute 2; 201 for the window of 200–300 tuples.

Then several functions are defined on each input tuple t to determine whether t is within or beyond the current window, e.g.

- $fw_{current}(t)$: returns the $w_{current}$; e.g. if t contains timestamp 100 (by second), the current window number (by minute) for t is 2.
- $fw_{next}(t)$: returns a boolean for detecting whether t belongs to the next window, and updates $w_{current}$ and $w_{ceiling}$ as appropriate.

4.3   Window-Based Checkpoint and Recovery

Aiming to support failure recovery by optimistic checkpointing, we incorporate the notion of synchronization point with the window semantics of stream processing, and propose the protocol of *Continued stream processing with Window-based Checkpoint* (**CWCR**), which allows a task to process data and emit results continuously on the per-tuple basis, but checkpoints state on the per-window basis.

With CWCR, the checkpointing is made once per-window (typically time-window) *asynchronously* with per-tuple execution. When a task T is re-established from a failure in a window boundary w, its last checkpointed state is restored; and the tuples T received from the beginning of w up to the most recent ones, from all input channels, are requested and resent to T. These resent tuples are processed in the recovery phase before T goes to the regular stream processing loop.

Compared with the pessimistic checkpointing approach, the benefit gained from CWCR consists in the enhanced overall performance by avoiding the overhead of per-tuple checkpointing in the absence of failures.

4.4   CWCR Synchronization Point

To describe CWCR more formally, let us denote a checkpoint of task T by S_T; denote the input *messageIds* (*mids*) and the output messages contained in S_T by μS_T and σS_T respectively; and denote the checkpoint history of T by ηS_T. Further, given a pair of source and target tasks A and B, the *messages* from A to B in σS_A and ηS_A are denoted by $\sigma S_{A \rightarrow B}$ and $\eta S_{A \rightarrow B}$ respectively; the input *mids* to B from A in μS_B and ηS_B are denoted by $\mu S_{B \leftarrow A}$ and $\eta S_{B \leftarrow A}$ respectively. Based on these notations we define the following concepts.

- **Checkpoint History:** the sequence of checkpoints of task T is referred to as T's checkpoint history.
- **Stable Checkpoint:** a checkpoint is *stable* if it can be reproduced from the checkpoint history of its upstream neighbors. More precisely, the checkpoint of task B. S_B, is *stable* wrt a source task A iff all the messages identified by $\mu S_{B \leftarrow A}$ are contained (denoted by $\propto$) in $\eta S_{A \rightarrow B}$, i.e.

$$\mu S_{B \rightarrow A} \propto \eta S_{A \rightarrow B}.$$

S_B is *stable* iff S_B is *stable* wrt all its source tasks.
- **Backtrack Recoverability:** given a pair of source and target tasks A and B, task B is backtrack recoverable from a failure wrt task A, if since B's last checkpoint, all the input tuples from A can be resent by A, even if in the case that A also fails.

  Then we compare the task recoverability wrt pessimistic and optimistic checkpointing.

Recoverability Rule with Pessimistic Checkpointing

With pessimistic checkpointing a task is backtrack recoverable if every input tuple is checkpointed by the corresponding source task *before emitting*.

A task with pessimistic checkpointing follows the above rule by first checkpointing and then emitting each output tuple, which ensures that the missing tuple during a failure can always be found and resent, even if the source task also fails. This is the strong criterion for recoverability.

With optimistic checkpointing, the above strong recoverability rule cannot be followed because the output tuples of a task are emitted continuously but checkpointed only occasionally; therefore we need to find a relaxed recoverability rule.

Intuitively, if task is reestablished from a failure and rolled back to its last checkpoint say p, to guarantee that the each missing tuple since p can be figured out and resent by the corresponding source task even if that source task also fails, p must be a stable checkpoint. This forms the basis of the following rule.

Recoverability Rule with Optimistic Checkpointing
With optimistic checkpointing a task B is backtrack recoverable iff B's checkpoints are stable, i.e. for each source task A of B, $\mu S_{B \leftarrow A} \alpha \eta S_{A \rightarrow B}$.

Ensure checkpoint stability is the key to avoid the domino effects in optimistic checkpoint based task recover. With CWCR we incorporate this with the window based chunking criterion. Specifically, for time series data, we provide a timestamp attribute for the stream tuples, and use a time window, such as per minute time window, as the basic checkpoint interval (although the concept of window is not limited to time window).

For example, given a pair of source and target tasks T_A and T_B, if the checkpoint interval of T_A is w_{delta} and that of T_B is $N \times w_{delta}$ where N is an integer, then the checkpoint of T_B is stable wrt T_A. For instance, if the checkpoint interval of T_A is per minute (60 s), and that of T_B is 1 min (60 s), 10 min (600 s) or 1 h (3600 s), then T_B's checkpoint is stable wrt T_A; otherwise if T_B's checkpoint interval is 90 s, it is not stable wrt to T_A, and in that case if T_B rollback to its latest checkpoint and requests T_A to resend the missing messages, there is no guarantee for T_A to identify and find them.

Based on these concepts we provide the algorithms for CWCR based failure recovery algorithms.

4.5 CWCR Algorithms

Overview. With the CWCR mechanism, a task, T, runs cycle by cycle to process stream data tuple by tuple. In each cycle before reaching a window boundary T takes an input tuple, records the *mid*, processes the tuple, records and emits the output tuples, but without checkpoint and acknowledgement. When a window boundary is reached, the task T checkpoints the current state, the latest seq# of all input channels, and all the output tuples as a *single checkpoint*; then T acknowledges each source task *only once* (per window) with the latest seq# in the corresponding input channel.

During failure recovery, a task T rolls back to the last checkpoint (at the end of the last window), then it sends *one message* to each source task, say T_s, asking for all the tuples T_s emitted to T since then in the current window boundary, then T_s would resend T these tuples in a single message through the *signal messaging hub* that is separate from the dataflow channel as explained above. In case T does not receive the resent tuple it would ask again, and again until receives. Then T will reprocess all the resent tuples first, before going to the regular stream processing cycles. Later the input tuples duplicated with the resent ones will be ignored.

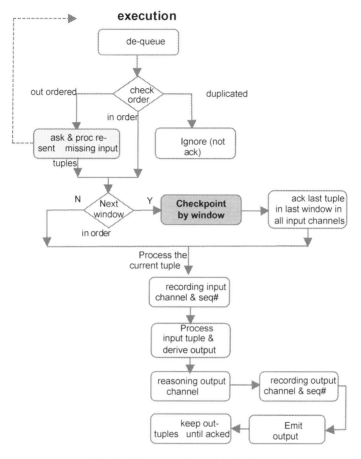

Fig. 6. Task execution with CWCR

A checkpoint contains information about

- the task-id, topology-id, number of tuples processed,
- the checkpoint window boundary - $w_{current}, w_{ceiling}$;
- the latest seq# of all input/output channels (kept in Maps M_i and M_o) from which the latest input/output *mids* in those channels can be derived),
- the current (final) computation state wrt the current window
- the output tuples emitted in the current window.

As mentioned above, a task, as an iteratively executed program for processing stream data tuple by tuple, is provided with two major methods: the **prepare()** method for instantiating the system facilities and the initial state, and the **execute()** for processing an input tuple in the main stream processing loop. Failure recovery, **recovery()**, is handled in *prepare()* since after a failed task restored it will experience the *prepare()* phase first. There exist other functions for interpreting the ACK for removing the pooled tuples no longer needed, and ASK for resending tuples.

Task Execution. The algorithm of **execute()** is illustrated in Fig. 6 with the following major steps.

- Resolve t's message id (mid), channel (c) and $seq\#$ (k_{curr}) of t, which may be virtual (described later) (*line 1*).
- Compare t's $seq\#$ (k_{curre}) and the expected $seq\#$ ($k_{last} + 1$); if t is duplicate (with smaller $seq\#$ than expected) it will not be processed again, i.e. ignored; if t is "jumped" (with $seq\#$ larger than expected), the missing tuples between the expected one and t will be requested, resent and processed first before moving to t (*line 2–8*).
- Update M_i with the current input channel and $seq\#$ (*line 9*).
- Given an input tuple t, $fw_{next}(t)$ is applied to check whether t falls into the next window boundary, and if true, the task T makes a single checkpoint for the state of the entire data processing in the current window, then T acknowledges each source task *only once* with the latest $seq\#$ in the corresponding input channel (*line 10–18*).
- Processing t and generating output tuples L_{out} (*line 19*).
- For each resulting tuple t_{out} in L_{out}, resolve its mid_{out} that may be virtual, embed mid_{out} in t_{out}, compose the carrying message m_{out}, and append m_{out} to the list of output messages L_{out_msg} (*line 21–26*).
- Emitting the output tuples (*line 27*).
- Pooling the output tuples (*line 28*), aiming to resend upon request. The pooled tuples will be removed upon acknowledgement on the per-channel basis where an ACK with $seq\#$ k causes the garbage collection of all the pooled tuples with $seq\# \le k$.
- Advance execution $cycle\#$ (*line 30*).

Algorithm 1. Task Execution (Tuple t)

```
1   extract mid, channel c, seq# k_curr from t
2   k_last ← get_seq (M_i, c);
3   if k_curr > k_last + 1 then
4       do_miss (c, k_last, k_curr);
5       k_last ← get_seq (M_i, c)
6   else if k_curr ≤ k_last then
7       return;
8   end if
9   put_seq(M_i, c, k_curr);
10  if (fw_next(t)) then
11      ck (S_ck)
12      ∀ c ∈ C_i do
13          mid_ack ← get_mid (c, M_i)
14          if mid_ack ≠ Ø then
15              ack (mid_ack);
16          end if
17      end do
18  end if
19  L_out ← processing(t);
20  if L_out ≠ Ø then
21      ∀t_out ∈ L_out do
22          mid_out ← getset_out_mid(M_o, t_out);
23          t_out ← embed (t_out, mid_out)
24          m_out ← compose (t_out, mid_out)
25          L_out_msg ← add (L_out_msg, m_out)
26      end do
27      emit_all(L_out_msg)
28      L_pool_msg ← append (L_pool_msg, L_out_msg)
29  end if
30  cycle++
```

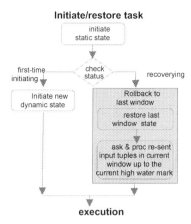

Fig. 7. Task recovery with CWCR handled in prepare()

Task Recovery. Supported by the underlying infrastructure, a failed task instance can be re-initiated on an available machine node by loading the serialized task class to the selected node and new an instance over there.

The algorithm of **recovery()**, as illustrated in Fig. 7, includes the following steps.

- The state S_{ck} of task T is restored from the checkpoint of last window (*line 1*).
- T sends one RESEND request to each source task in all the possible input channels C_i, asking for resending inputs starting from the first tuple (by *seq#*) of the current window; then T processes the resent tuples channel by channel sequentially before going to the normal execution loop (*line 2–10*).

In each source task, say T_s, upon receipt the above request, gets the latest, not yet emitted output seq#, t_h, and resends to T all the output tuples with seq# up to t_h *in a single message* from the dedicated signal messaging hub.

Algorithm 2. Task Recovery (ck_bytes)

1 $S_{ck} \leftarrow$ **restore**(ck_bytes)
2 $\forall c \in C_i$ **do**
3      $mid_{ask} \leftarrow$ **get**$_{mid}$ (c, M_i)
4   **if** $mid_{ask} \neq \emptyset$ **then**
5          $L_{resent} \leftarrow$ **ask_wait** (mid_{ask})
6          $\forall t \in L_{resent}$ **do**
7   **exec**(t)
8   **end do**
9   **end if**
10 **end do**

4.6   Failure in Failure

Recovering backwards chained failures is a recursive process, and we need a boundary condition – the event source S that feeds data stream to a streaming process topology, must be reliable, i.e. when requested, S can re-send the current tuple (wrt pessimistic checkpoint) or the tuples in the current window (wrt optimistic checkpoint) to the topology.

With pessimistic checkpointing, given a chained source and target tasks A and B, if B fails and restored, B would keep asking A to resent the last tuple; if A also fails, it will recover itself first, and after re-established it can always find and resend the requested tuple by B since any emitted tuple is checkpointed.

With optimistic checkpointing, the re-messaging in recovering single point failure and chained failures are different although the eventual results are consistent. Refer to Fig. 8, let us consider event source S and chained tasks A, B, C; in $window_1$ all the tasks processed 5 tuples, and in $window_2$ A processed input s_6, s_7, s_8 from S and output $a_6, a_7, a_8 \ldots$ etc. Assume task B fails after processing a_6, a_7, a_8 and emitting b_6, b_7, b_8, task B would ask A to resend the tuples in $window_2$ starting from a_6. In case A does not fail, A would resend them.

However, if task A also fails before resending, the following would happen.

- Task A must recover itself first by asking S to resend the tuples in $window_2$, eventually S re-emits s_6, s_7, s_8 to A for processing.
- As a result of A's recovery, A has already re-emitted a_6, a_7, a_8 to B through the regular data channel, which is recorded with A, but kept in B's in-queue without being processed before B receives and processes the resent tuples explicitly requested.
- Then in processing B's resend request, A would identify these already emitted tuples and resend them through the signal/resend channel. B will process the resent tuples and later ignored the previously re-emitted tuples.
- Since before B's failure, B might have emitted b_6, b_7, b_8 to task C, the same tuples emitted after failure recovery would be ignored by C.

Fig. 8. Recover chained failures

The above system behavior allows us to deal with failure-in-failure correctly. Since this situation is very rare, the overhead in additional messaging is insignificant.

In summary, compared with the pessimistic checkpointing based recovery approach, CWCR allows a task to checkpoint and acknowledge only once per window rather than on the per-tuple basis, but needs to process more resent tuples during failure recovery (although in each channel the resent tuples are carried by a single message), which constitute a beneficial performance trade-off in environments where failures are infrequent and failure-free performance is of primary concern. Further, under CWCR a task still emits output tuple by tuple continuously; therefore the latency requirement for real-time stream processing is retained. Since CWCR relies on window boundaries to synchronize the checkpoints of chained tasks to avoid the so called domino effects, therefore making the rollback propagation well controlled.

5   Tracking Message Channels Intelligently

5.1   The Messaging Channel Tracking Problem

In order to build a transaction layer on top of an existing parallel and distributed stream processing framework like Storm, rather than re-develop a new underlying framework from scratch, we have to solve some specific problems.

In a streaming process topology, a dataflow channel, or *messaging channel*, is identified by a pair of source and target tasks; a tuple is carried by a message and identified by the ***message-id*** (***mid***) composed with the channel and the corresponding sequence number. Supporting failure recovery based on checkpointing states and resending messages requires every task, when sending or receiving a message, to recognize the messaging channel; and specifically, to record the message-id ***before*** sending a message, in order to resend the right message to the right target task if the previously sent message is missing.

The challenge is, however, common to the modern component based distributed dataflow infrastructures, the data routing between tasks is handled by separate system components inaccessible to individual tasks. For example, in a Map-Reduce platform, passing a resulted tuple from a Map task, M_{task}, to a Reduce task, R_{task}, is handled by the platform but unknown to M_{task} before emitting. More generally, with a distributed stream processing infrastructure such as Storm, when a task emits an output tuple, the destination depends on the grouping type, the current system state or the data content, which is unknown to the task thus cannot be record by it *before* emitting, resulting the following ***messaging channel paradox***.

- If a task T failed after it emitted an output tuple t to a target task T_1, when T is restored, it would re-emit t anyway; however, under certain grouping criterion such as shuffle-grouping, the re-emitted tuple may go to a different target task, say T_2, since T_2 *never seen t*, it cannot determine whether t is duplicate and ignorable.
- If a task T failed and restored, the current input tuple may be missing, thus T, according to its records, would request each of its source tasks to resend its latest tuple; however, if a source task is unable to record its output channels *before emitting* every tuple, there is no way for it to know how to find the right tuple and resent it to the right target task.

Our solution to these problems is characterized by ***tracking the physical messaging channel logically*** by ***reasoning***; for that we introduce the notions of ***virtual channel***, ***task alias*** and ***messageId-set***, and use them in reasoning, tracking and communicating the channel information logically.

As mentioned previously, we ensure the regular order of data delivery not to be interrupted by the failure recovery process by providing a ***designated messaging hub*** that is separated from the regular dataflow channel, for signaling ACK/ASK and resending tuples.

5.2   Basic Notations

We first define the following notations.

- A topology-wise unique *task#* is assigned to each task by the underlying infrastructure.
- A *taskId* is composed by an *operationId* (name) and a *task#*, as *operationId.task#*; e.g. "`agg.2`" identifies a task of operation named "`agg`".
- A message *channel* is identified by the source and target *taskIds*, denoted by *srcTaskId^targetTaskId*; e.g. a message channel from task `tran.8` to `gemm.6` is expressed as `tran.8^gemm.6`.
- A *messageId*, or *mid*, is identified by a channel and the message sequence number, say *seq#*, via that channel, as *channel-seq#*, i.e. *srcTaskId^targetTaskId-seq#*; for instance, "`tran.8^gemm.6-134`" identifies the 134th tuple sent via the channel from "`tran.8`" to "`gemm.6`".

A tuple transmitted through a messaging channel is identified by the *messge-id* (or *mid*).

5.3   MessageId-Set and Virtual MessageId

We consider two kinds of "logical message identifiers", one for a set of recipients, another for a virtual recipient.

When an emitted tuple is delivered to multiple recipients through multiple message channels, we allow the tuple to be identified by a ***mid-set***. A *mid-set* contains multiple individual *mids* with the same source task but with different target tasks. On each recipient side, from the *mid-set* the target task picks up the *mid* with target taskId matching its own taskId, and records the corresponding input channel and seq#. This matched *mid* will be used for identifying both ACK and ASK messages. In the other words, *mid-sets* are recorded in the source task only with the output tuples to be sent; in the target task, only the matched single *mid* is recorded and used. A task identifies the buffered tuple matching the *mid* carried by an ACK or ASK message based on the set-membership relationship (as mentioned above, the tuple matches an ACK message will be garbage-collected, and the tuple matches an ASK message will be resent during failure recovery). A resent tuple is always identified by a single, matched *mid*.

Further we introduce the notions of ***task alias*** and ***virtual mid*** to resolve the destination of message sending with "fields-grouping", (or hash partition). In this case an output tuple only goes to one instance task of the given target operation which is determined by the routing component based on a unique number yield from the hash and modulo functions; the sending task has no knowledge about the physical desti-nation before emitting a tuple but can calculate that number, and can treat that number as the ***alias*** of the corresponding target task ID, and use the *alias* as the target task to create a ***virtual mid***. A virtual mid is directly recorded and used in both the sending and receiving tasks.

Below we illustrate how to use these notions to resolve the messaging channels wrt the typical grouping types.

All-Grouping. With "all-grouping", a tuple emitted by a task, e.g. gemm.6, is distributed to all tasks of the recipient operation (e.g. ana.11, ana.12), since there is only one emitted tuple but multiple physical output channels, we use ***mid-set*** to identify the emitted tuple. For instance, a tuple sent from gemm.6 to ana.11 and ana.12 is identified by

{gemm.6^ana.11-96, gemm.6^ana.12-96}

On the sender site (e.g. gemm.6), this *mid-set* is recorded and checkpointed; in each recipient task (e.g. ana.11) only the ***single mid*** matching itself (e.g. gemm.6^ana.11-96) will be extracted, recorded and used in ACK and in ASK messages. In the sender task (e.g. gemm.6) the match of an ACK or ASK message identified by a single *mid*, and a kept tuple identified by a *mid-set,* is determined by set membership. For example, the ACK or ASK message with *mid* gemm.6^ana.11-96 or gemm.6^ana.12-96 *matches* the tuple identified by {gemm.6^ana.11-96, gemm.6^ana.12-96}.

Fields-Grouping. With "fields-grouping", the tuples output from the source task are hash-partitioned to multiple target tasks, with one tuple going to one destination task; this is similar to have the Map results sent to the Reduce nodes. With the underlying streaming platform (common to most other platforms), the target task ID is mapped from the hash partition index, ***a***, calculated based on the selected key fields list, *keyList*, over the number of k tasks of the target operation, as

$$a = keyList.hashcode() \% k$$

On the source task, although it is impossible to figure out the physical target task and record the physical *mid* before emitting a tuple, it is possible to compute the above hash partition index, and use it as the ***task alias*** for identifying the target task. A task alias is denoted by

operationName.***a***@

such as *gemm.1@*, where ***a*** is the hash partition index.

In the example topology shown in Fig. 1, the output tuples of task "trans.9" to tasks "gemm.6" and "gemm.7" are under "fields-grouping" with 2 hash-partitioned index values 0 and 1, these values, 0 and 1, are used to create aliases of the recipient tasks. Then the target tasks "gemm.6" and "gemm.7" can be represented by aliases "gemm.0@" and "gemm.1@" without ambiguity. Although the task alias (gemm.1@) is different from the real target *taskId* (gemm.6), it is unique and all tuples sent to gemm.6 will bear the same *target task alias* under the given field-grouping.

Then an output tuple, say, from task *trans.9* to *gemm.6* under "fields-grouping" is identified by the ***virtual mid*** where the target taskId *gemm.6* is replaced the alias "gemm.1@"

trans.9^gemm.1@-35

A *virtual mid*, such as trans.9^gemm.1@-2, is directly recorded at both source and target tasks and used in both ACK and ASK messages. There is no need to resolve the mapping between a task-alias and its actual task-Id.

In case an operation has two or more target operations, such as in the above example, the operation "trans" has 2 target operations, "*gemm*" and "*trmm*", an output tuple can be identified by a *mid-set* containing *virtual-mids*; for instance, an output tuple from task "trans.9" is identified by the following *mid-set*

{trans.9^trmm.0@-30, trans.9^gemm.1@-35}

Indicating that the tuple is the 30th tuple sent from "trans.9" to a *trmm* task, and the 35th a *gemm* task. The recipient task with the recorded alias trmm.0@, can extract the matched *virtual-mid* trans.9^trmm.0@-30 based on the *match of operation name* "trmm", for recording the seq# 30 for that virtual channel.

Global-Grouping. With global-grouping, tuples emitted from a source task are routed to the same instance task of the target operation; and the selection of the recipient task is made by a separate routing component outside of the source task. Our goal is for the source task to record the messaging channel before each tuple is emitted. For this purpose we do not need to know what the exact task is, but create a single *alias* to represent the recipient task. In this case, all tuples go to the same recipient task that is represented by the same alias; the latest seq# is recoded on both the sender and receiving sides.

Direct-Grouping. With direct grouping, a tuple is emitted using the emitDirect API with the physical *taskId* (more exactly, task#) as one of the parameter. For channel specific recovery we extend the Topology Builder to turn all other grouping types to direct grouping where for each emitted tuple, the destination task is selected on-the-fly based on load balancing, i.e. the one currently with least load (i.e. least seq#) is chosen.

Shuffle-Grouping. Shuffle grouping is a popular grouping type. As mentioned above it is converted to direct grouping where a tuple is emitted to a designated task selected based on load balancing, i.e. the channel with least seq# is selected.

In summary, the combination of *mid-set* and *virtual mid* allows us to track the messaging channels of a task with multiple grouping criteria: for "all-grouping" the concept of *mid-set* is adopted; for "fields-grouping", *task-alias* and *virtual-mid* are used. We support "direct-grouping" systematically (rather than letting user to decide) based on load-balancing. Further we convert all other grouping types, which are random by nature, to our system-supported direct grouping.

5.4   System Support for Channel Tracking

For guiding channel resolution, we extract the topology information from the streaming process definition, and create the task specific meta-data objects: Task-Input-Context, *TIC*, and Task-Output-Context, *TOC*, for specifying input and output channels, grouping types, etc. Multiple *TIC* and *TOC* objects are associated with a task.

A task, T, has a list of TIC objects; with each specifying the input context of one source task of T; it comprises the following:

- task ID of source task T_s, that is the key field of TIC;
- operation ID (name) of source operation O_s, of that Ts is an instance;

- grouping type (shuffle, field, ... etc.);
- channel;
- stream ID (abstract dataflow between the source operation O_s, and the operation of this task);

A task, T, has a list of TOC objects; with each specifying the output context of one target operation (with one or more target task instances) of T; it comprises the following:

- operation ID (name) of target operation, O_t, that is the key field of TOC;
- grouping type (shuffle, field, ... etc.);
- key indices (int []) indicating the key fields of output tuples for hash partitioning in the field-grouping case;
- channel list comprising the channels from this task to all the tasks of the target operation, O_t.
- stream ID (abstract dataflow between the operation of this task and the target operation O_t.

While the TIC list and the TOC list provide static grouping information, the actual input and output < channel, seq# > are recorded in the HashMaps, inChannelBook and outChannelBook, of each task. Note that the seq# is the latest (largest) sequence number.

Tracking Output Channel in Sending Task. A single tuple emitted from a task may go to one or more target tasks. Using TOC, these target messaging channels can be traced operation by operation. The messaging channels and seq#s are represented with either actual or virtual, either single or set, mids, and recorded in the outChannelBook of the task.

For re-sending a tuple upon request (through a separate messaging channel) the task selects the buffered tuple with the tuple's *mid* matching the requested *mid*, or the tuple's *mid-set* containing the requested *mid*; but resend the tuple with the single, logically matched *mid*.

Tracking Input Channel in Recipient Task. When an input tuple is received, its *mid* or *mid-set* is extracted and an individual *mid* (possibly virtual) that logically matches the recipient task is singled out, that single *mid* is recorded in the inChannelBook, and used in ACK and ASK messages.

During failure-recovery, the restored task, T, would ask each source task to resend the possible next tuple wrt the latest one recorded in T's inputChannelBook, thus need to compose a *mid* for the requested tuple guided by its *TIC* and inChannelBook.

6 Experiments

We have built the *Fontainebleau* platform and provided the failure recovery capability described in the previous sections. In this section we briefly overview our experimental results. Our testing environment include 4 Linux servers with gcc version 4.1.2 20080704 (Red Hat 4.1.2–50), 32G RAM, 400G disk and 8 Quad-Core AMD Opteron Processor 2354 (2200.082 MHz, 512 KB cache). One server holds the coordinator daemon, others hold workers daemons, each worker supervises several worker processes, and each worker process handles one or more tasks. The experiments are designed on the streaming process example shown in Fig. 1 with simulated data stream. However, in these experiments we focus on the performance of one task in the streaming process topology, because our goal is to check the *latency ratios* of (a) checkpointing versus non-checkpointing, (b) ASK-based versus ACK-based recovery, and (c) optimistic versus pessimistic checkpointing. In these cases the overall performance of multiple parallel tasks with overlapping disk-writes, etc., cannot give clear measures for the above ratios.

In the streaming process example shown in Fig. 1, the heaviest computation is conducted by tasks of operations "*gemm*" and "*trmm*" which are similar so let us focus on "*gemm*". It is the abbreviation for "General Matrix Multiply (GEMM)", a subroutine in the Basic Linear Algebra Subprograms (BLAS) that calculates the new value of matrix *C* based on the matrix-product of matrices *A* and *B*, and the old value of matrix *C*, as

C = alpha*AB + beta*C

where *alpha* and *beta* are scalar coefficients. GEMM is often tuned by High Performance Computing (HPC) vendors to run as fast as possible, because it is the building block for so many other routines. It is also the most important routine in the LINPACK benchmark. For this reason, implementations of fast BLAS library typically focus on GEMM performance first. Our experiment results presented in this section is based on the *gemm* task.

6.1   Latency Overhead of Checkpointing

Let us first exam the impact of checkpointing to the performance of the streaming process involving GEMM operations. For this reason we focus on the performance ratio with and without checkpointing, particularly the turning point on the size of input matrices where checkpointing shows significant impact to the performance before it, and insignificant impact after it. As in the tuple by tuple stream processing the overall latency is nearly proportional to the number of input tuples, and we measure the performance ratio with and without checkpointing, the impact of the number of input tuples, say from 1 K to 1 M, is not significant.

In our testing, each original input tuple has 3 two-dimensional N × N matrices of float values, and we measure the above ratio wrt N. Our results shown in Fig. 9 indicate that when the matrix dimension size N is smaller than 600, checkpointing has visible impact to the latency of the stream processing; after the matrix dimension size N overpasses 600, that impact becomes insignificant, since in that case the latency is dominated by the computation complexity.

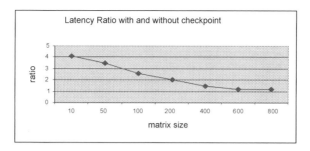

Fig. 9. Latency ration with and without checkpoint

6.2 ASK Versus ACK Based Recovery (Pessimistic)

In this experiment we compared the performance of the ASK-based transactional stream processing with the ACK based one, under pessimistic checkpointing. In our testing, the failure rate is set to 0.1 %. The matrix dimension size is fixed to 20. We measure the latency of a "*gemm*" task wrt its input tuples (a partition of tuples input to all "*gemm*" tasks) ranging from 1000 to 10000.

With the ACK based approach, a task does not move on to emit the next tuple until the success of processing the current tuple has been confirmed by the ACKs from all target tasks; otherwise the tuple will be re-sent after timeout. Such latency overhead is incurred during processing each tuple. However, under the proposed ASK based approach, a task does not wait for the acknowledgement to move forward as the acknowledgement is handled asynchronously to the task execution. In this case the corresponding latency overhead is only incurred during failure recovery which is rare. As a result, the ASK based approach can effectively improve the overall performance. Our comparison result shown in Fig. 10 has verified this observation.

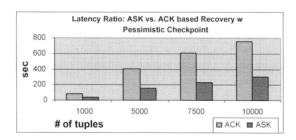

Fig. 10. Performance comparison of ASK and ACK based recovery mechanisms with pessimistic checkpointing

6.3 Optimistic Versus Pessimistic Checkpointing

In this experiment we compare the performance of optimistic and pessimistic check-pointing with the backtrack-based failure recovery mechanism. In our testing, the tuples are timestamped by seconds and the window boundary is set to 1 min with each containing approximately 100 tuples except the last window that contains less tuples;

the matrix dimension size is fixed to 20; and the failure rate is set to 0.1 %. The latency is measured on one "*gemm*" task with the input tuples (a partition of tuples input to all "*gemm*" tasks) ranging from 1000 to 10000. With pessimistic checkpointing, the output tuples must be persisted and acknowledged one by one (although asynchronous with execution), which incurs the performance penalty from both disk access and message delivery. With optimistic checkpointing, a task checkpoints, and is acknowledged, only once per window. Although the latency overhead incurred during failure recovery is higher, failures are rare thus the overall performance can be significantly enhanced. Our comparison result shown in Fig. 11 has verified this observation.

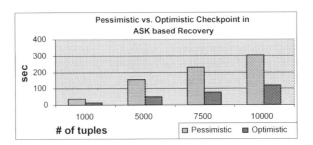

Fig. 11. Performance comparison of optimistic and pessimistic chepointing based recovery mechanisms

The performance comparison of optimistic and pessimistic checkpointing strongly depends on the computation complexity. The "*gemm*" tasks in our testing stream processing topology are computation-heavy compared with many event processing tasks thus the computation time contributes to a big portion of the elapse time, and the performance gain with the optimistic checkpoint mechanism is not very sharp. When the tasks are computation-lighter and the disk access cost for checkpoining is more dominated, the benefit of optimistic checkpointing becomes tremendous.

7   Conclusions

Fault-tolerance is the key requirement for applying stream processing to industry-scale and mission-critical applications; however the overhead for supporting fault-tolerance must be minimized to accommodate real-time analytics. This issue has been studied from various angles. The snapshot isolation model studied in the context of database transaction cares about stepwise state consistency but not failure recovery; the instant consistency of global state studied in the context of general distributed computing is too rigid for stream processing that is essentially based on eventual consistency. The checkpoint based failure handling is generally based on *pessimistic checkpoining* and *forward tracking*, i.e. a task checkpoints every output tuple before emitting, and waits for acknowledgement before rolling forward to emit the next one. The latency incurred by those approaches is too high to deal with real-time stream processing.

In this work we have taken an initial step to make transactional stream processing feasible to real-time stream processing. We integrated the *optimistic checkpointing* mechanism with the *backtrack-based failure recovery* mechanism for the combined benefits. With the proposed *Continued stream processing with Window-based Checkpoint and Recovery* (CWCR) approach, we allow a task to checkpoint and acknowledge only once per window but continuously emit tuples in real-time stream processing. We also incorporated the inter-tasks checkpoint synchronization with the window semantics of stream processing, to eliminate the possibility of uncontrolled rollbacks. To implement these mechanisms on top of an existing stream processing platform where message routing is handled by separate system components inaccessible to individual tasks, we track physical messaging channels logically with the notions of *virtual channel*, *task alias* and *messageId-set*. To ensure the regular order of data flows not to be interrupted by the failure recovery process, we provided a task with the *designated messaging hub*, separated from the regular dataflow channel, for signaling ACK/ASK messages and for resending tuples,

We have implemented these mechanisms on *Fontainebleau*, the distributed stream analytics infrastructure we develop by extending the open sourced Storm platform. Our experiment results reveal the novelty of the proposed technologies, and most significantly, the feasibility to support fault-tolerance with minimized overhead for real-time stream processing.

References

1. Arasu, A., Babu, S., Widom, J.: The CQL continuous query language: semantic foundations and query execution. VLDB J **15**(2), 121–142 (2006)
2. Abadi, D.J., et al.: The design of the Borealis stream processing engine. In: CIDR (2005)
3. Balazinska, M., Balakrishnan, H., Madden, S., Stonebraker, M.: Fault-Tolerance in the Borealis distributed stream processing system. In: SIGMOD 2005 (2005)
4. Botan, I., Fischer, P.M., Kossmann, D., Tatbu, N.: Transactional stream processing. In: EDBT 2012 (2012)
5. Johnson, D.B., Zwaenepoel, W.: Recovery in distributed systems using optimistic message logging and checkpointing. J. Algorithms **11**, 462–491 (1990)
6. Chen, Q., Hsu, M., Zeller, H.: Experience in continuous analytics as a service. In: EDBT 2011 (2011)
7. Chen, Q., Hsu, M.: Experience in extending query engine for continuous analytics. In: Bach Pedersen, T., Mohania, M.K., Tjoa, A.M. (eds.) DAWAK 2010. LNCS, vol. 6263, pp. 190–202. Springer, Heidelberg (2010)
8. Chen, Q., Hsu, M.: Query engine net for streaming analytics. In: Proceedings of 19th International Conference on Cooperative Information Systems (CoopIS) (2011)
9. DeWitt, D.J., Paulson, E., Robinson, E., Naughton, J., Royalty, J., Shankar, S., Krioukov, A.: Clustera: an integrated computation and data management system. In: VLDB 2008 (2008)
10. Franklin, M.J., et al.: Continuous analytics: rethinking query processing in a network-effect world. In: CIDR 2009 (2009)
11. Gedik, B., Andrade, H., Wu, K.-L., Yu, P.S., Doo, M.C.: SPADE: the system S declarative stream processing engine. In: ACM SIGMOD 2008 (2008)
12. Hwang, J.-H., Balazinska, M., et al.: High-availability algorithms for distributed stream processing. In: Proceedings of ICDE 2005, Washington, DC, USA (2005)

13. Johnson, D.B., Zwaenepoel, W.: Recovery in distributed systems using optimistic message logging and checkpointing. J. Algorithms **11**, 462–491 (1990)
14. Li, J., Karp, A.: Access control for the services oriented architecture. In: ACM Workshop on Secure Web Services (2007)
15. Shah, M.A., Hellerstein, J.M., Brewer, E.: Highly available, fault-tolerant, parallel datafows. In: Proceedings of SIGMOD, New York, USA (2004)
16. Prasad Sistla, A., Welch, J.L.: Efficient distributed recovery using message logging. In: Proceedings of the Eighth Annual ACM Symposium on Principles of Distributed Computing (1989)
17. Stiegler, M., Li, J., Kambatla, K., Karp, A.: Clusterken: A Reliable Object-Based Messaging Framework to Support Data Center Processing, HPL-2011-44 (2011)
18. Tweeter, Transactional topologies (2012). https://github.com/nathanmarz/storm/wiki/Transactional-topologies
19. Wang, Y.M., Fuchs, W.K.: Optimistic message logging for independent checkpointing in message-passing systems. In: IEEE Symposium on Reliable Distribution System, pp. 147–154 (1992)

LinkViews: An Integration Framework for Relational and Stream Systems

Yannis Sotiropoulos and Damianos Chatziantoniou[(✉)]

Department of Management Science and Technology,
Athens University of Economics and Business, Athens, Greece
{yannis,damianos}@aueb.gr

Abstract. Applications of stream data can be found in a wide variety of domains and settings, such as supply chain (RFID sensors), energy management (smart meters), social networks (status updates) and many others. While data stream management systems (DSMS) are technologically mature, they lack standardization in terms of modeling, querying and interoperability. In addition, so far, stream processing was confined within an organization. However, modern applications need to integrate and manage aggregates produced by a variety of stream engines, from complete DSMS to stand-alone stream-handling components. In this paper we discuss a relational-based framework that mix RDBMS' data and stream aggregates managed by different stream systems, a largely uninvestigated research area. We claim that this framework: (a) is transparent to naive database users, (b) addresses an important and useful class of queries, overlooked so far, (c) presents numerous optimization opportunities to minimize communication and processing costs, and (d) can serve as a standard for relational-stream interoperability.

Keywords: Data streams · Relational databases · Integration

1 Introduction

Many practical applications [8] need to process continuous flows of data in real-time. Well-known stream applications involve sensor networks, RFID product tracking, network and environmental monitoring, smart grids and others. In the era of Big Data, a wide range of analytics applications need to combine persistent and stream data in a simple and efficient way. For example, situational awareness [9] is a term used to describe the capability of an organization to become aware of what is happening in its immediate business environment and how internal or external events affect organization's daily operations. Situational aware applications require the collection of information from multiple data stream sources. This stream data must be combined with persistent data for analytic purposes.

The need for processing different types of data has led to the development of multiple and diverse systems. In the case of data streams, processing can be carried out by generic stream engines, standalone stream-handling components or custom stream applications. In the case of persistent data, relational technology has proven itself for reliably managing data for many decades now. In addition, SQL is a standard language

© Springer-Verlag Berlin Heidelberg 2015
M. Castellanos et al. (Eds.): BIRTE 2013 and 2014, LNBIP 206, pp. 65–80, 2015.
DOI: 10.1007/978-3-662-46839-5_5

for querying data with a wide acceptance from the IT industry and with a large base of knowledgeable users and resources. As a result, relational databases have a large market share and will continue to be used extensively, according to our view. As stream data will become more available and common, it will be important for database users to easily integrate it within the schema and transparently use it in their queries. However, there is no standard query language for streams [14] and as a result each stream system has its own features and specifications. This issue creates a three-fold problem for database users: First, they must learn a new system from scratch if they want to process and query stream data. Second, they must find a way to combine relational and stream data. Third, they need a query language to query integrated data.

In this paper we propose a view layer defined over standard relational systems to handle this mismatch. DBAs define a special type of views (called LinkViews) which combine relational data and stream aggregates. The columns of a LinkView are either columns of the relational schema (called *base* columns) or "placeholders" to be filled-in with stream values whenever necessary (called *linked* columns). A linked column L must be functionally dependent on one or more base column(s) B. As far as naive SQL users are concerned, a LinkView can be part of an SQL statement as any other relational view. We define a Key-Value interface between relational and stream systems and an API is proposed for the exchange of data (send keys, retrieve values). Our API follows a web-like approach where a web server executes programs/scripts using the parameters that receives from clients (web forms). Parameters in our case are distinct values (keys) found in the base columns of a LinkView. This is the common case in most operational business environments, as most of the time the analytic queries that utilize stream data use an identifying "persistent" value such as a tag ID, a location ID, a stock ID, or something else that is usually stored in a traditional database. Our goal is to create a framework that allows database users to be completely unaware of the implementation details and inner workings of stream systems but be able to use stream aggregates (i.e. the results of stream queries) in their relational analysis.

The paper is organized as follows: Sect. 2 provides motivating examples for the rest of the paper and presents the contributions of our work. Proposed SQL extensions to define LinkViews are given in Sect. 3. Section 4 presents the architecture of our framework and the primitives of the proposed API. Implementation details and experimental results are depicted in Sect. 5. Related work is discussed in Sect. 6. Finally, Sect. 7 summarizes our findings and describes future and ongoing work.

2   Motivation

A financial firm maintains in a relational system historical data on stock performance (opening and closing prices, variations, volumes, etc.) At the same time, it has access to two systems (e.g. Reuters and Bloomberg), lets call them A and B, that provide real-time information on stock prices and volumes respectively. These systems A and B could be anything, for example a SQL-based DSMS such as STREAM [2] or a Java-based component using sockets. Analysts would like to utilize in their relational queries real-time data (e.g. the running average price per stock) in a stream-transparent way, i.e. without knowledge either of the presence of stream systems or the continuous nature of the stream data. For example, to find the stocks with a previous day's closing price that is greater than their current running average price, one would like to write a SQL query similar to the following:

```
select stockID
from Historical H, Prices P
where H.stockID = P.stockID AND
      H.closingPrice > P.price AND
      H.date = date() - 1;
```

Historical is a relation containing historical data for the stocks and Prices is a relation with schema (stockID, price), where price is the running average price of the stockID. Whenever Prices is used within a query, price column is updated with the current value. While the transient nature of column price does not comply with the relational model, the "evaluate-whenever-used" approach is reminiscent of relational views, which are evaluated whenever used within a query. Let us now make Prices a little bit richer in information, by adding a couple more of these transient columns. The new schema would be:

```
Prices (stockID, price, price10, volume)
```

where price is the running average price, price10 is the average price of a 10-minute sliding window and volume is the running total volume of the stockID. While column stockID is a column found in the relational schema, columns price, price10 and volume do not involve relational data and represent aggregate values over stream data found in systems A and B. Figure 1 depicts the idea.

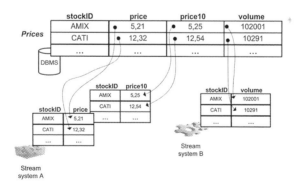

Fig. 1. Prices view and abstract representation of the linkage with stream systems

This figure suggests that the stream structures are handled by the stream systems, while the relational system has access to these structures through a *handler*, which returns a single value to be placed into the column. While this concept is simple and quite common in interoperability and collaborative systems, we must address who provides the definition of these stream structures, the DBA or the stream programmer (stream system expert)? In the first case (DBA), this definition should be part of the SQL defining statement of the LinkView and all stream systems should adhere to, i.e. be able to map to their own native language. The drawbacks of this approach are: (a) the case-specific stream processing that applications frequently require (e.g. different window types, peculiar pattern matching, exception handling), (b) complexities involved in mapping to specific systems and languages, and (c) acceptance of the proposed SQL syntax from the stream systems community. In addition, the DBA should be aware of the stream schema, something that is not always possible. Moreover, stream sources can change dynamically and as a result the declared views may become invalid. This tight coupling between DBMSs and stream systems makes view composition and evaluation hard. In the latter case, stream programmers define the required stream structures through programs written in the native language of their system. For example, if system A is STREAM, a CQL (Continuous Query Language) [3] statement should be issued to compute the running and window-based average prices. These programs should be able to have access to a set of input keys, supplied by the DBMS. In Fig. 1 we see that the stream structures of systems A and B are aware of the stockID keys, sent by the DBMS. Symmetrically, the DBA should be aware of the name of the programs that implements these stream structures, so s/he uses them in the SQL definition of the LinkView. A web-like paradigm, where the application logic programmer provides a program P to HTML form authors – who are completely unaware of how P manipulates form parameters – becomes very suitable. DBAs are informed by stream programmers of the name of the program(s) that handle stream structures. When a LinkView is *initiated*, these programs execute, receiving the distinct values of the appropriate base columns as input (the keys). Each program maintains a stream structure and computes an aggregate value for each input key. For example, Prices view in this case could be defined as:

```
create view Prices as
select  stockID
from    stocks
using   stockID
   exec program A.P₁() for price
   exec program A.P₂() for price10
   exec program B.P₃() for volume
```

P1(), P2() and P3() are programs written by stream programmers of systems A and B implementing stream structures. The using keyword defines the base column (stockID) whose values will be used as input to programs P1, P2, and P3: each program matches the input keys with values (stream aggregates), in a key-value structure, which then becomes a new column (*a linked column*) (price, price10, volume) in the view through an outer join on the base column (stockID). These key-value structures correspond to the stream structures mentioned above. Note that DBAs must only know the program names to define the view (in the previous approach DBAs needed to know the actual stream schemas). All these operations must be carried out through a well-designed API between the DBMS and stream systems.

2.1   LinkViews and SQL Query Examples

Example 2.1: Using LinkViews in SQL Queries: The motivation example uses the `Prices` view as shown in Fig. 1. We repeat `Prices` here.

LV1. `Prices(stockID, price, price10, volume)`

`price` and `price10` are computed from stream system A, while `volume` from stream system B. An example SQL query using LV1 is:

Q1. Find stocks with a previous day's closing price that is greater than their current running average price

Example 2.2: Stream Programs with Parameters: For example, instead of having two programs for columns `price` and `price10`, one can write a program that gets as parameter the sliding window size (in minutes), with size = 0 meaning a running average. In this case, there will be two execution instances of the same program. In both cases `Prices` schema is the same, but the LinkView definition is different.

LV2. `Prices2(stockID, price, price10, volume)`

Stream programs with parameters can be used for a wide range of tasks (provide filtering conditions, thresholds, window sizes, select which aggregate to output, etc.).

Example 2.3: Querying LinkView's Stream Columns: We assume the following view:

LV3. `MinMaxPriceCategory(categoryID, minPrice, maxPrice)`

Stocks belong to several categories, identified by a `categoryID`. For each category, `minPrice` (`maxPrice`) is the current minimum (maximum) price of the category's stocks. Both aggregates are computed by a single program in a stream system. Some SQL examples using LV3 are:

Q2. Find the `categoryIDs` having `minPrice` greater than 10

Q3. Show the `categoryIDs` and the `maxPrice` for categories that have `minPrice` above 10 and `maxPrice` below 12

2.2   Contributions

Our work contributes to a rather uninvestigated research area that deals with the integration of relational systems with heterogeneous stream systems [18]. The goal is to *standardize* the way a relational system interacts with several stream systems. Specifically, the main contributions of this work are:

- **Address an Overlooked Class of Queries.** Discuss a class of queries that hasn't been properly addressed in the past: ad hoc queries (no continuous semantics) using stream data in a database-oriented (pull) fashion.
- **LinkViews and Linked Columns.** We propose a new kind of view, called Link-View, where some columns are materialized with relational data and some columns are populated by external systems through a well-defined and efficient API. Link-Views can be implemented on top of any relational database system. Finally, end users can use LinkViews in their SQL statements as any other view.

- **Key-Value-Based Interfaces and Web-Like Protocol.** By introducing a key-value interface between DBMS and stream systems, we adequately handle scalability and efficiency issues. In addition, some query processing can be delegated to the key-value stores (e.g. pushing selections or even joins). By allowing LinkViews to specify stream programs to execute at the stream system's side, we offer a clean distinction between DBAs, naïve database users, and stream programmers. An approach similar to HTTP request and response protocol, but with the concept of sending keys and getting values is provided.
- **Prototyping.** We have built a prototype system over PostgreSQL, integrating with C/C++ programs managing synthetic stream data, to serve as a proof of concept.

3   Syntax and Examples

We propose the following extension of SQL syntax to facilitate LinkView definitions in relational systems:

```
create linkview name as
SQL statement
[using BaseCol link with P(c₁, …, cₘ) of S
      add column L₁ as (data-type) A₁
      ...
      add column Lₙ as (data-type) Aₙ
]+
```

A create linkview statement creates a LinkView database object. It consists of a standard SQL statement, which defines a materialized view, followed by one or more using statements. A using statement is used to define one or more linked columns, A_1, …, A_n, associated to *BaseCol* – an arbitrary subset of the schema of the materialized view – and sharing the same execution $P(c_1,..., c_m)$ at stream management entity S. A program P may produce several named output values per key, for efficiency and/or reusability reasons. For example, P may be a CQL [3] statement, computing the min, max and average price of a sliding window of size 10 for each stockID. It would be inefficient to have three distinct programs to separately compute min, max and average. For this reason the output values of P are named with labels L_1, …, L_n and correspond to A_1, …, A_n. Note that the LinkView author has to specify the datatype of the linked columns, since this information can not be retrieved by the stream system as semantics are completely transparent to database users. We provide below the syntactic definition of the LinkViews presented in Sect. 2.1:

Example 3.1: The definition of LV1 is:

```
create linkview Prices as
select stockID
from stocks
using stockID link with pPrice() of A
  add column priceL as (real)price
using stockID link with pPrice10() of A
  add column price10L as (real)price10
using stockID link with pVol() of B
  add column volumeL as (int)volume
```

LinkView LV1 uses two stream management systems named A and B. The actual connection information (e.g. network address/port) for each system is stored on LinkViews' metadata catalog. Stream system A can invoke executions of programs `pPrice()` and `pPrice10()`. `pPrice()` computes the running average price for each stock. `pPrice10()` computes the average price within a 10-minute sliding window for each stock. System B implements `pVol()` program that computes the running total volume for each stock. The DBMS can use programs' output by referring to the named outputs (labels) of each program. The label for `pPrice()` program is `priceL`, the label for `pPrice10()` program is `price10L` and the label for `pVol ()` program is volumeL. `price`, `price10` and `volume` are respectively the names of the linked columns corresponding to these outputs. The data type of each linked column is mentioned right before its name, using parentheses in the `add column` statements.

Example 3.2: The definition of LV2 is:

```
create linkview Prices2 as
select stockID
from stocks
using stockID link with pPriceV(0) of A
  add column priceL as (real)price
using stockID link with pPriceV(10) of A
  add column priceL as (real)price10
using stockID link with pVol() of B
  add column volumeL as (int)volume
```

In this case, stream system A has access to a *parameterized* program named `pPriceV(int size)`, where size denotes the size of the sliding window (size = 0 means a running average.) `pPriceV(0)` computes the running average price per stock and `pPriceV(10)` the running average price per stock within a 10-minute sliding window. `pVol()` is the same as in LV1. Note that parameterized executions allow for a wide range of options in terms of functionality. The parameters can have complex semantics, but a large number of stream applications can be supported with the use of simple parameters. For example such parameters may involve simple filtering conditions and threshold values that are easily understandable by LinkView writers.

Example 3.3: The definition of LV3 is:

```
create linkview MinMaxPriceCategory as
select categoryID
from categories
using categoryID link with pMinMax() of A
  add column min_priceL as (real)minPrice
  add column max_priceL as (real)maxPrice
```

`MinMaxPriceCategory` LinkView uses `pMinMax()` program of stream system A. `pMinMax()` computes two stream aggregates – the minimum and maximum price per category – and provides its results through two labeled outputs, `min_priceL` and `max_priceL`.

4 Architecture

The proposed architecture to support the LinkView integration framework is shown in Fig. 2.

The LinkView SQL (LV-SQL) Parser is responsible to parse out queries submitted by the users. A query can be either a LinkView definition, submitted by a user with administration privileges (e.g. DBA), or a standard SQL query, submitted by a naïve user. In the first case, the parsed query is passed to the LinkView Definition Interpreter (LDI) subcomponent. In the latter case, if the SQL statement involves LinkViews is directed to the Optimization Engine (OE), otherwise is directed to the database system's SQL component. LV-SQL also includes LinkViews management statements (e.g. init, cache policies) which are passed to the Commands Manager Module (COM).

The LinkView Manager is the core component of our architecture. It stores metadata for LinkViews and implements the API for DBMS/Stream systems communication. The Execution Engine (EE) of LVM is responsible for the execution of SQL queries involving LinkViews issued by naïve users. The Cache Manager (CM) is responsible for storing/caching linked columns, implementing various data refreshing policies, specified by the DBA. That means that linked columns may be refreshed with stream data at regular intervals and query processing may utilize cached linked

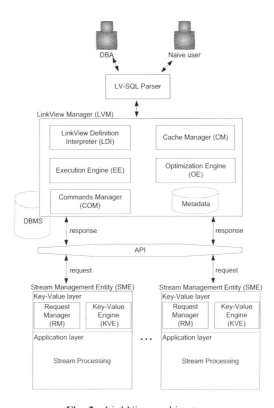

Fig. 2. LinkView architecture

columns instead of requesting actual stream data. Commands Manager (COM) handles statements for the management of LinkViews (e.g. init LinkView, drop LinkView, setting caching policies, etc.)

A Stream Management Entity is a module that process stream data and contains subcomponents that enable the communication with a DBMS. It consists of two layers. The Key-Value layer contains the Request Manager (RM) and the Key-Value Engine (KVE). The Request Manager receives requests from the LVM and implements the communication API. The Key-Value Engine manages the key-value system to realize the stream structures at the SME (Key-Value structures). The values of these structures are provided by the stream system (Application Layer). A KVE can be a Key-Value store, a custom solution, a database etc. In most cases Key-Value Engines support a simplistic query language to query keys and/or values, but it could also be a strict Key-Value store, only supporting key retrieval. The Application layer is the actual stream system that process data streams. Any stream system may exist in this layer. The only requirement is the ability of stream programs to access the keys and values of the Key-Value structures. This could be done either *natively* – i.e. the Key-Value structures reside *within* the stream system and are directly accessible by the stream programs – or *externally* – i.e. the Key-Value structures are accessible through an interface between the stream programs and the Key-Value store. Both approaches have pros and cons and our architecture does not assume the one or the other. In native implementations, the obvious benefits are performance and updatability – keys and values are always up to date, since programs directly manipulate these structures. The drawback is that one has to implement Key-Value structures' functionality within the stream system. In external implementations, one can use ready-to-use Key-Value stores, offering scalability and fault-tolerance. In fact, in many real applications this is the *only* possible approach – e.g. banking systems handling streams are application-specific and closed, offering a limited API, which could be used to update Key-Value structures.

Some well-known stream systems can easily support the implementation of Key-Value structures. For example the STREAM system [2] supports the CQL [3] language for the declaration of stream queries. STREAM supports the TableSource and QueryOutput interfaces [17] to import keys and output results. AURORA [1] can use connections points to static data sets to get keys from a DBMS and to output results to a Key-Value structure. For MapReduce Online [12] a possible solution is the usage of custom Java code to import keys from a DBMS and the usage of the online aggregation snapshots functionality to output computed aggregates.

4.1   API

Communication between the DBMS and a SME is carried out through a set of primitives implementing a request-response protocol. There are four different request types in order to define stream structures at the SME, initiate program execution at the SME and manage the Key-Value Engine (send keys and retrieve values). Table 1 summarizes the request types, along with the responses of the SME. Note that all communication is DBMS driven. In particular the DBMS-SME communication is guided by the LinkView Manager.

Table 1. Request types of DBMS-SME API

Request type: *define*

Description	Defines the Key-Value structure of a linked column at the SME.
Parameters	*handlerID*: a unique identifier assigned to each linked column by the LinkView Manager, *execName*: a string containing the program name and the parameters' values for the call, *label*: a string containing the named output of the execution.
Response	true/false

Request type: *sendKeys*

Description	Sends to the SME a (subset of) the values of the base column(s) of one (or more) linked columns.
Parameters	*H*: a list of handlerIDs, *K*: a set of keys.
Response	true/false

Request type: *getValues*

Description	Retrieves the values of the links of a linked column.
Parameters	*handlerID*: the handlerID of the linked column, θ : a logical expression, involving only the linked column and its base column(s).
Response	A list of key-value pairs.

Request type: *delKeys*

Description	Deletes entries of Key-Value structure according to a set of keys K and/or a logical expression θ.
Parameters	*handlerID*: the handlerID of a linked column, θ : a logical expression, involving only the linked column and its base column(s), *K*: a set of keys.
Response	true/false

define request defines the Key-Value structure of a linked column at the SME. It also sends a unique (cross-DBMS) identifier to the SME, the *handlerID*. All further communication between the DBMS and the SMEs are carried out through this *handlerID*. At the SME, a Key-Value structure is defined for each *handlerID* and is named using the *label* parameter. Stream programs output values to these labeled Key-Value structures.

sendKeys request sends a set of keys *K* that update (append mode) the Key-Value structure of those *handlerIDs* mentioned in *H*. The linked columns corresponding to the *handlerIDs* of *H* must have the same base column(s). Allowing a *sendKeys* request to affect several Key-Value structures is something useful performance-wise (bandwidth). When the *sendKeys* request is issued for the first time for a *handlerID*, it also initiates the program execution of that *handlerID*. Recall that the base columns of a LinkView correspond to a materialized view. When the base part of a LinkView is updated (i.e. during view maintenance, for example a new stock is inserted to the Stocks table) the *sendKeys* primitive is invoked to send the new keys to the SME.

getValues request is used during query processing for linked columns evaluation i.e. when a user submit a SQL query. It asks for the pairs of the Key-Value structure of *handlerID*. It may retrieve all key-value pairs corresponding to the submitted *handlerID* or it may retrieve key-value pairs according to a selection condition θ over the schema of the Key-Value structure (i.e. a condition mentioning keys and values.) For example, Query Q2 asks for the `categoryIDs` having `minPrice` greater than 10 using LinkView LV3 and its linked column `minPrice`. This filtering could be pushed to the Key-Value Engine using the above-mentioned condition. The SME may or may not support the mapping of θ to the native language of the Key-Value engine. In the latter case, θ is ignored and all key-value pairs are returned.

delKeys request is useful once again during view maintenance. It deletes the entries of the Key-Value structure of *handlerID* that exists in set K and according to the condition θ. This is feasible if the SME can map θ to the native language of the Key-Value Engine, otherwise θ is ignored and only keys mentioned in K are deleted.

5   Implementation and Performance

The proposed architecture can have different implementations based on the application we want to support. For example the need for real-time acquisition of stream data can be better supported by an in-memory DBMS, an in-memory Key-Value Engine and by a high-performance cluster based stream system (e.g. financial applications). On the other hand, for less critical applications (e.g. product information in a RFID supply chain environment) the requirement for near real-time acquisition of stream data can be achieved with a distributed architecture where SMEs are in different network locations than the LVM. In the following subsections we provide details on our prototype system and describe preliminary experimental results.

5.1   Prototype System

LinkView Manager (LVM) is implemented in C/C++ and operates over any relational database system using ODBC. In our prototype system we used the PostgreSQL DBMS. The default mode of LVM (prompt mode) accepts "`create linkview`" definitions and SQL queries. LVM supports a set of commands that define its operation. These commands are handled by the Commands Manager (COM) module. The commands are explained below:

- **init** *<LinkView name>*: it invokes the first *sendkeys* request for the LinkView.
- **drop** *<LinkView name>*: deletes a LinkView and stop associated stream program executions at the SMEs,
- **view** *<LinkView name>*: enables users to view the defined LinkViews and other miscellaneous statistics (e.g. linked column last update time etc.)
- **readQ** *<filename>*: reads and executes from a file a LinkView definition/command or a SQL query

API requests are XML-based messages. Requests and responses involving data (key-value pairs) use comma-separated format (CSV).

5.2 Performance Results

Our testing platform has the following characteristics: Windows 7, 2.13 GHz Intel Core i3 Processor i3-330M and 4 GB of RAM. We conducted our experiments in a single machine i.e. both LVM and SME run on the same node. LVM uses data stored in PostgreSQL DBMS and access is via ODBC. The financial database used in our experiments contains synthetic data sets. SME is a C/C++ process and is composed of an embedded in-memory Key-Value Engine implements C++ hash maps, natively accessible by C++ threads manipulating stream data (stream programs implementing LinkViews LV1 to LV3). SME is fed with tuples generated by a custom C/C++ stream generator running as a process in the same machine. The provided tuples have the following schema: <stock_id, category_id, stock_price≥. Stream generator-SME interprocess communication is achieved via shared memory. LVM-SME communication is done via sockets.

The most common operation in LinkView architecture is the execution of SQL queries involving LinkViews. So, we measured the execution time for two SQL queries. We used LV3 (`MinMaxPriceCategory`) and the following SQL queries in our experiment:

QE1. `select categoryID, minPrice`
    `from MinMaxPriceCategory`
QE2. `select categoryID, minPrice, maxPrice`
    `from MinMaxPriceCategory`

`MinMaxPriceCategory` uses `pMinMax()` from the SME to get values for `minPrice` and `maxPrice` columns. When an SQL query issued on LVM the *get-Values* request is called for each linked column and the SME returns a batch of key-value pairs to the LVM. These pairs of data are stored as CSV files in LVM machine and loaded in the DBMS as two-column Key-Value tables. We used the COPY command of PostgreSQL to load the CSV files. We annotate queries that use disk Key-Value tables with D and queries use memory Key-Value tables with M. The execution times of SQL queries (in seconds) are shown in Table 2. We varied key size (`categoryID`) from 50000 to 300000 for `MinMaxPriceCategory` with a step of 50000.

Table 2. SQL queries execution time (seconds)

Query	Number of keys					
	50000	100000	150000	200000	250000	300000
$QE1_M$	0.565	1.033	1.546	2.045	2.588	3.175
$QE1_D$	0.698	1.257	1.868	2.594	3.096	4.049
$QE2_M$	1.208	2.157	3.275	4.230	5.351	6.286
$QE2_D$	1.468	2.708	3.797	5.098	6.763	7.656

The results indicate that our system performs linearly as the number of keys increases. Note that queries using disk Key-Value tables ($QE1_D$, $QE2_D$) are slower than queries with in memory Key-Value tables ($QE1_M$, $QE2_M$). Also both versions of QE2 are slower than QE1. QE1 can be executed without a join i.e. all columns mentioned in the select clause can be retrieved by the created Key-Value table with schema <categoryID, minPrice>. On the other hand for QE2 a join between the Key-Value table with schema <categoryID, minPrice> and the Key-Value table with schema <categoryID, maxPrice> must be performed. In particular, QE2 evaluation requires the following tasks: (1) request of key-value data from SMEs (*getValues* API call) and storage as CSV files (2) create Key-Value tables and load the corresponding CSV files, (3) join of Key-Value tables and execution of the issued SQL query. Details on how these tasks affect linked columns evaluation can give better insights about performance bottlenecks in a LinkView system and will be the focus of future work.

6   Related Work

Data stream systems have attracted a lot of attention from the database research community. STREAM [2], Aurora [1], TelegraphCQ [10] and Gigascope [13] are some of the first systems built for processing stream data. Those systems support continuous queries [4] which are standing queries that provide results continuously as new data arrive. Continuous queries are used mainly in monitoring applications [8]. Commercial stream engines are also available: StreamBase, StreamInsight, InfoSphere etc. Similarly, Complex Event Processing engines [20] allow event pattern detection over streams of data. Most of these stream systems extend SQL [3] to support continuous queries or the queries are built as data flow graphs [14]. These graphs contain stream sources management elements, stream processing operators and output components. In addition, specialized stream handling components have been developed. For example MapReduce online [12] adds pipeline functionality between Map and Reduce operators to support stream data processing. Current authors in ·[11] describe a spreadsheet-like processing framework for streams. Finally a large number of stream applications are built from scratch using general purpose programming languages. Stream programming libraries [15, 19] can also be used for the development of custom stream applications. In this paper we propose an integration framework that enables database users to express SQL queries and retrieve stream data from all these stream platforms and applications.

Data integration has multiple applications and a wealth of techniques have been developed from database researchers. The main goal of data integration is to combine data residing at different sources and provide users with a unified view of the data. Our work is toward this goal and we focus specifically on relational and stream data. The challenges for DBMS and stream systems integration are presented in [18]. The author emphasizes that this is a new and challenging research area as current trend mostly focus on static data integration. Also the importance of integration of stream and stored data is analyzed in [16]. These authors discuss integration of stream and relational data from a stream system perspective i.e. how a stream system can use offline data, which is quite different than our approach, since we follow a DBMS-oriented view. In [7] authors propose a descriptive model to analyze the execution behavior of heterogeneous stream processing engines. The diversity of stream engines described in that paper motivates the creation of LinkViews framework. MaxStream [5] is a data integration system that can use multiple stream engines and databases for real-time business intelligence applications. MaxStream queries are translated into the native language of each stream system and the architecture is similar to federation database systems [6] i.e. it consists from a middleware and a set of data wrappers interacting with each stream engine. In our approach we want users to be able to use stream engines avoiding the translation of queries to the native query language of each stream system because stream heterogeneity makes that procedure complex. A framework for situation aware applications that use stream and stored data is described in [9]. A data flow interface is proposed for building situational aware applications. In our work a relational approach is proposed for integration of stream and stored data.

7   Conclusions and Future Work

We have presented an integration framework for relational database management systems and heterogeneous stream systems. In the proposed framework keys are managed by databases and stream data sets corresponding to these keys are managed by stream systems. A framework has been developed and a key-value based interface has been proposed. We argued for the advantages of such an approach. A prototype system has been implemented and can operate on top of any relational database management system. The goal of this work is to bring stream aggregates to naïve database users and analysts in a stream-transparent way. As most users are familiar with traditional relational systems and SQL, bringing stream support within such environments is of major importance.

Future work includes the identification of LinkViews theoretical semantics, optimizations and more performance results (e.g. materialization cost, keys update, etc.). Also we are going to use a cloud infrastructure for the implementation of our framework. Such an infrastructure can be used by stream providers to provide services (programs) to database users. Finally, LinkViews can be used to link to other non-stream systems, allowing the creation of a generic integration platform for different types of data and systems (e.g. MapReduce, Big Data platforms, etc.).

Acknowledgments. We would like to thank Yannis Kotidis for his helpful comments and suggestions during the preparation of this paper.

References

1. Abadi, D.J., Carney, D., Cetintemel, U., Cherniack, M., Convey, C., Lee, S., Stonebraker, M., Tatbul, N., Zdonik, S.B.: Aurora: a new model and architecture for data stream management. J. Very Large Databases **12**(2), 120–139 (2003)
2. Arasu, A., Babcock, B., Babu, S., Datar, M., Ito, K., Motwani, R., Nishizawa, I., Srivastava, U., Thomas, D., Varma, R., Widom, J.: Stream: the Stanford stream data manager. IEEE Data Eng. Bull. **26**(1), 19–26 (2003)
3. Arasu, A., Babu, S., Widom, J.: The CQL continuous query language: semantic foundations and query execution. J. Very Large Databases **15**(2), 121–142 (2006)

4. Babcock, B., Babu, S., Datar, M., Motwani, R., Widom, J.: Models and issues in data stream systems. In: Proceedings of the 21st ACM SIGACT-SIGMOD-SIGART Symposium on Principles of Database Systems, PODS 2002, pp. 1–16 (2002)
5. Botan, I., Cho, Y., Derakhshan, R., Dindar, N., Gupta, A., Haas, L.M., Kim, K., Lee, C., Mundada, G., Shan, M., Tatbul, N., Yan, Y., Yun, B., Zhang, J.: A demonstration of the MaxStream federated stream processing system. In: Proceedings of the 26th International Conference on Data Engineering, ICDE 2010, pp. 1093–1096 (2010)
6. Botan, I., Cho, Y., Derakhshan, R., Dindar, N., Haas, L., Kim, K., Tatbul, Nesime: Federated stream processing support for real-time business intelligence applications. In: Castellanos, M., Dayal, U., Miller, R.J. (eds.) BIRTE 2009. LNBIP, vol. 41, pp. 14–31. Springer, Heidelberg (2010)
7. Botan, I., Derakhshan, R., Dindar, N., Haas, L.M., Miller, R.J., Tatbul, N.: SECRET: a model for analysis of the execution semantics of stream processing systems. In: Proceedings of the Very Large Databases, PVLDB, vol. 3, iss. 1, pp. 232–243, September 2010
8. Carney, D., Cetintemel, U., Cherniack, M., Convey, C., Lee, S., Seidman, G., Stonebraker, S., Tatbul, N., Zdonik, S. B.: Monitoring streams - a new class of data management applications. In: Proceedings of 28th International Conference on Very Large Databases, VLDB 2002, pp. 215–226 (2002)
9. Castellanos, M., Wang, S., Dayal, U., Gupta, C.: SIE-OBI: a streaming information extraction platform for operational business intelligence. In: Proceedings of the ACM SIGMOD International Conference on Management of Data, SIGMOD 2010, pp. 1105–1110 (2010)
10. Chandrasekaran, S., Cooper, O., Deshpande, A., Franklin, M.J., Hellerstein, J.M., Hong, W., Krishnamurthy, S., Madden, S., Raman, V., Reiss, F., Shah, M. A.: TelegraphCQ: continuous dataflow processing for an uncertain world. In: Proceedings of the 1st Biennial Conference on Innovative Data Systems Research. CIDR 2003 (2003)
11. Chatziantoniou, D., Pramatari, K., and Sotiropoulos, Y.: COSTES: continuous spreadsheet-like computations. In: International Workshop on RFID Data Management, ICDE Workshops, RFDM 2008, pp. 82–87 (2008)
12. Condie, T., Conway, N., Alvaro, P., Hellerstein J. M., Elmeleegy, K., Sears, R.: MapReduce online. In: Proceedings of the 7th USENIX Symposium on Networked Systems Design and Implementation, NSDI 2010 (2010)
13. Cranor, C.D., Johnson, T., Spatscheck, O., Shkapenyuk, V.: Gigascope. A stream database for network applications. In: Proceedings of the ACM SIGMOD International Conference on Management of Data, SIGMOD 2003, pp. 647–651
14. Jain, N., Mishra, S., Srinivasan, A., Gehrke, J., Widom, J., Balakrishnan, H., Cetintemel, U., Cherniack, M., Tibbetts, R., Zdonik, S.B.: Towards a streaming SQL standard. In: Proceedings of the Very Large Databases, PVLDB vol. 1 iss. 2, pp. 1379–1390, August 2008
15. Spring, J.H., Privat, J., Guerraoui, R., Vitek J.: Streamflex: high-throughput stream programming in java. In: Proceedings of the 22nd Annual Conference on Object-Oriented Programming, Systems, Languages, and Applications. OOPSLA 2007, pp. 211–228 (2007)
16. Stonebraker, M., Cetintemel, U., Zdonik, S.B.: The 8 requirements of real-time stream processing. SIGMOD Record 34, 42–47 (2005)
17. STREAM: The Stanford Stream Data Manager, User Guide and Design Document (2013). http://infolab.stanford.edu/stream/code/user.pdf. Accessed 6 May 2013
18. Tatbul, N.: Streaming data integration: challenges and opportunities. In: 2nd International Workshop on New Trends in Information Integration, NTII 2010, pp. 155–158 (2010)

19. Thies, W., Karczmarek, M., Amarasinghe, S.: StreamIt: a language for streaming applications. In: Nigel Horspool, R. (ed.) CC 2002. LNCS, vol. 2304, pp. 179–196. Springer, Heidelberg (2002)
20. Wu, E., Diao, Y., Rizvi., S.: High-performance complex event processing over streams. In: Proceedings of the ACM SIGMOD International Conference on Management of Data, SIGMOD 2006, pp. 407–418 (2006)

OLAP for Multidimensional Semantic Web Databases

Adriana Matei$^{(\boxtimes)}$, Kuo-Ming Chao, and Nick Godwin

Faculty of Engineering and Computing, Coventry University,
Priory Street, Coventry CV1 5FB, UK
{adriana.matei,k.chao,csx0l4}@coventry.ac.uk

Abstract. Semantic Web (SW) and web data have become increasingly important sources to support Business Intelligence (BI), but it is difficult to manage due to its scalability in their volumes, inconsistency in semantics and complexity in representations. On-Line Analytical Processing (OLAP) is an important tool in analysing large and complex BI data, but it lacks the capability of processing disperse SW data due to the nature of its design. A new concept with a richer vocabulary than the existing ones for OLAP is needed to model distributed multidimensional semantic web databases. In this paper we proposed a new OLAP framework with multiple layers including additional vocabulary, extended OLAP operators, and SPARSQL to model heterogeneous semantic web data, unify multidimensional structures, and provide new enabling functions for interoperability. We present the framework with examples to demonstrate its capability to unify RDF Data Cube (QB) [2] and QB4OLAP [1] with additional vocabulary elements to handle both informational and topological data [3] in Graph OLAP. It is also able to compose multiple databases (e.g. energy consumptions and property market values etc.) to generate observations through semantic pipe-like operators.

Keywords: On-Line Analytical Processing · Business Intelligence · Semantic web · Data management · RDF vocabulary

1 Introduction

In today's business, the data (e.g. web data) obtained over the Internet and their semantics can play an important role as resources in enhancing data analysis, when used in combination with internal enterprise business information systems. The Semantic Web (SW) technologies provide the capability of annotating web data with semantics hence generating Semantic Web data.

The information and activities in a typical BI scenario can be modelled by three different layers [5]: the data source layer, the integration layer and the analysis layer. The combination of Data Warehouses (DWs) and On-Line Analytical Processing (OLAP) covers these layers in order to support BI efficiently. OLAP tools and

---

This research is carried out as a part of CASSANDRA Project, funded by the European Community's Seventh Framework Program FP7-ICT-2011-7 under grant agreement No. 288429.

© Springer-Verlag Berlin Heidelberg 2015
M. Castellanos et al. (Eds.): BIRTE 2013 and 2014, LNBIP 206, pp. 81–96, 2015.
DOI: 10.1007/978-3-662-46839-5_6

algorithms have been used successfully in BI to query large multidimensional (MD) databases or DWs for supporting decision making. In the middle layer the multidimensional model is used for normalizing and formatting the data, gathered from other sources, for subsequent analysis. The MD dataset representation is done through the OLAP Cube which is built from the data source using the ETL (extract, transform and load) process.

The evolution of the data management on SW data has recently showed an increase in the use of the OLAP approaches to improve efficiency. In order to perform OLAP over SW data, the data has to be modelled with a specific vocabulary and structure to comply with the facilities or engines that OLAP requires. Various MD models for enabling OLAP to operate over Semantic Web data resulted in the development of different structures and vocabularies which form autonomous and heterogeneous OLAP databases for handling semantic (linked) data [1, 2, 6, 7, 11, 12]. As a consequence, different OLAP databases based on proprietary structures with inconsistent query languages making it hard for individuals to communicate and share data with each other when joined datasets are required from multiple individuals.

There was no research conducted so far towards a method that enables multiple SW OLAP databases to be simultaneously accessible over the Internet, even though such demand is increasing. To respond to such queries is a complex task which needs a middleware with OLAP facilities and Semantic Web features to realize it. Furthermore, this type of system should provide explicit, expressive and consistent vocabulary for modelling data and offer full support for OLAP.

2 Research Context

An increasing number of large repositories containing semantically annotated data is available over Internet, but summarising the semantic data to support decision making is not a trivial task due to its scalability and complexity. The utilisation of OLAP capability in organising semantic web data into statistical or concise information can increase efficiency in analysis and visualisation. The implementation of OLAP analysis over a semantic web (SW), however, was understood differently and as such two main types of approach were adopted. Firstly, OLAP is performed after retrieving multidimensional information from the Semantic Web and stored in traditional databases. The second targets OLAP operations directly over RDF data. As for the first approach, storage of semantic web data in local DWs conflicts with the dynamic nature of web data, as OLAP is designed for static and batch offline processing. In addition, the manually built DWs cannot automatically reflect changes in the sources so it is hard to maintain the consistency between them.

On the other hand in order to perform OLAP over SW data there are a set of key aspects needed in the modelling process. There is a need for a precise, explicit describing vocabulary in order to represent OLAP data consistently. The key concepts of dimension and measure need to be introduced to support OLAP operations since they employ measures such as AVG, MIN, SUM etc. and dimension related actions such as roll-up, dice, slice, and drill.

SW data are, however, often published on the web in different cube representations for OLAP operations. As a consequence these generated multidimensional semantic web databases become standalone databases, so they only offer limited OLAP capabilities and only work with their own query languages. The information contained in these web databases can be incomplete for complex applications which may require information from multiple databases. Their proprietary specifications do not give the possibility to communicate or share with each other to compose appropriate responses. This is complicated when queries need to be performed over disparate data sources for new multidimensional semantic web databases.

2.1 Household Energy Consumption Profile Example

There are situations in which it is beneficial and desirable that multiple databases can be accessed simultaneously by complex queries in order to provide adequate answers. Below we introduce such an example in which we consider two different databases with complementary information, which if they are able to communicate, they can provide the data consumers with complete and valuable information.

One large Semantic Web OLAP database *DB1* contains detailed energy consumption information of households from different countries as well as properties of households like household income, accommodation size/layout (number of rooms), number of inhabitants, appliances and so on. A separate Semantic OLAP database *DB2* contains information about the historical value on the market of a specific property and its layout.

Energy consumption for households can be viewed in conjunction with different factors such as: number of inhabitants; household income; house size, or, house value, in order to analyse correlations in energy consumption. House energy efficiency profile can be a factor in a house acquisition or renting process, so it is desirable to have access to multiple databases. For example, a natural language version of a query relating to average energy consumption for houses within a selling price range and having a set of other characteristics may be issued by the users as follows:

The average electricity consumption per year of households in a specific area and with a specific layout, based on the number of occupants and the property market value is between a specific ranges (meaning both actual and historical).

This new aggregation can be materialized and stored as a new observation in the queried OLAP or in an independent OLAP structure. From the example, the following features are essential in order to satisfy the requests from users:

- Perform OLAP operations over the data
- Access to both databases without changing their structure but being able to generate the results
- Both databases have an OLAP structure in which basic OLAP operations such as AVG, SUM, COUNT can be applied as multi-level and multi-dimensionally
- Build OLAP observations in a common format
- Be able to perform data merging for building the response or to materialise it in a new database

In order to offer a solution for the above example, we need to provide a way in which the query is able to distribute to multiple databases, perform OLAP over each database and compose the results retrieved from them.

2.2 Related Work

On-Line Analytical Processing (OLAP) has been undeniably proven a successful approach to analysing large sets of data [5]. Furthermore OLAP is an approach that can be built on top of different database models and respond to multi-dimensional queries as long as they fall under some evaluation criteria regarding, but not limited to, multidimensionality, accessibility, transparency, dimensions and aggregation levels. Recently, a considerable stream of works [1–5, 9–11] was directed towards online analytical processing on informational network and mostly focusing on the Semantic Web data. Chen et al. [3, 9, 10] and Zhao et al. [4] both take the first step to introduce graphs in a multidimensional and level context by proposing conceptual frameworks for graph data cubes and a data warehousing model able to support graph OLAP queries. They both consider attribute aggregations and structure summarization, where the authors in [3] classify their framework into topological and informational OLAP based on the dimension. They proposed different aggregation functions to build summarisations and these cannot be mutually applied.

Kämpgen and Harth [12] introduce linked data transformations for OLAP analysis and they [6] try to map statistical Linked Data to an OLAP to conform to the RDF Data Cube Vocabulary [2] but they did not provide sufficient semantics that are required from the topological elements to build parts of the multiple dimensions. Etcheverry and Vaisman [11] introduce Open Cubes which focus on the publication of multidimensional cubes on the Semantic Web and they found the limitation of the RDF Data Cube [2] which can only address statistical data. Their work revolves around informational OLAP aggregations. Furthermore they revisit RDF Data Cube (DC) by extending DC's capabilities to support multidimensional levels to build hierarchies and to implement other OLAP operators beside the sole *Slice* operator offered by DC. Beheshti et al. [7] continue the work from [3, 4, 9, 10] and offered a graph data model for OLAP informational networks. The approach supports the description of entities and relationships between them and provides both topological aggregations. They use three levels of partitioning conditions to implement their proposed model as well as an adapted query language extended from SPARQL in order to support necessary n-dimensional computations. The aforementioned works do not only show the diversity of the approaches towards online analytical processing of Semantic Web but also the rapid change in the research direction.

RDF Data Cube Vocabulary (QB) [2] focuses on the adherence to Linked Data principles while publishing statistical data and metadata using RDF. QB4OLAP [1] introduces an extended vocabulary of QB in order to support OLAP operators directly over RDF representation. As it will be seen in Sect. 3.1. QB4OLAP introduces levels, members and aggregated functions in order to represent OLAP dimension structure which is not offered by QB vocabulary.

With all these, QB4OLAP, however, does not support a vocabulary to model online analytical processing on graphs introduced by Chen et al. [3]. Zhao et al. [4] introduced a data warehousing model that supports OLAP queries on graph and Graph Cube. None of these [7] provides a semantic-driven framework considering both informational and topological dimensions of graphs.

Beheshti et al. concentrate their approach on topological graphs without considering informational graphs. This is an important factor as semantic data is usually found in a mix of topological and informational graphs. Furthermore, in order to address topological dimensions constrains for OLAP, they use partitioning and an adapted SPARQL query to operate over the data. This approach hinders the published datasets being reused or being queried by applications and users against other datasets offering automated OLAP observations.

In order to reuse and extend existent implementations while extending OLAP capabilities to both topological and informational dimensions, we used the vocabulary in QB and QB4OLAP as basis to form a new vocabulary. Furthermore we introduced new elements and relationships able to model the topological OLAP. By describing topological and informational elements in the same vocabulary and identifying the relationships between entities we enable OLAP to operate over both aspects.

Research on bringing the pipe concept to the Semantic Web was introduced by Morbidoni et al. [8], where their focus was to build RDF-mashups by fetching RDF models on the Web and producing an accessible output. While the Semantic Pipes operators can access different RDF graphs and produce outputs to be consumed by other pipes, they do not offer means to access summary data or support OLAP operations.

The brief introduction of the up-to-date research in the Semantic Web's data management shows that a new model is required to answer computational intensive semantically queries but no existing OLAP system is capable of accessing, retrieving, and reusing semantic OLAP databases efficiently. In order to address this challenge we introduce a new model which can interpret a query based on the OLAP concept. The model offers standard OLAP functionalities with a built-in Pipe concept by extending existing OLAP systems with observations generated from individual RDF graphs or other SW OLAP. This new model is equipped with facilities for composing multiple queries to operate on multiple OLAP databases. It also provides an extended vocabulary for modelling semantic data for OLAP operations.

3 Conceptual Framework

A key factor in successfully performing OLAP over Semantic data is to acknowledge the characteristics and the relationship of data. The relationships between the data can be divided in two categories: *informational* (dimensions are coming from node attributes) and *topological* (when dimensions are coming from node and edge attributes). Some databases may be structured using one type (e.g. DB2) while others may have a mix of structures with the information offered from different dimensions (e.g. DB1). An example of a mix structure can be found in Fig. 1.

A middleware system is needed to perform collective OLAP operations over multiple databases to store the newly generated views in a multidimensional database as well as having an expressive vocabulary to model both topological and informational structure. Even though multiple semantic OLAP databases are accessible, composing retrieved data from them is a complex process. A pipe architectural style can be designed to handle RDF and summary data that can be fed into OLAP functions to support decision making.

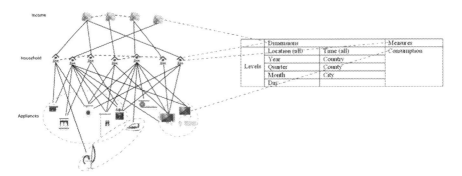

Fig. 1. Connections between topological and informational dimensions

This paper asserts that the key elements for composing such complex results are not yet fully available. Some related work, presented in the next subsection, has been proposed but each approach has limitations.

In order to provide OLAP functionality over multiple Semantic databases, our proposed model (IGOLAP) in Fig. 2 presents a three level contribution:

- An integrated system for collective querying over multiple multidimensional databases
- An extended vocabulary for multidimensional data representation
- A materialization of semantic OLAP database capability

The proposed conceptual framework with multiple layers is to address the issues identified and discussed in the previous sections.

On the bottom layer we have the raw data from relational databases and web data in different forms. In the case of data stored in relational databases, the layer on top of it provides multidimensional modelling of data. For the web data, there is an intermediate layer between raw data and data modelling for OLAP. This layer is described by linked data, which is a specific type of the semantic web data. This layer can also be an intermediate layer between data in relational databases and the modelling layer, when data is transformed from relational databases to linked data [12] before further OLAP analysis. Regarding the multidimensional modelling layer, the data is transformed into cubes for multidimensional models. It contains a series of different vocabularies which trigger different semantic OLAP databases, so this layer can have different representations of data for OLAP. We introduce an extended representation with an enhanced vocabulary and functionalities lacking in other existing vocabularies on the layer to support it. The proposed vocabulary and the functionalities are presented in subsection 3.1.

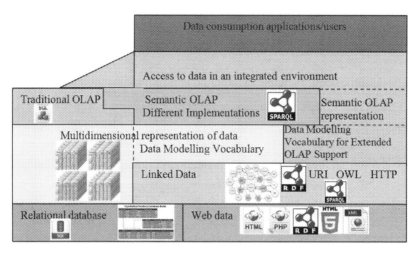

Fig. 2. Conceptual framework

The proposed framework is a multiple layer Semantic OLAP database which is able to handle data in dimensions, levels and measures in order to respond to OLAP related queries.

The top layer in the framework provides users with interfaces to specify queries and visualise the retrieved information in relation to business intelligence or decision making. The other layers provide necessary mechanisms and functions to transform the requests into executable syntax. The framework also increases interoperability among different semantic OLAP databases. So, a query can be executed to locate datasets, retrieve data, summarise information and compose semantics from various semantic OLAP databases. In order to support this functionality we introduce a pipe architecture and distributed query processing as detailed in Sect. 3.2.

3.1 Vocabulary for Modelling Multidimensional Graph Data

As mentioned in Sect. 2, there is existing work regarding a vocabulary for multidimensional data modelling for OLAP support. We consider that the QB vocabulary does not have sufficient capabilities to handle OLAP, but it has adequate structure. The QB4OLAP vocabulary is an extended version of QB, offering more functionality to support OLAP. Both vocabulary sets have missing facilities in relation to modelling two groups of data: Informational (dimensions are coming from node attributes) and Topological (when dimensions are coming from node and edge attributes). Their vocabulary needs to be extended and altered in order to provide full OLAP capabilities. Since an informational graph is modelled by dimensions and hierarchical levels and the topological graph is modelled in dimensions, members and defined relationships, the type of aggregations over their measures are very different. On the informational graphs the standard measure aggregations such as SUM, AVG, and COUNT are used to summarise the data, but the topological graphs require relationship type of aggregations. To design a unified semantic OLAP to handle both graphs is not trivial.

Considering that the dimensions in the topological structure do not have levels but direct members we introduced two different classes to model it: ***igolap:InfoDimension*** and ***igolap:TopoDimension*** as subclasses of the ***qb:DimensionProperty*** class. The property that connects these two classes to their superclass is: ***igolap:dimensionType***. The new vocabulary is presented in Fig. 3 and the comparison of the vocabularies' capabilities is presented in Table 1.

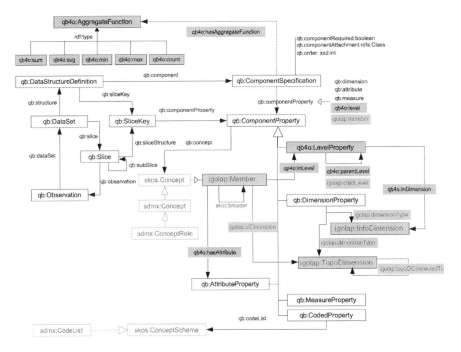

Fig. 3. IGOLAP vocabulary

The existing ***qb4o:LevelMember*** has to be altered in order to handle the topological dimension. We introduced the modified ***igolap:Member*** which while keeping the connection with qb4o:LevelProperty it also has a new connecting property to the topological dimension: ***igolap:ofDimension***. Since both topological and informational dimension have attributes, the property ***qb4o:hasAttribute*** had to be altered to reflect this. The informational dimension has levels which have members and the topological dimension has direct members. In order for the property ***qb4o:hasAttribute*** to apply to both topological and informational dimension, it has to connect the ***igolap:Member*** to ***qb:AttributeProperty***.

The topological dimensions can be connected to each other through a topological property and each member of the dimension holds the property. We introduced the ***igolap:topoDConnectedTo*** property to define those connections.

QB4OLAP introduces ***qb4o:parentLevel*** property which connects levels and can support the roll-up operation, but in order to offer a better support the Drill-down

Table 1. The differences between these three vocabularies, on both classes and properties

	QB	QB4O	IGOLAP
New classes	Attachable; DataSet;	LevelProperty	Member
	CodedProperty; AttributeProperty;	LevelMember	InfoDimension
	ComponentProperty; ComponentSet;	AggregateFunction	TopoDimnsion
	ComponentSpecification; SliceKey; Observation; MeasureProperty;		
	DataStructureDefinition; Slice;		
	DimensionProperty		
Properties	attribute; codeList; componenet; componentAttachment; component Property; dimension;	level inLevel	dimensionType, of Dimension, topo DConnectedTo
	componentRequired; measure;	inDimension	
	concept; dataSet; slice; sliceKey;	parentLevel	member
	measureDimension; subSlice;	hasAggregate Function	childLevel
	measureType; observation; order; sliceStructure; structure;		
Altered Classes	–	LevelMember	Member
Properties	–	has Attribute	hasAttribute
		inDimension	inDimension

operation we introduced the ***igolap:childLevel*** property which also connects levels and is an inverse function to qb4o:parentLevel.

3.2   Integrated System for Collective Query of Semantic OLAP Databases

The proposed framework is based on a set of specialized OLAP operators (Federated OLAP operators) that can operate over multiple semantic OLAP databases, merge the outputs into a common format and translate them according to the desired output which can be materialized or viewed.

The Federated OLAP operators need to interpret the requests according to a specific OLAP database in order to retrieve the data and convert it to a requested output format. The Federated OLAP operators represent an extension of the classic OLAP operations as: roll-up, dice, drill down or slice.

A **roll-up operation** assumes a data summarization inside a given cube alongside a given dimension such as a given Cube C, a dimension D ∈ C and a dimension level lu∈ D, the Roll-up (C,D, lu) will return a new cube C' where measures are aggregated along D up to the level lu.

In the **dice operation** a new cube C' is generated from a given cube C and a set of constrains along its dimensions. The emerging cube has the same schema as the initial cube C and the instances in C' are also instances of C.

Slice operation receives a cube C, and a dimension D ∈ C and returns a sub cube C', with the same schema except the dimension D.

Drill down is considered to be the reverse of Roll up and assumes the disaggregation on a previously stored aggregation.

The dimension operations that are used in our approach are defined as F_Operators. These include the standard dimension operators as F_ROLL_UP, F_DICE, F_SLICE and F_DRILL. They are derived from the standard OLAP dimension operations, but they are adapted to have the necessary functions to access multiple semantic databases.

The standard OLAP measure operations are used as restriction functions in the dimension operations that include AVG for retrieving the arithmetical mean of a set of numerical values, SUM for the sum of a set of numerical values, COUNT for the cardinality of a set of elements and MIN and MAX for the minimum and maximum element of a set of elements.

We briefly introduce the F_ROLL_UP operator in the following subsections.

3.2.1   F_ROLL_UP Overview

The F_ROLL_UP operator includes a set of processes. For the retrieval stage, the operator identifies the targeted databases, builds the SELECT operators for each database with given constraints and gathers information from multiple databases by applying the built operators to specific datasets. In the building stage, the CON-STRUCT operator is initiated to compose the response from the retrieved data. When the datasets retrieved by each SELECT operator are in the same format, the CON-STRUCT operator is applied directly, but if the datasets have different formats, data normalisation is performed before generating the output. In order to handle the data exchange, the F_ROLL_UP operator is described as a pipe architecture containing a CONSTRUCT operator and a number of SELECT operators. If data normalisation is required before the output is generated the third operator, the MERGE operator, is included in the F_ROLL_UP pipe construction. The MERGE operator is used to structure the partial RDF triple results from the SELECT operators using the same vocabulary for the output construction. Even though the MERGE concept has some similarity with the one in the semantic web pipes, the MERGE from semantic web pipes is a simple join of the CONSTRUCT and/or SELECT operators output without normalisation capabilities and facilities to support OLAP.

Since F_OPERATOR's are designed to access one or more than one OLAP database, they require a set of arguments in order to interpret the requests. Based on the arguments received, F_ROLL_UP distinguish between:

* single or multiple database access;
* formatted or unformatted output;
* request for view or request for materialization of the output, and, so on

This means that the parameters can be divided into two main categories: the mandatory and the optional ones (e.g. materialised or immaterialised output represents an optional parameter). The mandatory parameters that need to be passed on are: location of accessed SW OLAP implementation(s) (URIs or IRIs), dimensions (and dimension level for F_ROLL_UP) and some others.

Assuming the example of a request of a ROLL-UP operation across two databases, defined by a F_ROLL_UP, the following steps describe the full process:

Input: *olapds1* is the data set of an implemented OLAP data cube *C*;
olapds2 is the data set of an implemented OLAP cube K
constructSet is the observation building requirements set;
constrs1 is the observation constrains for building for C,
constrs2 is the observation constrains for building for K,
swOimpl1 represents the first SW OLAP that needs to be queried
swOimpl2 represents the second SW OLAP that needs to be queried

Output: *o1* is an observation generated by roll-up OLAP operation, from a specific
a given level which can be materialized or not. Since in this example there is no request
for materialization, the observation is outputted as a onetime view.

```
1.     Validate the f_roll-up request, search for valid call
implementation (set of checks as:  if (Count(swOimpl)=i) then
(Count(olapds)=i)||(Count(constrs)=i))
2.     Call of roll-up operator as:f_rollup(swOimpl1, swOimpl2,
olapds1, olapds2, constrSet, constrs1, constrs2)
3.     If the number of swOimpl parameters is bigger than "1"
then the f_rollup call is for multiple database access.
4.     If swOimpl1 equals swOiml2 then {
         Build f_rollup pipe as:
5.        CONSTRUCT(constrSet) <-   (SELECT(olapds1,constrs1),
SELECT(olapds2,constrs2))}
6.        Else{ Build f_rollup pipe as:
7.         CONSTRUCT(constrSet) <-  MERGE((SELECT(olapds1,
constrs1), SELECT(olapds2,constrs2)))}
8.      If materlize_view request exists
9.      Then MATERIALIZE(graph_location, graph_name)
10.     Else step 11 is skipped and standard RDF Graph returned
```

Firstly the request is validated by verifying the number of parameters and their
types. The second step is to determine if F_ROLL_UP needs to access a single database or a multiple semantic OLAP databases. According to the outcomes of the previous steps, the operators decide the next tasks, to which a set of given parameters is
passed. Step 4 and 5 show the construction of roll-up operator accessing a single
database. Step 6 and 7 describe the multi-database access. In the above example no
parameter is given to instruct the production of a materialised output. In this case Step 9
and 10 are skipped and the response is produced only for visualisation.

3.3   Multidimensional and Multi-databases OLAP

In this section, we will use the scenario presented in Sect. 2 to show how both
informational and topological structures can be implemented using our new vocabulary
elements. The content and structure of DB1 in the scenario are described in Figs. 4 and
5 and it contained curated data of both type of structures. Due to space restrictions, we
omit the dataset prefixes, only introduce F_ROLL_UP operator, and demonstrate its
application to DB1. The descriptions of other operators will be covered in future
publications.

Figure 4 shows the structure of informational dimensions of an energy consumption
database, DB1. It shows the representation of time and location dimensions structure as
well as instances of the location. The structure of informational dimension is very similar

```
e:location a golap:InfoDimension.

e:country a qb4o:LevelProperty;
    qb4o:inDimension e:location;
    golap:childLevel e:firstAdministrativeDivision.
e:firstAdministrativeDivision a qb4o:LevelProperty;
    qb4o:inDimension e:location;
    golap:childLevel e:secondAdministrativeDivision;
    qb4o:parentLevel e:country.
e:secondAdministrativeDivision a qb4o:LevelProperty;
    qb4o:inDimension e:location;
    golap:childLevel e:city;
    qb4o:parentLevel e:firstAdministrativeDivision.
e:city a qb4o:LevelProperty;
    qb4o:inDimension e:location;
    qb4o:parentLevel e:secondAdministrativeDivision.

e:time a golap:InfoDimension.

e:year a qb4o:LevelProperty;
    qb4o:inDimension e:time;
    golap:childLevel e:quarter;
e:quarter a qb4o:LevelProperty;
    qb4o:inDimension e:time;
    golap:childLevel e:month;
    qb4o:parentLevel e:year.
e:month a qb4o:LevelProperty;
    qb4o:inDimension e:time;
    golap:childLevel e:day;
    qb4o:parentLevel e:quarter.
e:day a qb4o:LevelProperty;
    qb4o:inDimension e:time;
    qb4o:parentLevel e:month.
```

```
gn:2635167 a golap:Member;
    qb4o:inLevel e:country;
    rdfs:label "United Kingdom@en";
    golap:childLevel gn:6269131.
gn:6269131 a golap:Member;
    qb4o:inLevel e: firstAdministrativeDivision;
    rdfs:label "England@en";
    golap:childLevel gn:3333134;
    golap:childLevel gn:3333125.
gn:3333134 a golap:Member;
    qb4o:inLevel e:secondAdministrativeDivision;
    rdfs:label "City of Bristol@en";
    golap:childLevel gn:2654675.
gn:2654675 a golap:Member;
    qb4o:inLevel e:city;
    rdfs:label "Bristol@en";
    qb4o:parentLevel gn:3333134.
gn:3333125 a golap:Member;
    qb4o:inLevel e:secondAdministrativeDivision;
    rdfs:label "City and Borough of Birmingham @en"
    golap:childLevel gn:2655603.
gn:2655603 a golap:Member;
    qb4o:inLevel e:city;
    rdfs:label "Birmingham@en";
    qb4o:parentLevel gn:3333125.
```

Fig. 4. Informational dimensions: time and location schema and location instances

to the QB4OLAP vocabulary, but the igolap:childLevel in association with qb4o:parentLevel property give the possibility of bidirectional navigation in order to support both roll-up and drill-down OLAP operations.

Figure 5 shows the representation of the topological dimensions that include three dimensions: income, household and appliances. These dimensions are connected by a connecting property. These dimensions do not have a well-defined hierarchical structure but they define aggregations based on common attributes (e.g. number of bedrooms, or number of inhabitants, in the household dimension). We present in Fig. 5 instances of each dimension, with the necessary attributes to populate DB1, producing possible observations.

```
te:incomeRange a golap:TopoDimension;
  golap:TopoConnectedTo te:household.

te:ukI04 a golap:Member;
  golap:ofDimension te:incomeRange;
  golap:TopoDConnectedTo te:hhBrs01;
  golap:TopoDConnectedTo te:hhBhm73;
  te:min 25000;
  te:max 35000;
  te:currency "GBP".

te:household a golap:TopoDimension;
  golap:TopoDConnectedTo te:incomeRange;
  golap:TopoDConnectedTo te:appliances.

te:hhBrs01 a golap:Member;
  golap:ofDimension te:household;
  golap:TopoDConnectedTo te:ukI04;
  golap:TopoDConnectedTo te:fridge_ZZRB934FW2Brs01;
  golap:TopoDConnectedTo te:tv_SUE22D5003Brs01;
  te:hasCity gn:2654675;
  te:hasPostCode "BS35";
  te:size    57;
  te:bedrooms 3;
  te:bathrooms 2;
  te:houseType    "detached";
  te:built    1987.
```

```
te:appliance a golap:TopoDimension;
  golap:TopoDConnectedTo te:household.

te:fridge_ZZRB934FW2Brs01 a golap:Member;
  golap:ofDimension te:appliances;
  golap:TopoDConnectedTo te:hhBrs01;
  te:hasModel "ZRB934FW2";
  te:hasMake "Zanussi";
  te:consumption e:fridge_ZZRB934FW2_20090522;
  te:consumption e:fridge_ZZRB934FW2_electricCons20090523;
  te:consumption e:fridge_ZZRB934FW2_electricCons20090527;
  te:consumption e:fridge_ZZRB934FW2_electricCons20090612;
  te:consumption e:fridge_ZZRB934FW2_electricCons20090719.

te:tv_SUE22D5003Brs01 a golap:Member;
  golap:ofDimension te:appliances;
  golap:TopoDConnectedTo te:hhBrs01;
  te:hasModel "ZRB934FW2";
  te:hasMake "Zanussi";
  te:consumption e:fridge_ZZRB934FW2_20090522;
  te:consumption e:fridge_ZZRB934FW2_electricCons20090523;
  te:consumption e:fridge_ZZRB934FW2_electricCons20090527;
  te:consumption e:fridge_ZZRB934FW2_electricCons20090612;
  te:consumption e:fridge_ZZRB934FW2_electricCons20090719.
```

Fig. 5. Topological dimensions: income, household, appliance and instances

```
e:consumptionYCity a qb:DataStructureDefinition;        e:consumption a qb:MeasureProperty
        qb:component [qb4o:level e:year];
        qb:component [qb4o:level e:city];               e:electricMeasureUnit a qb:AttributeProperty.
        qb:component [qb4o:measure e:consumption;       e:kWh a e:electricMeasureUnit;
qb4o:hasAggregateFunction qb4o:sum];                            rdfs:label "Kilowatt-hour@en".
        qb:component [qb:attribute e:electricMeasureUnit].
                                                        e:o1 a qb:Observation;
e:datasetYCC a qb:DataSet;                              qb:dataSet e:datasetYCC;
rdfs:label "Yearly consumption in a city@en";           e:year db:2009;
qb:structure e:consumptionYCity.                        e:city gn:2654675;
                                                        e:consumption 600000;
e:consumptionMHAC a qb:DataStructureDefinition;         e:electricMeasureUnit e:kWh.
        qb:component [qb4o:level e:month];
        qb:component [golap:member te:household];       e:o2 a qb:Observation;
        qb:component [golap:member te:appliance];       qb:dataSet e:datasetMHC;
        qb:component [qb4o:measure e:consumption;       e:month tl:05_2009;
qb4o:hasAggregateFunction qb4o:sum];                    te:household te:hhBrs01;
        qb:component [qb:attribute e:electricMeasureUnit].  te:appliance te:fridge_ZZRB934FW2Brs01;
                                                        e:consumption 000;
e:datasetMHAC a qb:DataSet;                             e:electricMeasureUnit e:kWh.
rdfs:label "Monthly consumption of household by appliance@en";
qb:structure e:consumptionYCity.
```

Fig. 6. Observations structure definitions and instances

We define the measure for the database and include attribute property which are used in generating observations. In our scenario, we define a measure for consumption (line 23) and its attribute which is measurement unit (e.g. kWh, line 26).

Using the structures, instances, measures and attributes mentioned we can obtain different observations over both topological and informational dimensions, as shown in Fig. 6. We use additional constraints over topological dimensions' attributes and/or different levels of the informational dimensions to structure the observations.

Assume that the proposed system needs to satisfy a query on *yearly energy consumption* of *households* from a specific *city*, based on a set of constraints such as no. of bedrooms and property price range. DB1 can only provide partial information and DB2 with informational dimensions regarding properties' market values in different years, based on the location and property layout details, can offer the complimentary information. This requires federated OLAP operations to retrieve, summarise and compose data from multiple semantic databases.

But the dimensions from different databases can have mismatched structure such as different level of detail in modelling. The location dimension in DB2 has a level called *area* which is a smaller division of *city* in DB1. Another mismatch in structure among them is the existence of a redundant level secondAdministrationDivision from DB1. Figure 7 provides the structure and an instance of area level observation.

```
z:area a qb4o:LevelProperty;          z:BS3 a golap:member;
        qb4o:inDimension z:location;          qb4o:inLevel z:area;
        qb4o:parentLevel z:city.              rdfs:label "Area covering
                                                    Bristol BS3 postcode@en";
                                              qb4o:parentLevelgn:2654675.
```

Fig. 7. Structure and instance of DB2's location dimension level

Other dimensions used in this database include time and property with the property price as measure. Figure 8a shows observations over the price of a certain type of property, based on the year and the layout of the property.

```
z:pricebyAreaProperty a qb:DataStructureDefinition;
    qb:component [qb4o:level z:area];
    qb:component [qb4o:level z:Year];
    qb:component [qb4o:level z:bedno];
    qb:component [qb4o:measure z:propertyPrice;
                  qb4O:hasAggregateFunction qb4o:avg];
    qb:attribute [qb:attribute z:currency].

z:datasetPriceAreaProperty a db:DataSet;
    rdfs:label "Propertis prices by Area, number of
               bedrooms and year@en";
    qb:structure z:pricebyAreaProperty.

z:obsBS3B1Y2009 a qb:Observation;
    qb:dataSet z:datasetPriceAreaProperty;
    z:area z:BS3;
    z:year db:2009;
    z:bedno 1;
    z:propertyPrice 120236;
    z:currency z:GBP.
```

Fig. 8a. Observation instance of DB2

```
d:consByYearHousehold a qb:DataStructureDefinition;
    qb:component [qb4o:level z:city];
    qb:component [qb4o:level e:year];
    qb:component [qb4o:topoDimension te:household];
    qb:component [qb4o:measure e:consumption;
                  qb4o:hasAggregateFunction qb4o:sum];
    qb:component [qb:attribute e:electricMeasureUnit].

d:datasetConsByYearHouseholdCMBI a qb:DataSet;
    rdfs:label "Yearly consumption for households from
               a specific area by number of bedrooms and
               inhabitants and restricted by market
               value@en";
    qb:structure d:consByYearHousehold.
```

Fig. 8b. Observation structure over DB1 and DB2

These standalone observations from both databases give useful overviews of the data but their combination can provide the complete output to the query, for example, on yearly energy consumption of households by performing roll up operations over these databases from and to different levels.

The structure of the desired observation that reflects our query is showed in Fig. 8b and contains information extracted from both DB1 and DB2. The following is an example showing the use of the federated roll-up operator to execute on the semantic databases against a set of constraints.

```
F_roll_up(swOimpl1, swOimpl2, olapds1, olapds2, constructSet,
constrs1, constrs2, true, materialize_location)
```

The following parameters passed to F_ROLL_UP are:

swOimpl1 = "igolap"
swOimpl2 = "igolap"
olapds1 = "http://www.energydb.eu/YearlyByAppliances#"
olapds2 = "http://www.zooplainfodb.org/PriceByArea#"
constructSet = observationStructure.rdf
materialize_location = "http://www.energydb.eu/mixObservations#"

The target of the operator is to perform roll-up operation on *olapds1* to summarise energy consumption from yearly by-appliance to yearly by-household and from area to city level over *olapds2*. The *swOimpl* parameter represents the type of the database, which also identifies the vocabulary used to structure the data. The *olapds1* and *olapds2* give the locations of data and *constructSet* sets the schema for the CONSTRUCT operator, describing how the observation needs to be built. The *constr1* and *constr2* represent a set of constrains for each database in order to build the appropriate SELECT pipe to retrieve data (e.g. city, price range and number of bedrooms for *olapds2* and household, year, consumption for *olapds1*).

The operator also has the capability to materialise the OLAP observations in datasets that can be used for more complex processing. These can be published with dataset attributes that show the level and type of summarisation performed.

The materialisation capability provides a big advantage when it comes to reanalysing data, or building a new database containing summarised information from different databases.

The F_ROLL_UP operator above is required through the boolean "true" value, to materialise the generated observations in a given location identified by the URI passed through materlize_location parameter.

One of the observations generated from the F_ROLL_UP operator above is:

```
d:oYHCMBI01 a qb:Observation;
      qb:dataSet d:datasetConsByYearHouseholdCMBI;
      z:city gn:2654675;
      e:year db:2009
      te:household te:hhBrs01;
      e:consumption 8800;
      e:electricMeasureUnit e:kWh.
```

This example gives a brief introduction about how the vocabulary can describe observations and use those observations or datasets to provide more meaningful information through OLAP operators over multiple semantic databases.

4   Conclusion and Future Work

The need for accessing multiple Semantic Web multidimensional databases increases, but there is a lack of effective and efficient solutions due to their complexity and inconsistency, and the difficulty in providing scalability. We have shown that there are cases in which standalone semantic web OLAP databases need to communicate with each other, but the diversity of the existing designs on their structures has complicated their interoperability. The incompatibility between informational and topological graph OLAP has deepened the issue of having unified OLAP semantic system.

We proposed an OLAP framework with a multiple-layers mechanism in order to address the challenges.

The requirements for designing the proposed framework have been identified and addressed with a set of new federated OLAP operators, vocabulary and semantic pipe like functions that can retrieve and merge the data from heterogeneous semantic web OLAP databases. We presented one of the operators, F_ROLL_UP, in detail and walked through the steps with an example to demonstrate how it executes queries, locates the data, retrieves the information, and composes the outputs for visualisation.

The proposed new operators and the extended interpreter capabilities to handle multiple OLAP databases have been partially implemented and tested. The rest of the outstanding operators will be implemented and applied to the complex case study in order to evaluate its effectiveness and efficiency.

We recognise the need for querying and analysing data from semantic web and relational multidimensional databases in the future. Our proposed framework is extendable to include retrieval and composition to meet this need and to provide a basis for further analysis. These functions can be realised from the composition of the OLAP operators and the translation of SPARQL queries into specific SQL queries in order to provide complex query responses.

References

1. Etcheverry, L., Vaisman, A.: QB4OLAP: a new vocabulary for OLAP cubes on the semantic web. In: Proceedings of COLD 2012: 3rd International Workshop on Consuming Linked Data, 11–12 November 2012
2. The RDF Data Cube Vocabulary. http://www.w3.org/TR/2012/WD-vocab-data-cube-20120405/. Accessed 5 April 2012
3. Chen, C., Yahn, X., Zhu, F., Han, J., Yu, P.S.: Graph OLAP: towards online analytical processing on graphs. In: Proceedings of the Eighth IEEE International Conference on Data Mining (2008)
4. Zhao, P., Li, X., Xin, D., Han, J.: Graph cube: on warehousing and OLAP multidimensional networks. In: Proceedings of the Sigmod Conference, Athens, Greece (2011)
5. Berlanga, R., Romero, O., Simitsis, A., Nebot, V., Pedersen, T.B., Abelló, A., Aramburu, M.J.: Semantic web technologies for business intelligence. In: Zorrilla, M.E., Mazón, J.-N., Ferrández, Ó., Garrigós, I., Daniel, F., Trujillo, J. (eds.) Business Intelligence Applications and the Web: Models, Systems and Technologies, pp. 310–339 (2012). doi:10.4018/978-1-61350-038-5.ch014
6. Kämpgen, B., O'Rain, S., Harth, A.: Interacting with statistical linked data via OLAP operations. In: Proceedings of the International Workshop on Interacting with Linked Data, pp. 36–49 (2012)
7. Beheshti, S.-M., Benatallah, B., Motahari-Nezhad, H.R., Allahbakhsh, M.: A framework and a language for on-line analytical processing on graphs. In: Wang, X., Cruz, I., Delis, A., Huang, G. (eds.) WISE 2012. LNCS, vol. 7651, pp. 213–227. Springer, Heidelberg (2012)
8. Morbidoni, C., Polleres, A., Tummarello, G., Phuoc, D.L.: Semantic Web pipes. Technical report DERI-TR-2007-11-07, DERI Galway. December 2007
9. Chen, C., Yan, X., Zhu, F., Han, J., Yu, P.S.: Graph OLAP: a multi-dimensional framework for graph data analysis. Knowl. Inf. Syst. **21**, 41–63 (2009). Springer, London
10. Qu, Q., Zhu, F., Yan, X., Han, J., Yu, P.S., Li, Hongyan: Efficient topological OLAP on information networks. In: Yu, J.X., Kim, M.H., Unland, R. (eds.) DASFAA 2011, Part I. LNCS, vol. 6587, pp. 389–403. Springer, Heidelberg (2011)
11. Etcheverry, L., Vaisman, A.A.: Enhancing OLAP analysis with Web cubes. In: Simperl, E., Cimiano, P., Polleres, A., Corcho, O., Presutti, V. (eds.) ESWC 2012. LNCS, vol. 7295, pp. 469–483. Springer, Heidelberg (2012)
12. Kämpgen, B., Harth, A.: Transforming statistical linked data for use in OLAP systems. In: Proceedings of the 7th International Conference on Semantic Systems, Graz, Austria, pp. 33–40, 07–09 September 2011

Detecting the Temporal Context of Queries

Oliver Kennedy[1]([⊠]), Ying Yang[1], Jan Chomicki[1], Ronny Fehling[2],
Zhen Hua Liu[2], and Dieter Gawlick[2]

[1] University at Buffalo, SUNY, Buffalo, NY 14260, USA
{okennedy,yyang25,chomicki}@buffalo.edu
[2] Oracle Corporation, Redwood Shores, CA 94065, USA
{ronny.fehling,zhen.liu,dieter.gawlick}@oracle.com

Abstract. Business intelligence and reporting tools rely on a database
that accurately mirrors the state of the world. Yet, even if the schema and
queries are constructed in exacting detail, assumptions about the data
made during extraction, transformation, and schema and query creation
of the reporting database may be (accidentally) ignored by end users, or
may change as the database evolves over time. As these assumptions are
typically implicit (e.g., assuming that a sales record relation is append-
only), it can be hard to even *detect* that a mistaken assumption has been
made. In this paper, we argue that such errors are consequences of unin-
tended *contextual dependence*, i.e., query outputs dependent on a variable
characteristic of the database. We characterize contextual dependence,
and explore several strategies for efficiently detecting and quantifying
the effects of contextual dependence on query outputs. We present and
evaluate our findings in the context of a concrete case study: Detecting
temporal dependence using a database management system with versioning capabilities.

1 Introduction

The goal of analytical modeling is to reflect as accurately as possible the real
world. However, with data often being machine-generated, people are increasingly realizing that "a single version of the truth ceases to be absolute and
becomes relative and contextual."[1] Being able to relate the results of a query to
the contextual assumptions on which the base data is built is thus increasingly
critical for providing accurate and timely results.

In this paper, we explore the notion of data context: First, we identify *contextual dependence* as a relationship between query outputs and *implicit* contextual
filters on the data being used. Then, we address a concrete class of contextual
dependence: *temporal dependence*, which occurs when a query result depends on
data that changes over time. Finally, we survey and evaluate multiple strategies
for what we call *dependence analysis*: the detection of contextual dependence in
query results.

---

[1] http://blogs.forrester.com/boris_evelson/12-12-12-top_10_bi_predictions_for_2013_
and_beyond.

© Springer-Verlag Berlin Heidelberg 2015
M. Castellanos et al. (Eds.): BIRTE 2013 and 2014, LNBIP 206, pp. 97–113, 2015.
DOI: 10.1007/978-3-662-46839-5_7

1.1   Motivation

The root challenge of contextual analysis arises across a variety of domains. We will discuss three specific domains that directly benefit from contextual analysis.

Contextual Dependence Errors in ETL Processes. Extract, Tranform, Load (ETL) is the process by which data is typically introduced into a data management system. Because of the nature of ETL, contextual assumptions about or dependencies in a data set or its structure can be omitted or misrepresented. ETL processes typically mask the source data and the transformation — only the final result is loaded into the analytical warehouse. For example when an ETL process aggregates data, individual values are lost and an outlier might skew the results in a misleading way. As a consequence, end-users who are not aware of such masked properties of the original data may inadvertently issue queries that mischaracterize it.

Example 1. Consider an ETL process that periodically dumps an OLTP customer database to an OLAP database for analysis. At the moment the ETL process runs, Alice's credit account balance might be $10,000. This simplified representation is natural, but might be misleading for analysts — for example, Alice's typical credit balance of $0 might be masked by a recent purchase.

Dependence analysis is a first step towards ensuring user awareness of masked properties (e.g., by visually annotating query results). Identifying tuples and attributes that change with variations in the ETL process can serve as a quick mental sanity check for end-users, to ensure that these variations are expected and/or within acceptable tolerances. Note that this issue could be addressed by a carefully designed ETL process *if* queries are known apriori, or handled aposteriori in query logic *if* this dependence can be identified or tracked. Context analysis *eases the burden* of detecting dependence in the first place.

Optimizing Operational Business Intelligence. Operational business intelligence, sometimes referred to as real-time business intelligence uses the analysis of real-time or low latency data to enable a continual view into what is happening, and to support decision making for a company. While integration, processing and analysis of near-real-time information is needed across the board, it can require significant cost in software, hardware and staff to develop and deploy [9].

We believe that a *fully* real-time decision query support system might not always be the best answer for operational BI. For example, consider a threshold on the inventory of certain items. In order to decide whether new items need to be ordered, there is no real need to constantly evaluate the exact number of items currently on the shelves until an inflection point is crossed which marks the boundary of inventory. In the past, such thresholds have been determined manually and were typically static. Predicting the optimal thresholds based on live sales data has resulted in higher efficiency and profits. However, creating these models can be very challenging and costly. Contextual analysis on the time domain could suggest models, again easing the burden on end users.

Volatility Analysis. Similarly, by analyzing the historic volatility for certain columns, a system could autonomously provide insight into another big BI data quality problem: missing data. For example, if a column historically has a certain update rate, and suddenly that rate changes outside of the norm, the system can notify the user accordingly.

In this paper, we characterize the notion of contextual analysis using time as a context in Sects. 3 and 4. In Sect. 5 we survey and adapt multiple strategies, both exact and approximate, for detecting and quantifying the extent of temporal dependence in a query result. We implement these strategies on a commercial database system and present the result of our evaluation of their performance and accuracy in Sect. 6.

2   Related Work

There has been much work on the use of database versioning to track the evolution of data over time [7,8,18,21], and on providing low latency access to temporal and versioned data using temporal indexing methods [16,22]. Many existing production-grade databases support SQL 2011's bi-temporal features [15]; This and related research efforts are basic technology enablers for our own work. Our primary focus is on performing query analysis *in-situ over existing database applications* by using transaction-time support already in the database. We evaluate and compare a range of strategies based on Monte-Carlo sampling, temporal queries, and provenance.

Our first approach uses Monte-Carlo sampling [11], a technique used in approximate query answering [19], and for probabilistic data [13]. We employ similar strategies to estimate the evolution of a query result over time.

We also explore the use of temporal database techniques [5,17,24] to optimize query evaluation. Point-in-time semantics allow non time-aware queries to be posed over temporal data, but do not admit an efficiently queryable data representation. Techniques for compiling point-in-time queries into interval-semantics queries [17] are a potential strategy for us, as they allow non-temporal queries to be evaluated efficiently over a version history.

Finally, we consider CTables and related work on provenance and incomplete information [4,12,26]. These strategies modify query execution to be aware of annotations tracking provenance [4,26] or missing information [12]. We employ a simplified form of these techniques to connect pre-computed summaries of data variability in query inputs with the corresponding query outputs.

3   Data Context

In this paper we adapt the model of context proposed by Bertossi et al. [2], and treat the relations of a database as views over a "global" database instance extended with additional contextual metadata. The Bertossi model classifies data as being of either high or low quality using a set of predicates over both the database and its surrounding context. Different quality metrics are achieved by varying the set of predicates considered. Rather than using a binary classifier, we instead consider context as establishing an *enumerable* space of possible interpretations.

The space of possible interpretations is captured by a *singleton* relation C with attributes encoding factors *implicitly* assumed by a database developer and/or the user posing a query. For example, the context relation might consist of a user's current location, a database designer's choice of Fahrenheit or Celsius, and/or a vector of exchange rates over time. Let G be a global database instance with schema S_G. We define a context-aware database instance D_C as a database instance with schema S_G and relations $R_C \in D_C$ defined as views over G:

$$R_C(x) \Leftarrow \phi_G(x) \wedge C(x)$$

Here $\phi_G(x)$ is an arbitrary conjunctive query over G. We refer to the relation C as the *context* of D_C. D_C captures the effects of context C under the set of assumptions that form C.

Given a query $Q(D_C)$ and a set $\mathcal{C}$ of contexts (i.e., instances of C), the goal of context analysis is to determine if and how $Q(D_C)$ depends on C. We refer to such dependencies as table-, tuple-, or attribute-level *dependence* in Q, depending on what parts of $Q(D_C)$ are affected.

Example 2. An analyst is working with a database G which includes temperature readings, and poses a query $Q(G)$. Using units of temperature as an assumption, there might be two possible contexts: one in which G's temperatures are in Celsius, and another in which they are in Fahrenheit. This gives us two instances D_c, D_f, respectively. The query $Q(G)$ can now be restated as a choice between the results of either $Q(D_c)$ or of $Q(D_f)$, depending on which contextual assumption is true. If $Q(D_c) \equiv Q(D_f)$, we say that Q does not have a contextual dependence. Similarly, a tuple present only one of $Q(D_c)$ and $Q(D_f)$ exhibits a tuple-level context dependence.

We are not only interested in the presence of context dependence, but in quantifying its *impact*. Following the literature on representing and querying incomplete information [1,12–14], one form of impact is to measure the subset of $\mathcal{C}$ for which a given tuple is present in $Q(D_C)$ (the tuple's *confidence*). Another is to generate visualizations and analytical summaries (moments, boundaries, or trends) for individual attribute values in the output. Such analyses generally take the form of a query aggregating over all possible contexts. This common, simple structure admits a range of different evaluation strategies. Our goal in this paper is to enumerate and evaluate four such strategies: (1) A naive, evaluation for each context, (2) a monte-carlo based sampling strategy, (3) a strategy based on query rewriting, and (4) an approximation strategy that composes precomputed partial analyses.

Time as Context. A particularly important instance of contextual dependence occurs when a relation's context changes over time. This class of dependence is frequently opaque to users, making it extremely hard for humans to detect. Moreover, many commercial databases already have transaction time and/or versioning capabilities and natively provide support for views of data parameterized by time. This makes the detection of contextual dependences feasible to implement, *even for databases already deployed in production.*

Example 3. Returning to Example 1, an analyst decides to run a new promotion for customers with low balances. Without realizing the volatility of the balance attribute, the analyst queries for all customers with a balance under \$1000 and mistakenly excludes Alice due to her recent purchase. The OLTP database's version history can be used to correctly answer the analyst's query, only after the analyst comes to realize that an error has occurred. Temporal dependence analysis can serve as a quick sanity check for the analyst, allowing her to quickly discover the potential error.

To define the view R_C, we take a context C consisting of a single attribute: *time* chosen from an enumerable *time horizon of interest.* The view R_t defines the state of relation R at the *point in time t.* We refer to a contextual dependence where time is the primary feature of the context as a *temporal dependence.* For the remainder of this paper we will focus on detecting temporal dependence in queries.

4   Detecting Temporal Dependence

We consider three levels of detail when searching for temporal dependence in query results: (1) Detecting temporal dependence in the entire result relation: *Does the set of customers with balances under \$1000 change over time?*, (2) Detecting temporal dependence in individual result attributes: *Does Alice's balance change over time?*, and (3) Quantifying the effects of temporal dependence on the results: *How much does Alice's balance change over time?*.

Naive Temporal Dependence Analysis. As a baseline, we consider a naive strategy based on a process called *temporal query normalization* [5,17,24]. Normalization identifies a minimal set of time intervals over which the results of a query Q are guaranteed to be unchanged. This is accomplished by enumerating the full list of versions at which a change is applied to any base relation referenced by Q (*versions*(Q) for short). The query is evaluated once for each version in *versions*(Q), producing a set of result relations (a set of sets) $R_Q = \{Q(D_t) \mid t \in versions(Q)\}$. Clearly, if $|R_Q| > 1$ then Q has a temporal dependence.

   This approach presents two immediate challenges: First, detecting (and quantifying) row-level changes with respect to time requires matching corresponding rows between relations in R_Q. Second, this approach can require substantial wasteful re-evaluation of large portions of the query, especially if each version makes only minor changes to the base relation. We first consider the question of row matching, and return to evaluation strategies in Sect. 5.

4.1   Row Matching

We would like to be able to identify not only row-level differences (i.e., insertions and deletions), but also cell-level differences (i.e., updates to individual data values). To accomplish this, it is necessary to match rows across query evaluations on different versions of the database — Was a row of the output modified (i.e., a cell-level change) or replaced in its entirety (i.e., a row-level change)?

We would like to match query output rows according to conceptual equivalence if at all possible, pairing two outputs if they correspond to the same conceptual entity. We consider three classes of queries for which it is possible to exactly detect conceptual equivalence:

Aggregate Queries. The group-by attributes of an aggregate query act as a unique identifier, or key for each output tuple.

Distinct Queries. The distinct attributes of a query act as a key.

Single-Relation Queries. The key (if available) of the relation being queried is used to identify each output tuple. For base relations that do not have keys (i.e., bags), we use the relation's physical row identifier attribute as a key.

For queries that do not fall into one of the above categories, we approximate conceptual equivalence through a form of why-provenance [3,6]. To support non-aggregate join queries, we compute a new key for each query output by composing the keys of each input source. The projection targets of the query are then extended with the key. Throughout the rest of this paper, we will assume that all queries have been transformed according to this process, and that the key is known.

4.2   Impact Assessment and Visualization

A copy of the query is evaluated over each version in a user-specified time horizon of interest: $t_1 \ldots t_N$. We abuse notation and treat t as the entire contextual interpretation C, and define AS-OF [18] queries as $Q^t(D) := Q(D^t)$ Visual annotations such as colored highlights (or asterisks in a purely text-based setting) on the query output convey two pieces of information to users:

1. Rows present in the current output are marked if they were not present in the output at some point in the time horizon of interest. The entire output table is marked if rows in the table were removed at some point in the time horizon of interest.
2. Individual (non-key) cells are marked if their values have changed at some point in the past.

In addition to highlighting temporal dependence in results, we wish to present the user with a significance metric for each case of temporal dependence. This is accomplished by grouping tuples together by key with an aggregate function of the form:

```
SELECT key, AGG(...) FROM Q¹ UNION ... UNION Qᴺ GROUP BY key
```

We focus on two aggregate metrics in this paper: row confidence, and attribute boundaries. More general aggregate summaries like average, standard deviation, and even plots over time can also serve as useful metrics or visualizations of the significance of a specific temporal dependence.

Confidence. We use confidence to capture the significance of a row-level temporal dependence. The confidence of a given row r is the fraction of time during which it is present in the database. This may be defined in terms of versions (e.g., as the percent of versions during which the row is present in the output), or by weighting (e.g., by wall-clock time):

```
SELECT key, COUNT(*) / N FROM Q¹ UNION ... UNION Qᴺ GROUP BY key
```

Boundaries. Boundaries or ranges capture the significance of an attribute-level temporal dependence. The upper and lower bounds for each attribute are computed by matching key attribute values across all results.

```
SELECT key, MakeRange(MIN(A₁), MAX(A₁)) AS A₁, ...
FROM Q¹ UNION ... UNION Qᴺ GROUP BY key
```

Example 4. Returning to Example 3, we would like to make it possible for the OLAP interface to signal the analyst in one of three ways: (1) By marking the analyst's balance query as time-dependent, (2) By marking Alice's presence in the result set as time-dependent, and/or (3) By indicating that Alice is part of the result set 99 % of the time.

5   Practical Temporal Dependence Detection

This naive strategy requires many complete evaluations of the query. We now survey a variety of specialized query evaluation techniques designed for related scenarios, and discuss how they may be applied to support efficient detection of temporal dependence in results. We consider three strategies: approximation algorithms including *Monte-Carlo Approximation*, and one we call *Analysis Composition*, as well as an exact algorithm that we call *Dynamic Analysis*.

5.1   Monte-Carlo Approximation

Our first approach attempts to limit the amount of work performed during temporal dependence detection by using Monte-Carlo approximation. Instead of evaluating the query at every version, the query is only evaluated on a fixed set of randomly selected sample versions S. In other words:

$$\left(\bigcup_{1 \leq t \leq N} Q^t \right) \approx Q^S := \left(\bigcup_{t \in S} Q^t \right)$$

Statistical metrics for the result set are computed as in the naive approach, but on a smaller set of sample points. Confidence values, expectations, and range boundaries are independent of result-set size; The process for computing these metrics is entirely unchanged. The time complexity of detecting temporal dependence in Q^S scales linearly in $|S|$, which we can control directly, rather than in N, which we can not. The improved performance comes at the cost of result accuracy.

5.2 Dynamic Analysis

The normalization process described previously operates at a coarse granularity. A separate instance of the query is executed for every version where *any* output changes. Instead of discarding query instances to produce an approximation, computation can be shared across successive versions.

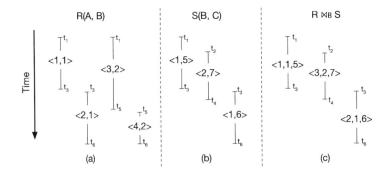

Fig. 1. An example dataset illustrating the value of dynamic analysis. The histories of relations $R(A, B)$ and $S(B, C)$ contain (respectively) 4 and 3 tuples over the interval (t_1, t_6). The join of both relations is shown under dynamic analysis. Under static analysis, tuple $\langle 2, 1, 6 \rangle$ would be partitioned into 3 intervals: (t_3, t_4), (t_4, t_5), and (t_5, t_6).

Consider the temporal database shown in Fig. 1. Naively, evaluating $R \bowtie S$ completely for each version where R or S changes (i.e., for each of (t_1, t_2), (t_2, t_3), ..., (t_5, t_6)) involves redundant computation. For example, $\langle 1, 1 \rangle \in R$ must be joined with tuple $\langle 1, 5 \rangle \in S$ twice, once for the interval (t_1, t_2), and again for the interval (t_2, t_3), even though neither input tuple changes at version t_2.

In this section, we adapt temporal query compilation techniques developed by Lessa [17] to our substantially simpler setting, and present an optimized form of temporal query normalization that we call *dynamic analysis*. Instead of partitioning tuple intervals prior to query evaluation, intervals are partitioned on-demand, as needed. Because tuples are partitioned independently, the number of partitions created is much smaller.

Each tuple is annotated with a new pair of *interval* attributes *start* and *end*, denoting the first and last version during which the tuple is present in the database. Queries are rewritten to properly map the interval attributes of their input relations to their output tuples.

Select, Project. Selections do not interact with intervals, and remain unchanged. Projections are modified to preserve the interval annotating each input tuple. For example, the query `SELECT A FROM R` would be rewritten to preserve the interval annotation: `SELECT A, start, end FROM R`

Join. Joins normalize output tuples on a tuple-by-tuple basis. The joined tuple is only present in the database so long as both tuples that generated it are present; The output tuple's interval is the intersection of the intervals of its sources. If this interval is empty, the tuple can be dropped immediately. For example, the query `SELECT A FROM R, S WHERE R.B = S.B` is rewritten as:

```
SELECT A, GREATEST(R.start,S.start) AS start,
        LEAST(R.end,S.end) AS end
FROM R, S WHERE R.B = S.B
        AND GREATEST(R.start,S.start) < LEAST(R.end,S.end)
```

This process generalizes to any number of relations and projection attributes.

Aggregate. Unlike joins, an aggregate requires its inputs to be normalized first. Consider a query of the form `SELECT A, SUM(B) AS B FROM R GROUP BY A` For each version in which R is modified, the aggregate value of the group containing the modified tuple also changes. We embed this transition into the aggregate query through a synthetic relation: `VSET(A, B, vers)`, which includes every version where $\pi_{A,B}(R)$ changes. We compute the aggregate value for each interval, using the versions in `VSET` to mark the **end** of each generated interval.

```
SELECT R.A, V.vers, SUM(B) AS B FROM R, VSET V
WHERE V.A = R.A AND vers BETWEEN R.start AND R.end GROUP BY A
```

Each interval is now annotated with only the end-point. We construct a simple window query to obtain the matching start points for each interval. In the following query, the `NTH_VALUE` aggregate is used to obtain the endpoint of the previous interval for group A.

```
SELECT A, B, NTH_VALUE(vers, 1) OVER
        (PARTITION BY A ORDER BY vers ROWS 1 PRECEDING) AS start,
        V.vers AS end FROM QPOINT
```

This process generalizes trivially to multiple group-by attributes, or multiple aggregate values. If the aggregate query involves multiple source relations, the join component of the query is first isolated in a separate nested-from clause and then rewritten as a normal non-aggregate query.

Acct	Name	Balance	ROWID	XID
	Alice	100	r1	v1
	Bob	200	r2	v1
	Carol	5000	r3	v1

(a)

Acct	Name	Balance	ROWID	XID
	Alice	10,000	r1	v2
	Carol	5000	r3	v1
	Carol	55	r4	v2

(b)

Fig. 2. The table Acct extended with row id ROWID and transaction id XID metadata (a) before updates, and (b) after updates.

Example 5. Recall our running example, and consider the example Accounts relation Acct shown in Fig. 2a. A sequence of updates is applied to this relation as follows, and the final relation is shown in Fig. 2b.

```
UPDATE Acct SET Balance = Balance + 9900 WHERE Name = 'Alice';
INSERT INTO Acct VALUES ('Carol', 55); COMMIT; -- Creates v2
DELETE~FROM Acct WHERE Name = 'Bob'; COMMIT;   -- Creates v3
```

Acct	Name	Balance	RID	start	end
	Alice	100	r1	$-\infty$	v2
	Alice	10,000	r1	v2	∞
	Bob	200	r2	$-\infty$	v2
	Carol	5000	r3	$-\infty$	∞
	Carol	55	r4	v2	∞

(a)

Q	Name	Balance	start	end
	Alice	100	$-\infty$	v2
	Alice	10,000	v2	∞
	Bob	200	$-\infty$	v2
	Carol	5000	$-\infty$	v2
	Carol	5055	v2	∞

(b)

Fig. 3. An interval encoding of the history of the relation Acct from Fig. 2 and the result of query Q on Acct.

The analyst poses a query $Q :=$ SELECT Name, SUM(Balance) FROM Acct GROUP BY Name, and wishes to detect temporal dependence in the output. To begin, the internal representation of Acct uses an interval encoding as shown in Fig. 3a. Following the dynamic analysis rules, Q is rewritten as follows.

```
SELECT Name, Balance, NTH_VALUE(pt, 1) OVER
        (PARTITION BY Name ORDER BY pt ROWS 1 PRECEDING) AS start,
     pt AS end
FROM (SELECT A.Name, V.pt, SUM(Balance) FROM Acct, (
             SELECT DISTINCT Name, start AS pt FROM Acct
          UNION SELECT DISTINCT Name, end   AS pt FROM Acct
       ) V WHERE V.A = R.A AND V.pt BETWEEN R.start AND R.end
        GROUP BY Acct.Name, V.pt
     ) QPOINT
```

Finally, the impact assessment process of Sect. 4.2 aggregates the result to obtain confidence and range values. Name is a key for Q, resulting in the following summary relation:

Q	Name	Balance	confidence
	Alice	[100, 10000]	1
	Bob	[200, 200]	0.75
	Carol	[5000, 5055]	1

Alice's balance is highly volatile, but her account is open for all four versions resulting in a confidence of 1. Bob's account balance is stable, but he closes his account in v3. Carol opened a new account in v2, but the query only returns the total balance for each customer; The small fluctuation in her balance reflects this.

5.3   Analysis Composition

Finally, we consider an approach inspired by the C-Tables [12] encoding for incomplete information. Instead of analyzing queries directly, this approach instead *composes* already precomputed results to approximate the result of a full analysis.

A C-Table encodes many possible instantiations of a base relation in a compact encoding using labeled nulls to represent missing attribute values, and tuple annotations to mark tuples that only exist in a subset of all instantiations. Although originally targeted at representing incomplete information, C-Table-style encodings have been applied to other forms of partial information, including probability distributions [1,14,20] and generalized provenance [10]. Exact probability computations for C-Table queries can be #P complete [1], so we instead use a simpler uncertainty model based on pessimistic error bounds.

Precomputation. For each base relation R, we precompute a summary relation $S(R)$, which contains the output of a full temporal dependence analysis of the trivial query SELECT * FROM R as described in prior sections. As an additional optimization before analyzing each base relation, we determine which columns are fixed, and which are time-dependent within the time horizon of interest by performing a COUNT DISTINCT grouping by the full relation schema.

Based on the sets of fixed and time-dependent columns, $S(R)$ tracks ranges for each time-dependent attribute and confidence values for each row. Concretely, the schema $sch(S(R))$ includes: (1) a confidence attribute, which we label $CONF$, (2) all of the fixed attributes in $sch(R)$, and (3) two attributes a_{min} and a_{max} for each time-dependent attribute $a \in sch(R)$ representing upper and lower bounds for the attribute, respectively.

This compact encoding discards the specific distribution of values that each time-dependent attribute can take, as well as any temporal correlations that might exist between attributes. When querying this data, we make two simplifying assumptions: First, we compensate for discarding correlations by computing only pessimistic, worst-case bounds on the ranges output for each attribute. Second, for confidence computations, we assume a uniform distribution for values in each range.

SPJ Query Rewriting. Consider a query $Q(R_1, \ldots, R_n)$ which we wish to analyze for temporal dependence. Given summary relations $S(R_1), \ldots, S(R_n)$, we wish to construct a query $Q'(S(R_1), \ldots, S(R_n))$ that approximates the results of a full temporal dependence analysis on Q. We initially consider SPJ queries:

SELECT F_1, ..., F_j, D_1, ..., D_k FROM R_1, ..., R_n WHERE $\phi \wedge \psi$

where F and D are fixed and time-dependent attributes, respectively, and ϕ is a boolean formula over both types of attributes, while ψ is a boolean formula exclusively over fixed attributes. Adapting the rules for C-Tables query rewriting [12] to our simplified model, the following three transformations are applied. (1) Time-dependent attributes are replaced by their corresponding range attributes D_{min}, D_{max}, (2) The confidence of the output relation is computed as the product of confidences of the input relations, and (3) The expression ϕ does not produce a binary truth value, but rather a confidence value that is combined with confidence values from the input sources. The above query is rewritten as:

SELECT $F_1, \ldots, F_j, D_{1,min}, D_{1,max}, \ldots, D_{k,max}$,
        COMPUTE_CONF$(\phi) \times R_1$.CONF $\times \ldots \times R_n$.CONF
FROM $R_1, \ldots, R_n$ WHERE ψ

Here, COMPUTE_CONF(ϕ) computes the probability of ϕ being satisfied, assuming that each D_i uniformly takes values in the range $[D_{i,min}, D_{i,max}]$.

SPJA Query Rewriting. Aggregation is handled differently based on the aggregate function. Non-group-by aggregates always have a single row as output, fixing their confidence at 1. The confidence of a group is the cumulative probability that at least one tuple belonging to the group exists. Aggregates over time-dependent attributes are replaced with an expressions that compute hard upper and lower bounds of each as follows:

- MAX(D): The pessimistic upper bound on the maximum aggregate is the maximum of all D_{max} in the group. A lower bound could be computed similarly, but we must also account for the possibility that tuples may be removed from the aggregated value if they do not have 100 % confidence. The pessimistic lower bound is the lowest value of D_{min} contained in a tuple with 100 % confidence, or $-\infty$ if no such tuple exists.
- MIN(D): The upper and lower bounds are computed as the inverse of MAX.
- SUM(D): The pessimistic upper (resp., lower) bound includes contributions from all positive (resp., negative) integers D_{max} (resp. D_{min}), as well as all negative (resp., positive) integers in tuples with a 100 % confidence.
- COUNT$(*)$: The pessimistic upper and lower bounds are the total number of tuples, and the total number of tuples with 100 % confidence respectively.
- AVG(D) is computed as $\frac{\text{SUM}(D)}{\text{COUNT}(D)}$.

6   Experiments

System Configuration. Experiments were performed on a commercial database system[2] with temporal query support and our query-rewriting front-end. The commercial database system was deployed on 2x8-core 2.6 GHz Intel Xeon processor system with 32 GB of RAM, RHEL 6.5, and 4 300 GB 10kRPM HDDs in a RAID 5 configuration. The front-end was deployed on a 3.7 GHz Intel i7 with 16 GB of RAM, OS X 10.9, and a 256 GB SDD, connected to the server through a 100 mb/s ethernet network.

Benchmark Workload. We based our evaluation on the TPC-H benchmark [25] workload and dataset generators. In order to simulate real-world temporal dependence in the data, we extended TPC-H's synthetic update generator with additional events as follows:

- **(a) Place Order** (44 %): An `orders` row and its matching `lineitem` rows as generated by the TPC-H update generator are inserted into the database. The `customer` who placed the `orders` has their `acctbal` debited the price of the order, and the `availqty` fields of matching `part` records are also adjusted.
- **(b) Cancel Order** (9 %): An `orders` row and its matching `lineitem` rows as selected by the TPC-H delete generator are deleted from the database.
- **(c) Pay Supplier** (9 %): The `acctbal` field of a `supplier` row selected uniformly at random is set to 0.
- **(d) Customer Pays** (9 %): The `acctbal` field of a `customer` row selected uniformly at random is set to 0.
- **(e) Buy Part** (9 %): An *amount* is selected uniformly in the range $[1, 1000]$, and a `partsupp` row is selected uniformly at random. The `availqty`, and `supplier.acctbalance` fields are updated accordingly.
- **(f) Change Part Price** (9 %): A `part` row is selected uniformly at random, and its `retailprice` field is multiplied by a value uniformly chosen in the range $[0.95, 1.1]$.
- **(g) MSRP Changes** (2 %): A `part.brand` value is selected uniformly at random, and all matching `part` rows have their `retailprice` fields multiplied by a value uniformly chosen in the range $[0.95, 1.1]$.
- **(h) Supplier Price Change** (9 %): A `supplier` row is selected uniformly at random, and all corresponding `partsupp` fields have their `supplycost` multiplied by a value uniformly chosen in the range $[0.95, 1.1]$.

Experiments were run on a database initialized with a 1 GB TPC-H Dataset (Scaling Factor 1.0). The database's temporal features were then activated, and a sequence of approximately 100,000 events from the synthetic workload were applied to the database with a new version created after each event.

---

[2] The commercial database system remains anonymous due to its licensing agreement.

Algorithms. We consider the four temporal dependence detection strategies strategies presented in Sects. 4 and 5. `Naive` denotes naive normalization, `MonteCarlo-X` denotes Monte Carlo sampling with X versions chosen uniformly at random, `Dynamic` denotes dynamic normalization, and `Composable` denotes composable analyses.

6.1   Performance Evaluation

Our experiments used a representative set of the TPC-H query workload including queries 1, 3, 9, and a lightly modified version of query 20. These queries cover a spread of functionality, requirements, and base relation update classes. Performance results are presented in Fig. 4. We used each algorithm to analyze a single query for both confidence and attribute bounds, changing the time horizon of interest. For composable analysis, the pre-computation of each base-relation's analysis is not counted by our results, however even for the largest relation the process took less than two minutes. Results are presented in in Fig. 4.

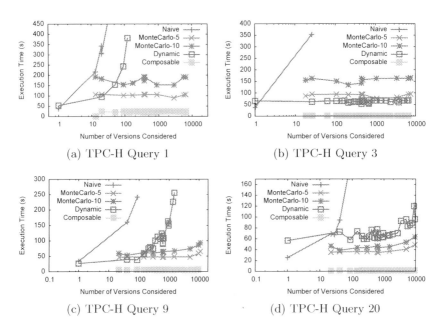

Fig. 4. Algorithm performance relative to size of the time horizon of interest. Note the log scale on the x axis.

Query 1 is an aggregate query over a single table and consistently produces a set of four output rows. Without temporal query logic enabled, the query takes approximately 3 S to evaluate. As shown in Fig. 4a, the approximate algorithms outperform the exact ones. Recall that for aggregates, dynamic analysis subdivides the versions created across all groups being output. Correspondingly,

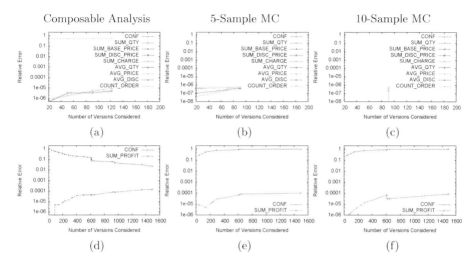

Fig. 5. Accuracy of the approximate algorithms on TPC-H Queries 1 (a-c) and 9 (d-f). Each line represents the relative error introduced by the algorithm on a single attribute query output or the tuple confidence (CONF).

Dynamic analysis remains a constant factor (approximately 3–4 times) faster than the Naive strategy. Both approximate strategies show an expected near constant-time performance. The bulk of the work for the Monte Carlo approach is in generating a constant number of samples, while the size of each base relation summary remains roughly constant as the number of versions grows — note that the cost of generating the summaries is linear in the number of versions considered.

Query 3 is an aggregate query over a three-way hierarchical join. Without temporal query logic enabled, the query takes approximately 1.5 S to evaluate. As before, the approximate methods show linear scaling. However, Dynamic analysis also shows linear scaling. This is due to the hierarchical nature of the query. The query produces one output for each row of orders that satisfies the predicate. Update classes (a) and (b) insert and remove orders together with their corresponding lineitem, ensuring no attribute-level temporal dependence in the aggregate values.

Query 9 is an aggregate query over a six-way join grouping on a dimension attribute. Without temporal query logic enabled, this query takes approximately 3.5 S to compute. The number of groups is capped at the 25 nations in the TPC-H Schema, all of which are affected by updates in the base data. As before, Dynamic analysis is a constant factor faster than Naive analysis. We also note a slight linear increase in the cost of the Monte Carlo approach as the number of versions considered approaches 10,000. As this same pattern appears in our results for query 20 experiment, we suspect that this slight increase is due to the join width.

Query 20 is a non-aggregate query over multiple tables. We made two minor modifications to this query: (1) We manually applied a standard decorrelation rewrite [23], and used a `SELECT DISTINCT` query to emulate the `EXISTS` predicate. (2) We avoid non-numeric values in the query results, and compute the set of supplier account balances rather than the set of supplier addresses. Without temporal query logic enabled, this query takes approximately 5 S to compute.

6.2 Accuracy

Figure 5 shows a comparison of accuracy metrics for the approximation methods. Composable analysis is quite accurate, generating estimates to within four nines for most aggregate values. In Query 1, a significant error appears in the `COUNT_ORDER` attribute. This is a consequence of composable analysis' pessimistic lower bound estimate. Any row with a confidence value lower than 1 is dropped from the lower bound; The upper bound is accurate. For Query 9, the accuracy actually increases as more versions are considered: this is an artifact of the actual confidence getting closer to the pessimistic bound. The monte-carlo methods fared significantly better at estimating the aggregate values computations. However, they did not identify some output groups, creating an extremely high confidence error.

7 Conclusions

In this paper, we identified an important class of queries: Context analysis queries, which vary one or more contextual attributes to identify dependence on the context. We explored context analysis in the domain of versioned/temporal databases, and identified three strategies for leveraging temporal features in existing database systems to detect temporal dependence *in existing queries*: Sampling, Dynamic Analysis, and Composable Analysis. We evaluated these strategies on a commercial database system and found that Composable Analysis substantially out-performs the other strategies. This performance comes at the cost of accuracy, in particular when computing confidence values. As expected, Dynamic Analysis provided the best performance of the non-approximate strategies.

References

1. Antova, L., Koch, C., Olteanu, D.: $10^{(10^6)}$ worlds and beyond: efficient representation and processing of incomplete information. VLDBJ **18**(5), 1021–1040 (2009)
2. Bertossi, L., Rizzolo, F., Jiang, L.: Data quality is context dependent. In: Löser, A. (ed.) BIRTE 2010. LNBIP, vol. 84, pp. 52–67. Springer, Heidelberg (2011)

3. Buneman, P., Khanna, S., Tan, W.-C.: Why and where: a characterization of data provenance. In: Van den Bussche, J., Vianu, V. (eds.) ICDT 2001. LNCS, vol. 1973, pp. 316–330. Springer, Heidelberg (2001)
4. Buneman, P., Tan, W.-C.: Provenance in databases. In: SIGMOD (2007)
5. Chomicki, J., Toman, D.: Temporal databases. Found. Artif. Intell. **1**, 429–467 (2005)
6. Cui, Y., Widom, J., Wiener, J.L.: Tracing the lineage of view data in a warehousing environment. ACM TODS **25**(2), 179–227 (2000)
7. Dadam, P., Lum, V.Y., Werner, H.D.: Integration of time versions into a relational database system. In: VLDB (1984)
8. Dittrich, K.R., Lorie, R.A.: Version support for engineering database systems. IEEE TOSE **14**(4), 429–437 (1988)
9. Gartner. Predicts 2014: Business intelligence and analytics will remain cio's top technology priority. http://www.gartner.com/document/2629220
10. Green, T.J., Karvounarakis, G., Tannen, V.: Provenance semirings. In: PODS (2007)
11. Hastings, W.K.: Monte carlo sampling methods using markov chains and their applications. Biometrika **57**(1), 97–109 (1970)
12. Imieliński, T., Lipski Jr., W.: Incomplete information in relational databases. JACM **31**(4), 761–791 (1984)
13. Jampani, R., Xu, F., Wu, M., Perez, L.L., Jermaine, C., Haas, P.J.: MCDB: a monte carlo approach to managing uncertain data. In: SIGMOD (2008)
14. Kennedy, O., Koch, C.: PIP: a database system for great and small expectations. In: ICDE (2010)
15. Kulkarni, K., Michels, J.-E.: Temporal features in SQL:2011. SIGMOD Rec. **41**(3), 34–43 (2012)
16. Kumar, A., Tsotras, V.J., Faloutsos, C.: Designing access methods for bitemporal databases. IEEE TKDE **10**(1), 1–20 (1998)
17. Lessa, D.: Temporal model for program debugging and scalable visualizations. Ph.D. thesis, University at Buffalo, SUNY (2013)
18. Lomet, D., Barga, R., Mokbel, M.F., Shegalov, G.: Transaction time support inside a database engine. In: ICDE, April 2006
19. Olken, F.: Efficient methods for calculating the success function of fixed-space replacement policies. Technical report, Lawrence Berkeley Lab., CA (USA) (1981)
20. Olteanu, D., Huang, J., Koch, C.: Lazy vs. eager query plans for tuple-independent probabilistic databases. In: ICDE, Sprout (2009)
21. Oracle. Oracle flashback. http://www.oracle.com/technetwork/database/features/availability/flashback-overview-082751.html
22. Šaltenis, S., Jensen, C.S.: R-tree based indexing of general spatio-temporal data. Technical report TR-45, TimeCenter (1999)
23. Seshadri, P., Pirahesh, H., Leung, T.Y.C.: Complex query decorrelation. In: ICDE, February 1996
24. Toman, D.: Point-based temporal extensions of sql and their efficient implementation. In: Etzion, O., Jajodia, S., Sripada, S. (eds.) Temporal Databases: Research and Practice. LNCS, vol. 1399, pp. 211–237. Springer, Heidelberg (1998)
25. Transaction Processing Performance Council. Tpc-h benchmark specification. http://www.tpc.org/tpch/
26. Widom, J.: Trio: a system for integrated management of data, accuracy, and lineage. Technical report, Stanford InfoLab (2004)

Towards Exploratory OLAP Over Linked Open Data – A Case Study

Dilshod Ibragimov[1,2]([✉]), Katja Hose[2], Torben Bach Pedersen[2],
and Esteban Zimányi[1]

[1] Université Libre de Bruxelles, Brussels, Belgium
{dibragim,ezimanyi}@ulb.ac.be
[2] Aalborg University, Aalborg, Denmark
{diib,khose,tbp}@cs.aau.dk

Abstract. Business Intelligence (BI) tools provide fundamental support
for analyzing large volumes of information. Data Warehouses (DW) and
Online Analytical Processing (OLAP) tools are used to store and analyze
data. Nowadays more and more information is available on the Web in
the form of Resource Description Framework (RDF), and BI tools have
a huge potential of achieving better results by integrating real-time data
from web sources into the analysis process. In this paper, we describe a
framework for so-called exploratory OLAP over RDF sources. We propose a system that uses a multidimensional schema of the OLAP cube
expressed in RDF vocabularies. Based on this information the system
is able to query data sources, extract and aggregate data, and build a
cube. We also propose a computer-aided process for discovering previously unknown data sources and building a multidimensional schema of
the cube. We present a use case to demonstrate the applicability of the
approach.

Keywords: Exploratory OLAP · LOD · QB4OLAP

1 Introduction

In the business domain, there is a constant need to analyze big volumes of
information for intelligent decision making. Business intelligence tools provide
fundamental support in this direction. In general, companies use data warehouses
to store big volumes of information and OLAP tools to analyze it. Data in
such systems are generated by feeding operational data of enterprises into data
warehouses. Then, OLAP queries are run over data to generate business reports.
Multidimensional Expressions (MDX) query language is the de-facto standard
for OLAP querying.

Traditionally, such analyses are performed in a "closed-world" scenario, based
only on internal data. With the advent of the Web, more and more data became
available online. These data may be related to, for example, the market, competitors, customer opinions (e.g., tweets, forum posts), etc. Initially, these data
were not suitable for machine processing. Later, a framework that extends the

© Springer-Verlag Berlin Heidelberg 2015
M. Castellanos et al. (Eds.): BIRTE 2013 and 2014, LNBIP 206, pp. 114–132, 2015.
DOI: 10.1007/978-3-662-46839-5_8

principles of the Web from documents to data converting the Web of Documents into the Web of Data was proposed. According to the standards, to facilitate a discovery of the published data, these data should comply with the Linked Data principles [32]. RDF was chosen as a standard model for data interchange on the Web [34]. With these principles in action, the whole Internet may be considered as one huge distributed dataspace.

With data being publicly available, businesses see the benefits of incorporating additional, real-time data into the context of information received from data warehouses or analyzing these data independently. Companies may explore new data opportunities and include new data sources into business analyses. A new type of OLAP that performs discovery, acquisition, integration, and analytical querying of new external data is necessary. This type of OLAP was termed *Exploratory* OLAP [2].

In the past years the scientific community has been working on bringing these new BI concepts to end-users. The main focus of research was providing an easy and flexible access to different data sources (internal and external) for non-skilled users so that the users can express their analytical needs and the system is able to produce data cubes on-demand. Optimally, the internal complexity of such systems should be transparent to end-users.

In [1] a vision to new generation BI and a framework to support self-service BI was proposed. The process, according to this framework, is divided into several steps and consists of query formulation, source discovery and selection, data acquisition, data integration, and cube presentation phases. Based on this framework, we propose our approach to performing exploratory OLAP over Linked Open Data (LOD). For the sake of simplicity, our scenario considers only data available in RDF format and accessible over SPARQL endpoints [35].

The novel contribution of this paper are:

- We define a multidimensional schema of an OLAP cube exclusively in RDF. This multidimensional schema allows to define remote data sources for querying during the OLAP analysis phase.
- We propose a computer-aided approach to deriving the schema of the OLAP cube from previously unknown sources.

The remainder of the paper is structured as follows: in Sect. 2, we introduce a case study for exploratory OLAP scenario where the multidimensional schema and sources of data are already known. We show how we can retrieve data and build an OLAP cube. In Sect. 3, we propose ideas for sources discovery and schema generation for such cases. In Sect. 4, we present a conceptual framework for achieving exploratory OLAP over LOD. In Sect. 5, we discuss the related work. Finally, in Sect. 6, we conclude this paper and identify future work.

2   A Movie Case Study

This scenario is based on the dataset originating from the Linked Movie Database[1] (LinkedMDB) website, which provides information about movies.

---
[1] http://data.linkedmdb.org.

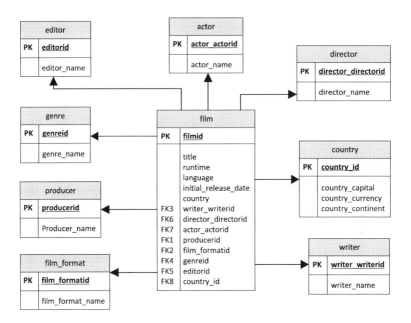

Fig. 1. Partial LinkedMDB logical schema

LinkedMDB publishes Linked Open Data for movies, including a large number of interlinks to several datasets on the LOD cloud and references to related webpages. Data can be queried using a SPARQL endpoint[2].

A typical movie record contains information about the movie, the actors who played in the movie, the director of the movie, the genre, the initial release date, the runtime, the country where it was produced, etc. An example record for the movie "The Order"[3] stored in LinkedMDB is as follows (all the prefixes used in the paper are listed in the appendix):

```
<http://data.linkedmdb.org/resource/film/1005> rdf:type movie:film ;
  movie:actor <http://data.linkedmdb.org/resource/actor/32063> ;
  movie:actor <http://data.linkedmdb.org/resource/actor/42288> ;
  foaf:based_near <http://sws.geonames.org/2921044/> ;
  movie:country <http://data.linkedmdb.org/resource/country/DE> ;
  dc:date ''2003,2003-09-05'' ;
  movie:director <http://data.linkedmdb.org/resource/director/9091> ;
  movie:film_cut <http://data.linkedmdb.org/resource/film_cut/15031> ;
  movie:filmid ''1005''^^xsd:int ;
  movie:genre <http://data.linkedmdb.org/resource/film_genre/28> ;
  movie:initial_release_date ''2003,2003-09-05'' ;
  rdfs:label ''The Order'' ;
  movie:language <http://www.lingvoj.org/lingvo/en> ;
  foaf:page <http://www.imdb.com/title/tt0304711> ;
  movie:runtime ''102'' ;
  dc:title ''The Order'' .
```

---

[2] http://data.linkedmdb.org/sparql.
[3] http://data.linkedmdb.org/resource/film/1005.

A partial logical schema of the LinkedMDB is given in Fig. 1. LinkedMDB also contains links to other datasets using the property `owl:sameAs`. For example, a country information is interlinked to GeoNames[4]. Based on the analysis of GeoNames, the partial logical schema of GeoNames is illustrated in Fig. 2.

Suppose a user wants to analyze data about movies. Examples of typical queries could be:

– Average runtime for movies by movie director and country
– Number of movies by continent and year

N.B.: She may want to do it in the context of information retrievable from GeoNames.

For this purpose, the user may want to construct a virtual data cube. Data will be retrieved from two sources: LinkedMDB and GeoNames. The data cube is considered virtual because data are not materialized in the local system. This data cube accepts user queries, queries the data sources,

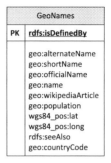

Fig. 2. Partial GeoNames logical schema

retrieves the information, processes it, and answers user queries. The multidimensional schema of such a data cube is given in Fig. 3. The schema describes the dimensions: Country (Population, Country Name), Release Date (Year, Quarter, Month), Director, Actor, Script Writer and the measure: Runtime.

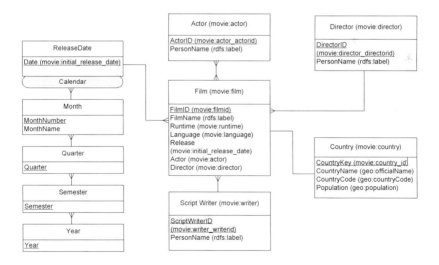

Fig. 3. Conceptual schema of the data cube

[4] http://www.geonames.org/.

Knowing the structure of the cube, a user wants to find the average runtime for movies by director and country. She issues an MDX query as shown in Listing 1.1:

```
WITH MEMBER Measures.AvgRuntime AS Avg(Film.Director.CurrentMember, Measures.Runtime)
SELECT NON EMPTY {Film.Director.Members} ON COLUMNS,
       NON EMPTY {Film.Country.Members} ON ROWS
FROM [MoviesDataWarehouse] WHERE (Measures.AvgRuntime);
```

Listing 1.1: MDX Query on the Data Cube

Data on the Web are mostly stored and retrieved as RDF and not as relational data. Therefore, we propose to use a fully RDF-based approach for exploratory OLAP over LOD sources and to analyze data without converting them to relational data and storing them in a local data warehouse. Additionally, loading and storing highly volatile, real-time data in a local system may not be practical.

In our case study we use RDF vocabularies such as QB4OLAP [5] and VoID [31] to describe the multidimensional schema. QB4OLAP is an RDF vocabulary that allows the publication of multidimensional data. QB4OLAP can represent dimension levels, level members, rollup relations between levels and level members, etc. QB4OLAP can also associate aggregate functions to measures. VoID is an RDF Schema vocabulary for expressing metadata about RDF datasets. The vocabulary may specify how RDF data can be accessed using various protocols. For example, the SPARQL endpoint location can be specified by the property `void:sparqlEndpoint`. Based on the information from the multidimensional schema, the system will be able to identify the sources and query them. An excerpt of the multidimensional schema for our running example, expressed in the QB4OLAP and VoID vocabularies, is given in Listing 1.2.

```
## Data structure definition and dimensions      ## Dimension Properties and Hierarchies
exqb:FilmCube a qb:DataStructureDefinition ;      exqb:year a qb4o:LevelProperty ;
    void:sparqlEndpoint                               skos:closeMatch db:Year ;
        <http://data.linkedmdb.org/sparql> ;         rdfs:comment "Film release year"@en ;
## Dimensions                                         qb4o:inDimension exqb:ReleaseDate .
qb:component [qb:dimension exqb:Actor];           exqb:quarter a qb4o:LevelProperty ;
qb:component [qb:dimension exqb:ReleaseDate];         rdfs:comment "Film release quarter"@en ;
qb:component [qb:dimension exqb:Director];            qb4o:inDimension exqb:ReleaseDate .
qb:component [qb:dimension exqb:Country];          exqb:ReleaseDate a qb:DimensionProperty .
## Definition of measures                          exqb:Actor a qb:DimensionProperty ;
qb:component [qb:measure exqb:Runtime];               skos:mappingRelation movie:actor ;
## Attributes                                         rdfs:seeAlso owl:sameAs ;
qb:component [qb:attribute exqb:FilmName] .            qb4o:hasAttribute exqb:PersonName .
```

Listing 1.2: Multidimensional Schema Expressed in QB4OLAP

To answer the MDX query, the system needs to send SPARQL queries to remote data endpoints for data retrieval. To do this, it first finds appropriate information for the measures and the dimensions specified in the MDX query from the multidimensional schema. The system finds the sources of data for dimensions /measures (`void:sparqlEndpoint`), all the attributes (`qb4o:hasAttribute`), the mapping information to map these attributes to the source equivalents (`skos:mappingRelation`), etc. For instance, for the MDX query given in

Listing 1.1 the system needs to find the information about the `Runtime` measure and the `Director` and the `Country` dimensions. Then, the system sends SPARQL queries to the LinkedMBD and the GeoNames SPARQL endpoints. The query that is sent to LinkedMDB to retrieve the information regarding dimensions, attributes, and measures is given in Listing 1.3.

```
### Retrieving attributes, dimensions, and measures
CONSTRUCT {
    ?movieUrl exqb:Runtime ?runtime . ?movieUrl exqb:FilmName ?movieName .
    ?movieUrl exqb:Country ?country . ?country owl:sameAs ?owlCountry .
    ?movieUrl exqb:Director ?directorID . ?directorID exqb:PersonName ?directorName .
} WHERE {
    ?movieUrl rdf:type movie:film . ?movieUrl movie:country ?country .
    ?country owl:sameAs ?owlCountry . ?movieUrl rdfs:label ?movieName .
    ?movieUrl movie:runtime ?runtime . ?movieUrl movie:director ?directorID .
    ?directorID rdfs:label ?directorName .
}
```

Listing 1.3: SPARQL Query to LinkedMDB

This query uses the `CONSTRUCT` clause to automatically create triples. These triples specify the dimension attributes and therefore can easily be copied to the final QB4OLAP structure. An excerpt from the result returned to the system for the query is as follows:

```
<rdf:Description rdf:about="http://data.linkedmdb.org/resource/film/930">
  <exqb:FilmName>Godfather</exqb:FilmName>
  <exqb:Director rdf:resource="http://data.linkedmdb.org/resource/director/448"/>
  <exqb:Country rdf:resource="http://data.linkedmdb.org/resource/country/IN"/>
  <exqb:Runtime>158</exqb:Runtime>
</rdf:Description>
<rdf:Description rdf:about="http://data.linkedmdb.org/resource/film/2939">
  <exqb:Director rdf:resource="http://data.linkedmdb.org/resource/director/10494"/>
  <exqb:Runtime>120</exqb:Runtime>
  <exqb:FilmName>Raincoat</exqb:FilmName>
  <exqb:Country rdf:resource="http://data.linkedmdb.org/resource/country/IN"/>
</rdf:Description>
<rdf:Description rdf:about="http://data.linkedmdb.org/resource/director/448">
  <exqb:PersonName>K. S. Ravikumar (Director)</exqb:PersonName>
</rdf:Description>
<rdf:Description rdf:about="http://data.linkedmdb.org/resource/director/10494">
  <exqb:PersonName>Rituparno Ghosh (Director)</exqb:PersonName>
</rdf:Description>
<rdf:Description rdf:about="http://data.linkedmdb.org/resource/country/IN">
  <owl:sameAs rdf:resource="http://sws.geonames.org/1269750/"/>
</rdf:Description>
```

Then, the data from GeoNames may be downloaded. In our running example the system uses the URI received from the "`owlCountry`" property and use it in the `VALUES` statement of the SPARQL query. We use a `VALUES` statement to group several arguments together in one query. Our goal is to send as few queries as possible. Since GeoNames does not have an associated SPARQL endpoint, the query is sent to the mirrored endpoint (http://lod2.openlinksw.com/sparql):

```
CONSTRUCT {
    ?s geo:countryCode ?o1 . ?s geo:name ?o2 . ?s geo:population ?o3 .
} WHERE {
    ?s geo:countryCode ?o1 . ?s geo:name ?o2 . ?s geo:population ?o3 .
    VALUES (?s){ (<http://sws.geonames.org/1149361/>) ... (<http://sws.geonames.org/1269750/>) }
}
```

Listing 1.4: SPARQL Query to GeoNames

This query returns information about the country's population, name, and code. A sample answer may look as follows:

```
<http://sws.geonames.org/1149361/>  geo:countryCode "AF" ;
    geo:name "Islamic Republic of Afghanistan" ;
    geo:population "29121286" .
```

The data obtained from the two sources are merged into a QB4OLAP structure: all received facts may be stored as qb:Observation instances (in OLAP terminology this corresponds to facts indexed by dimensions), all dimension instances are stored as triples. The aggregated values for measures are computed based on the qb4o:AggregateFunction function type. A sample QB4OLAP structure is given in Listing 1.5:

```
<http://data.linkedmdb.org/resource/film/810> a qb:Observation;
  qb:dataSet exqb:MoviesDataWarehouse ;
    exqb:Director < http://data.linkedmdb.org/resource/director/8629> ;
    exqb:Runtime 188;
    exqb:Country < http://data.linkedmdb.org/resource/country/IN> .
http://data.linkedmdb.org/resource/film/930> a qb:Observation;
  qb:dataSet exqb:MoviesDataWarehouse ;
    exqb:Director < http://data.linkedmdb.org/resource/director/448> ;
    exqb:Runtime 158;
    exqb:Country < http://data.linkedmdb.org/resource/country/IN> .
<http://data.linkedmdb.org/resource/country/IN>
        exqb:CountryName "India" ;
        exqb:CountryCode "IN" ;
        exqb:Population "1173108018" .
<http://data.linkedmdb.org/resource/director/448>
        exqb:PersonName "K. S. Ravikumar (Director)" .
```

Listing 1.5: Observations in QB4OLAP

In case the number of returned triples is large and cannot be handled by a SPARQL endpoint or transferred over the Internet, the system can send aggregate subqueries to the sources. The aggregation can be performed on the graph patterns used for joining several federated SPARQL subqueries. This will help to reduce the number of records for which the values from the endpoints will be transferred. For example, the following subqueries return aggregate values (left) and additional information (right) on the runtime of the movies by director and country. The results can be connected via the values of the ?owlCountry.

```
SELECT AVG(?runtime) ?dirName ?owlCountry          SELECT ?owlCountry ?code ?c_name ?pop
WHERE {                                            WHERE {
  ?movUrl exqb:Runtime ?runtime .                    ?owlCountry geo:countryCode ?code .
  ?movUrl exqb:Country ?country .                     ?owlCountry geo:name ?c_name .
  ?cntr owl:sameAs ?owlCountry .                      ?owlCountry geo:population ?pop
  ?movUrl exqb:Director ?dirID .                    }
  ?dirID exqb:PersonName ?dirName .
} GROUP BY ?dirName ?owlCountry
```

Listing 1.6. Aggregate and Informational Subqueries

The intermediate results of the execution of the subqueries may be stored in an in-memory table. Then, the results of the execution of the subqueries will be merged into the QB4OLAP structure.

Based on these data, the computed aggregated values are returned back to a user of the system. A sample answer to the previous MDX query may look as shown in Table 1:

Table 1. Aggregated Values

	Great Britain	India	United states	Venezuela	Pakistan	Russia	Netherlands
Sally Potter (Director)	86						96
Robert Aldrich (Director)			88				
Román Chalbaud (Director)		93					
Roland Joffé (Director)				87			
Gerald Thomas (Director)	78		83				

3 Source Discovery and Schema Building for Exploratory OLAP

In the case study introduced in Sect. 2 we assume that the data sources and the multidimensional schema of the OLAP cube are known. However, in reality the discovery of essential data sources is not a trivial task. Despite the fact that the publication of Linked Data has gained momentum in recent years, there is still no single approach on how these data should be published to be easily discoverable. We identified three potentially interesting data source discovery approaches for further investigation. In all three approaches described below we show how we can derive a schema of the OLAP cube for the scenario discussed in Sect. 2.

3.1 Querying Knowledge Bases

The first approach is querying large knowledge bases such as DBpedia[5], Yago[6], or Freebase[7] to find relevant information. Data from such knowledge bases are usually freely accessible over SPARQL endpoints. Querying these endpoints for the term of interest may lead to the discovery of useful sources of data or the necessary information itself. Since the number of answers that come from these sources may be extremely large and not always relevant, there is a need for filtering the answers. Also, since the user entry may be ambiguous due to the ambiguity and complexity of natural languages, the end user needs to guide the process of source discovery by selecting most appropriate alternatives for further investigation.

To find some relevant information about the term "Film", we can send the following SPARQL query to the Freebase SPARQL endpoint:

---

[5] http://dbpedia.org/About.

[6] http://www.mpi-inf.mpg.de/yago-naga/yago/.

[7] http://www.freebase.com/.

Table 2. Freebase Query Partial Results

?s	?l	?count
http://rdf.freebase.com/ns/m.02nsjl9	Film character	2001832
http://rdf.freebase.com/ns/film.film/character	Film character	1384754
http://rdf.freebase.com/ns/film.actor	Film actor	874840
http://rdf.basekb.com/ns/m.0jsg30	Film performance	673398
http://rdf.freebase.com/ns/film.film	Film	557505
http://rdf.freebase.com/ns/m.0jsg4j	Film actor	492249
http://rdf.freebase.com/ns/film.film_crew_gig	Film crew gig	456500
http://rdf.basekb.com/ns/m.02nsjl9	Film character	410669
http://rdf.basekb.com/ns/m.0jsg4j	Film actor	215777
http://rdf.freebase.com/ns/m.02_6zn1	Film crewmember	205938

Table 3. Freebase Movie Instances

?s	?p	?o
http://rdf.freebase.com/ns/m.0pj5t	rdfs:label	Falling Down
http://rdf.freebase.com/ns/m.0swhj	rdfs:label	A Charlie Brown Christmas
http://rdf.freebase.com/ns/m.0m2kd	rdfs:label	Stand by Me
http://rdf.freebase.com/ns/m.07cz2	rdfs:label	The Matrix
http://rdf.freebase.com/ns/m.0c296	rdfs:label	Amélie
http://rdf.freebase.com/ns/m.0prk8	rdfs:label	Hamlet
http://rdf.freebase.com/ns/m.0j90s	rdfs:label	Guess Who's Coming to Dinner
http://rdf.freebase.com/ns/m.02yxx	rdfs:label	Fearless
http://rdf.freebase.com/ns/m.0p9rz	rdfs:label	Romeo and Juliet
http://rdf.freebase.com/ns/m.0symg	rdfs:label	Dead Man

```
SELECT ?s ?l COUNT(?s) as ?count
    WHERE { ?someobj ?p ?s .  ?s rdfs:label ?l .
    FILTER(CONTAINS(?l,"Film") && (lang(?l) = 'en') && (!isLiteral(?someobj))) .
} ORDER BY DESC(?count) LIMIT 20
```

This query is optimized to allow sorting by relevance using the COUNT function so that the user sees the most relevant answers first. The partial result of the query is given in Table 2.

By examining the returned answer, the user may find some interesting triples and may want to explore these triples further. The system at this stage helps the user to do so. For example, several triples should be retrieved for further exploration. In our case, one of the triples has a subject equal to <http://rdf.freebase.com/ns/film.film>. The following query returns several instances related to the triple pattern of interest:

```
SELECT ?s ?p ?o
    WHERE {
    ?s ?p ?o . ?s ns:type.object.type ns:film.film . FILTER (lang(?o) = 'en').
} LIMIT 10
```

The result of the execution of the query is given in Table 3.

If the user decides that the selected samples satisfy the needs, the user is aided in building a multidimensional model of the OLAP cube. Our proposition for building a graph representation of the source is based on characteristic sets (CS) (Neumann and Moerkotte [19]), which contain the properties of RDF data triples for triple subjects. The system should also offer possible candidates for measures, dimensions, and dimensional attributes, identifying all triples related to the instances, their data types, etc. Then the user chooses the schema that most closely reflects the needs or directs the system for further search. In our example, the user may encounter properties of interest such as runtime, director, actors, and country by exploring the instance properties of the class `ns:film.film`:

```
ns:m.0c296  ns:film.film.country     ns:m.0345h;
ns:film.film.directed_by     ns:m.0k181;
ns:film.film.edited_by ns:m.07nw1y6;
ns:film.film.genre     ns:m.05p553;
ns:film.film.initial_release_date     "2001-04-25"^^xsd:datetime;
ns:film.film.runtime..film.film_cut.runtime     ns:122.0;
ns:film.film.starring..film.performance.actor    ns:m.01y9t4;
ns:film.film.starring..film.performance.actor    ns:m.0jtcpc;
```

The whole process of discovering the sources and building the multidimensional schema needs to be guided by a user.

3.2   Querying Data Management Platforms

The second approach for source discovery is querying so-called data management platforms. One such platform is the Datahub[8]–the platform based on the CKAN[9] registry system. CKAN is an open source registry system that allows storing, distributing, and searching of the contents for spreadsheets and datasets. Search and faceting features allow users to browse and find the data they need. CKAN provides an API that can be used for searching the data by applications. For instance, CKAN's Action API provides functions for searching for packages or resources matching a user query. Using the Action API, we can list all the datasets (packages) residing in the system (http://datahub.io/api/3/action/package_list), view the dataset descriptions (http://datahub.io/api/3/action/package_show?id=linkedmdb), or search for datasets matching the search query (http://datahub.io/api/3/action/package_search?q=Film). The answer is returned in JSON format.

Querying the Datahub for a "Film" string returns 99 results, where 5 results have SPARQL endpoints: Prelinger Archives (http://api.kasabi.com/dataset/prelinger-archives/apis/sparql), Linked Movie Database (http://data.linkedmdb.

---

[8] http://datahub.io.

[9] http://ckan.org/.

org/sparql), DBpedia-Live (http://live.dbpedia.org/sparql), Europeana Linked
Open Data (http://europeana.ontotext.com/sparql), and DBpedia (http://
dbpedia.org/sparql). By retrieving several instances of triple patterns and identifying corresponding properties (the same process as proposed for querying knowledge bases), we may define the multidimensional schema needed for the OLAP
cube.

3.3 Querying Semantic Web Search Engines

The third approach for sources discovery is querying semantic web search engines.
An example of such search engines is Sindice[10], which also provides a Search API
(http://sindice.com/developers/searchapiv3) using a query language (http://
sindice.com/developers/queryLanguage). The Search API provides programmatic
access to search capabilities of the search engine and returns the result in one of
three formats: JSON, RDF, or ATOM. This API supports a keyword search to
facilitate the discovery of relevant documents that contain either a keyword or a
URI. The query language supports filtering the search results by URL, domain,
class, predicate, ontology, etc. and grouping the search results by datasets.

Querying Sindice for the "Film" string returns many results (582,883), mostly
individual triples, but grouping the results by datasets allows identifying the
datasets for further exploration. The following query to Sindice reveals the
Linked Movie Database dataset (http://data.linkedmdb.org) for further exploration among others:http://api.sindice.com/v3/search?q=Film&format=json&
fq=format%3ARDF&page=6&facet.field=domain.

After discovering a proper source of information, we should apply the process
of building the multidimensional schema of the OLAP cube.

4 Conceptual Framework

The main functionality of an exploratory OLAP system is illustrated in Fig. 4.
Here we assume that there may (optionally) exist some internal data depicted as
a cube with dotted lines. These data may serve as a foundation for further exploration. A user may want to enrich/supplement these data by external data from
the Web. Ideally, the system should be able to retrieve data stored in any format (HTML, XML, CSV, RDF, etc.). In Fig. 4 these data are depicted as small
colored cubes which extend the internal cube. This requirement imposes additional complexity over the system, so the part of the system that is responsible for
exploratory OLAP can be further subdivided into several subparts, each handling
another data format. In this paper we concentrate on Linked Open Data and we
describe our vision on how to achieve exploratory OLAP over Linked Open Data.

The envisioned architecture for the exploratory OLAP over Linked Open
Data system is sketched in Fig. 6. The system consists of four main modules.
The Global Conceptual Schema module contains information about the schema

---

[10] http://sindice.com/.

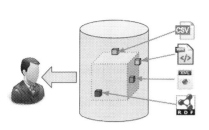

Fig. 4. Functional View

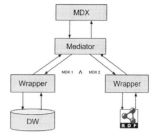

Fig. 5. Data Integration

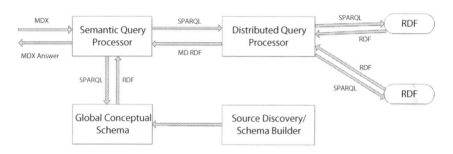

Fig. 6. System Architecture

of the specified data cube. In particular, it contains information about the measures, the dimensions and hierarchies in the dimensions, the potential aggregation functions over the measures, and pointers to data sources where the data are located. To represent this information, we propose to use the combination of QB4OLAP and VoID vocabularies. QB4OLAP allows defining dimensions, measures, and aggregations. The access and linkset metadata sections of the VoID vocabulary allow to describe data sources. An example of the multidimensional schema expressed in QB4OLAP that is part of the Global Conceptual Schema module can be found in Listing 1.2.

This combination of vocabularies is robust w.r.t. the schema complexity, the number of data sources, and the data volume. The schema complexity is handled by the QB4OLAP vocabulary as demonstrated in [30]. Recent changes to the QB4OLAP vocabulary [4] aid in defining complex multidimensional schemas with different hierarchies of levels in dimensions (balanced, recursive, ragged, many-to-many), different cardinalities between level members (one-to-many, many-to-many, etc.), levels belonging to different hierarchies, etc. A number of data sources can be referenced in a multidimensional schema of a data cube with the help of the VoID vocabulary. Regarding the data volume, recent experiments show that triple stores per se are not worse for analytical queries than RDBMS [15], so we expect our approach to be sufficiently scalable.

The Semantic Query Processor is a module of the system that accepts an MDX query as input and produces a multidimensional SPARQL query using the QB4OLAP vocabulary for further processing. For this purpose, it queries the Global Conceptual Schema to find appropriate information – the measures and the dimensions specified in the MDX query. After having received the requested information, the Semantic Query Processor will formulate SPARQL queries to all data endpoints and send these queries to the Distributed Query Processing module for data retrieval. Examples of such SPARQL queries can be found in Listings 1.3 and 1.4. The Distributed Query Processor in turn queries all data endpoints, collects and merges all data, and returns the result back to the Semantic Query Processor (Listing 1.5). The returned answer is then either displayed to the user or passed to the calling module for the integration with data from the internal data warehouse.

The integration of external dimensional data with an internal data warehouse has been studied before. For instance, Pedersen et al. [21] present an approach to the logical federation of OLAP and XML data sources. Following the same pattern, we envision that the system will have the mediator/wrappers to split and translate initial MDX query to other query languages. This is a common approach in distributed database systems [27]. The results received from the wrappers will then be merged by the mediator and shown to the user. The data integration architecture is depicted in Fig. 5.

The Source Discovery/Schema Builder module is responsible for deriving a schema of the OLAP cube based on the user requirements. This module interacts with the user during the schema construction phase. The user specifies the domain/key concept of interest; the module searches for appropriate data sources and proposes the most relevant of them to the user. The module uses the approaches described in Sect. 3 to find interesting data sources. We propose to use all three approaches because none of these approaches alone guarantees full reliability. After identifying data sources, the system proposes a list of potential facts, dimensions, and measures, constructs possible multidimensional schemas, and presents them to the user for confirmation. This multidimensional schema is then used in the Global Conceptual Schema module.

5   Related Work

In the following, we review previous research in semantic web warehousing, source discovery, and distributed SPARQL query processing.

5.1   Semantic Web Data Warehousing

Related work for semantic web data warehousing can be divided into two categories. In the first category of approaches, the data is loaded into a local data warehouse that is built over a relational database management system. The schema of the data warehouse is generally determined by an administrator of the system and the data from the Linked Data sources are loaded into the defined tables. Then, the OLAP queries are run against the data stored in a star or snowflake schema. In the second category of approaches the OLAP operations are executed directly over RDF stores via SPARQL.

Determining schema information for a discovered data source helps in building a multidimensional model of a data cube. In an RDF dataset, the subjects that share the same properties can be grouped together. The result is a list of property sets with associated subjects. These property sets are called Characteristic Sets. Neumann et al. [19] used the knowledge about these sets for the estimation of the result cardinality for join operations in triple stores. In comparison, we instead employ characteristic sets as a basis for building a multidimensional data cube schema.

Romero et al. [25] defined a semi-automatic general-purpose method of building a multidimensional schema for a data warehouse from a domain ontology. The method aims to propose meaningful multidimensional schema candidates. The method defines main steps that lead to identifying facts, dimensions, and dimension hierarchies. The system is semi-automatic in the sense that it expects a user confirmation for suggested concepts proposed as potential facts. Once the user selects a concept as a fact concept, it will give rise to a multidimensional schema. The disadvantage of this approach is the requirement to have a corresponding domain ontology. This may not be the case for all data sources.

Similarly, a semi-automatic method for the identification and extraction of data expressed in OWL is defined in [18]. OWL/DL is used to transfer valid data into fact tables and to build dimensions. According to the proposed method, an analyst defines a multidimensional star schema based on the known ontology of the source of data. Then, the data from the sources are loaded into the data warehouse. Overall, this method does not allow populating a multidimensional schema with semantic web data from the newly discovered sources with previously unknown structures.

A framework to streamline the ETL process from Linked Open Data to a multidimensional data model is proposed in [13]. In contrast to [18], this work does not require previous knowledge and an ontology to collect the data. The data that are retrieved from Linked Open Data sources are first stored in an intermediate storage, where these data are partitioned based on the type. Then, the analyst investigates the tables and chooses measures and dimensions for the multidimensional data model. Afterwards, the system generates the schema for the fact table, selects dimensions, and dumps data into relational tables for performing OLAP analysis. The disadvantage of this method is the requirement to have a high-level analyst for intermediate result investigation and multidimensional schema construction.

The approach proposed in [14] uses an ETL pipeline to convert statistical Linked Open Data into a format suitable for loading into an open-source OLAP system. The data are presented using the RDF Data Cube (QB) vocabulary [33] suitable for statistical data. The data that are stored in a QB file are loaded, via an ETL process, into the data warehouse. Then, the OLAP queries can be executed over the data. The advantage of the data stored as QB is that the measures and dimensions are already partly defined, so the transformation of data into the multidimensional model is easier. However, the method is not suitable for data expressed in other RDF vocabularies.

The execution of OLAP queries directly over an RDF store is explained in [16]. Statistical data defined with the help of on RDF Data Cube (QB) vocabulary are used. These data are loaded to a triple store. OLAP queries are translated to SPARQL queries and are run over the triple store. However, the proposed approach is applicable only to the data presented in QB. Moreover, the observations in the data should not include any aggregated values, otherwise the computation is incorrect.

In the majority of the current approaches [13,14,18] Linked Open Data are loaded into the relational tables of a data warehouse for further analysis. Our approach does not require a relational database for the OLAP analysis of web data. Additionally, our approach handles all types of RDF data unlike the proposal of [16], where only data stored as RDF Data Cubes (QB) are processed. Furthermore, our approach retrieves data from multiple sources whereas other approaches work with a single source of information at a time.

5.2   RDF Source Discovery

Heim et al. [10] propose an approach that automatically reveals relationships between two known objects in a large knowledge base such as DBpedia and displays them as a graph. They use properties in semantically annotated data to automatically find relationships between any pair of user-defined objects and visualize them. Although this approach is not relevant to source discovery the idea of searching through knowledge bases may be applicable to it.

Exploring Linked Data principles for finding data sources is proposed in [9]. One of these principles includes the usage of HTTP-based URIs as identifiers, which may be understood as a data link that enables the retrieval of data by looking up the URI on the Web. Hence, by exploring data during the query execution process one can obtain potentially relevant data for the system. However, this technique is less suitable for bulk retrieval of RDF data, which is needed for OLAP processing.

The publication of Linked Data as services is investigated in [22,23]. The use of Web Services and Service Oriented Architecture (SOA) is explored in this work. SOA facilitates easier data exchange between parties. A key component of SOA is the service repository, which serves the purpose of publishing and discovering services for future use. Research on service repositories for Web Services were extensive but the approach did not receive widespread adoption and was discontinued later. The main problem was the lack of support for expressive queries to identify and automate the discovery and consumption of services [23]. To address this problem, researchers propose to semantically annotate service descriptions to aid automatic discovery. Unfortunately, this technology did not receive widespread adoption either. If such a universal registry for services that publish Linked Data is created, a discovery and consumption of Linked Data from previously unknown sources will become easier.

An architecture of creating an up-to-date database of RDF documents by involving user participation in discovery of semantic web documents is described in [3]. This database can be used by search engines and semantic web applications to provide search and user-friendly services over the discovered documents. However, the service does not support discovery of SPARQL endpoints – this part of the process is left for future work. Scalability issues are not considered and are left for future as well.

Search engines for the semantic web [11,20] index the semantic web by crawling RDF documents and offer a search API over these documents. Different search engines use different index types: some index triples/quads, some index RDF documents. These search engines create an infrastructure to support application developers in discovering relevant data by performing lookup using, for example, full-text search over the literals. In this paper we propose to use semantic web search engines to support the discovery of SPARQL endpoints.

In this paper we further enhance existing approaches. We elaborate on ideas from [13,19,25] to build a multidimensional schema from previously unknown RDF data sources. Moreover, we extend principles from [10,20] for SPARQL endpoint discovery by grouping related results by datasets. For increased reliability in source discovery, we propose to employ a combination of approaches. Additionally, we target our approach to non-professional data analysts.

5.3   Indexing and Distributed Query Processing

As Linked Data are scattered over the Web, efficient techniques for distributed query processing become an important part of the system. Regarding distributed query processing over multiple SPARQL endpoints, several approaches and frameworks were proposed in the past years. In contrast to the systems for source discovery mentioned above, most systems for distributed query processing over SPARQL endpoints rely on the presence of pre-computed indexes or statistics to identify the relevance of sources [6–8,24,28] and only a few frameworks can avoid the need of pre-computed information [26]. Whereas most systems specialize in one type of data access, exploratory data access or SPARQL endpoints, hybrid systems propose handling different types of native access [17], often in combination with local caching [29].

In addition to determining the relevance of sources for a given SPARQL query based on the binary decision whether a source provides data that is relevant to answer any part of a query, sources can be selected based on their benefit [12]. In doing so, additional aspects are considered such as the overlap of the data provided by available sources. As a result, the minimum number of sources that still produce the complete answer to the query can be selected.

6   Conclusions and Future Work

In this paper, we presented a framework for exploratory OLAP over LOD sources. We introduced a system that uses a multidimensional schema of the data cube expressed in QB4OLAP and VoID. Based on this multidimensional schema, the system is able to query data sources, extract and aggregate data, and build an

OLAP cube. We proposed to store multidimensional information retrieved from external sources in a QB4OLAP structure. We also introduced a computer-aided process for discovering previously unknown data sources necessary for the given data cube and building a multidimensional schema. We presented a use case to demonstrate the applicability of the proposed framework. In the future, we plan to finish the prototype of the proposed framework and test the solution on large-scale case studies.

Acknowledgment. This research is partially funded by the Erasmus Mundus Joint Doctorate in "Information Technologies for Business Intelligence – Doctoral College (IT4BI-DC)".

Appendix

A   Prefixes Used in the Paper

```
PREFIX rdf: <http://www.w3.org/1999/02/22-rdf-syntax-ns#>
PREFIX rdfs: <http://www.w3.org/2000/01/rdf-schema#>
PREFIX exqb: <http://example.org/exqb#>
PREFIX owl: <http://www.w3.org/2002/07/owl#>
PREFIX movie: <http://data.linkedmdb.org/resource/movie/>
PREFIX lmdbres: <http://data.linkedmdb.org/resource/>
PREFIX geo: <http://www.geonames.org/ontology#>
PREFIX wgs84_pos: <http://www.w3.org/2003/01/geo/wgs84_pos#>
PREFIX qb: <http://purl.org/linked-data/cube#> .
PREFIX qb4o: <http://purl.org/olap#> .
PREFIX xml: <http://www.w3.org/XML/1998/namespace> .
PREFIX xsd: <http://www.w3.org/2001/XMLSchema#> .
PREFIX skos: <http://www.w3.org/2004/02/skos/core#> .
PREFIX foaf: <http://xmlns.com/foaf/0.1/> .
PREFIX dc: <http://purl.org/dc/elements/1.1/> .
PREFIX db: <http://dbpedia.org/resource/> .
PREFIX ns: <http://rdf.freebase.com/ns/> .
```

References

1. Abelló, A., Darmont, J., Etcheverry, L., Golfarelli, M., Mazón, J., Naumann, F., Pedersen, T.B., Rizzi, S., Trujillo, J., Vassiliadis, P., Vossen, G.: Fusion cubes: towards self-service business intelligence. IJDWM **9**(2), 66–88 (2013)
2. Abelló, A., Romero, O., Pedersen, T.B., Berlanga, R., Nebot, V., Aramburu, M.J., Simitsis, A.: Using semantic web technologies for exploratory OLAP: a survey. TKDE **99** (2014)
3. Bojars, U., Passant, A., Giasson, F., Breslin, J.G.: An architecture to discover and query decentralized RDF data. In: SFSW (2007)
4. Etcheverry, L., Vaisman, A., Zimányi, E.: Modeling and querying data warehouses on the semantic web using QB4OLAP. In: Bellatreche, L., Mohania, M.K. (eds.) DaWaK 2014. LNCS, vol. 8646, pp. 45–56. Springer, Heidelberg (2014)
5. Etcheverry, L., Vaisman, A.A.: QB4OLAP: a vocabulary for OLAP cubes on the semantic web. In: COLD (2012)
6. Görlitz, O., Staab, S.: SPLENDID: SPARQL endpoint federation exploiting VOID descriptions. In: COLD (2011)

7. Hagedorn, S., Hose, K., Sattler, K., Umbrich, J.: Resource planning for SPARQL query execution on data sharing platforms. In: COLD (2014)
8. Harth, A., Hose, K., Karnstedt, M., Polleres, A., Sattler, K., Umbrich, J.: Data summaries for on-demand queries over linked data. In: WWW, pp. 411–420 (2010)
9. Hartig, O.: Zero-knowledge query planning for an iterator implementation of link traversal based query execution. In: Antoniou, G., Grobelnik, M., Simperl, E., Parsia, B., Plexousakis, D., De Leenheer, P., Pan, J. (eds.) ESWC 2011, Part I. LNCS, vol. 6643, pp. 154–169. Springer, Heidelberg (2011)
10. Heim, P., Hellmann, S., Lehmann, J., Lohmann, S., Stegemann, T.: RelFinder: revealing relationships in RDF knowledge bases. In: Chua, T.-S., Kompatsiaris, Y., Mérialdo, B., Haas, W., Thallinger, G., Bailer, W. (eds.) SAMT 2009. LNCS, vol. 5887, pp. 182–187. Springer, Heidelberg (2009)
11. Hogan, A., Harth, A., Umbrich, J., Kinsella, S., Polleres, A., Decker, S.: Searching and browsing linked data with SWSE: the semantic web search engine. J. Web Semant. 9(4), 365–401 (2011)
12. Hose, K., Schenkel, R.: Towards benefit-based RDF source selection for SPARQL queries. In: SWIM, pp. 2:1–2:86 (2012)
13. Inoue, H., Amagasa, T., Kitagawa, H.: An ETL framework for online analytical processing of linked open data. In: Wang, J., Xiong, H., Ishikawa, Y., Xu, J., Zhou, J. (eds.) WAIM 2013. LNCS, vol. 7923, pp. 111–117. Springer, Heidelberg (2013)
14. Kämpgen, B., Harth, A.: Transforming statistical linked data for use in OLAP systems. In: I-SEMANTICS, pp. 33–40 (2011)
15. Kämpgen, B., Harth, A.: No size fits all - running the star schema benchmark with SPARQL and RDF aggregate views. In: ESWC, pp. 290–304 (2013)
16. Kämpgen, B., O'Riain, S., Harth, A.: Interacting with statistical linked data via OLAP operations. In: ILD, pp. 336–353 (2012)
17. Ladwig, G., Tran, T.: Linked data query processing strategies. In: Patel-Schneider, P.F., Pan, Y., Hitzler, P., Mika, P., Zhang, L., Pan, J.Z., Horrocks, I., Glimm, B. (eds.) ISWC 2010, Part I. LNCS, vol. 6496, pp. 453–469. Springer, Heidelberg (2010)
18. Nebot, V., Berlanga, R.: Building data warehouses with semantic web data. Decis. Support Syst. 52(4), 853–868 (2012)
19. Neumann, T., Moerkotte, G.: Characteristic sets: accurate cardinality estimation for RDF queries with multiple joins. In: ICDE, pp. 984–994 (2011)
20. Oren, E., Delbru, R., Catasta, M., Cyganiak, R., Stenzhorn, H., Tummarello, G.: Sindice.com: a document-oriented lookup index for open linked data. IJMSO 3(1), 37–52 (2008)
21. Pedersen, D., Riis, K., Pedersen, T.B.: XML-extended OLAP querying. In: SSDBM, pp. 195–206 (2002)
22. Pedrinaci, C., Domingue, J.: Toward the next wave of services: linked services for the web of data. J.UCS 16, 1694–1719 (2010)
23. Pedrinaci, C., Liu, D., Maleshkova, M., Lambert, D., Kopecky, J., Domingue, J.: iServe: a linked services publishing platform. In: ORES (2010)
24. Prasser, F., Kemper, A., Kuhn, K.: Efficient distributed query processing for autonomous RDF databases. In: EDBT, pp. 372–383 (2012)
25. Romero, O., Abelló, A.: Automating multidimensional design from ontologies. In: DOLAP, pp. 1–8. ACM (2007)
26. Schwarte, A., Haase, P., Hose, K., Schenkel, R., Schmidt, M.: FedX: optimization techniques for federated query processing on linked data. In: Aroyo, L., Welty, C., Alani, H., Taylor, J., Bernstein, A., Kagal, L., Noy, N., Blomqvist, E. (eds.) ISWC 2011, Part I. LNCS, vol. 7031, pp. 601–616. Springer, Heidelberg (2011)

27. Sheth, A., Larson, J.: Federated database systems for managing distributed, hetero-geneous, and autonomous databases. ACM Comput. Surv. **22**(3), 183–236 (1990)
28. Umbrich, J., Hose, K., Karnstedt, M., Harth, A., Polleres, A.: Comparing data summaries for processing live queries over linked data. WWWJ **14**(5–6), 495–544 (2011)
29. Umbrich, J., Karnstedt, M., Hogan, A., Parreira, J.X.: Hybrid SPARQL queries: fresh vs. fast results. In: Cudré-Mauroux, P., et al. (eds.) ISWC 2012, Part I. LNCS, vol. 7649, pp. 608–624. Springer, Heidelberg (2012)
30. Vaisman, A., Zimányi, E.: Data Warehouse Systems: Design and Implementation. Springer, New York (2014)
31. W3C. Describing linked datasets with the VoID vocabulary (2010). http://www.w3.org/TR/void/
32. W3C. Data W3C (2013). http://www.w3.org/standards/semanticweb/data
33. W3C. The RDF data cube vocabulary (2013). http://www.w3.org/TR/2013/CR-vocab-data-cube-20130625/
34. W3C. W3C semantic web activity homepage (2013). http://www.w3.org/2001/sw
35. Semantic Web. SPARQL endpoint (2013). http://semanticweb.org/wiki/SPARQL_endpoint

Efficient Pattern Detection Over a Distributed Framework

Ahmed Khan Leghari$^{(\boxtimes)}$, Martin Wolf, and Yongluan Zhou

Institute of Mathematics and Computer Science (IMADA),
University of Southern Denmark, Odense, Denmark
{ahmedkhan,zhou}@imada.sdu.dk, mawo09@student.sdu.dk

Abstract. In recent past, work has been done to parallelize pattern
detection queries over event stream, by partitioning the event stream on
certain keys or attributes. In such partitioning schemes the degree of parallelization totally relies on the available partition keys. A limited number of partitioning keys, or unavailability of such partitioning attributes
noticeably affect the distribution of data among multiple nodes, and is a
reason of potential data skew and improper resource utilization. Moreover, majority of the past implementations of complex event detection
are based on a single machine, hence, they are immune to potential data
skew that could be seen in a real distributed environment. In this study,
we propose an event stream partitioning scheme that without considering any key attributes partitions the stream over time-windows. This
scheme efficiently distributes the event stream partitions across network,
and detects pattern sequences in distributed fashion. Our scheme also
provides an effective means to minimize potential data skew and handles
a substantial number of pattern queries across network.

1 Introduction

Complex event detection is a growing field and a lot of work has been done to
efficiently detect sequence patterns [1–12]. Much of the past implementations
and research are aimed to process complex events on a single machine. Some
work has also been done to detect complex events in distributed environment
[1,13–15]. The focus of that work is partitioning the event stream on certain keys
or attributes, such as stock symbols. If no such partitioning attribute exists in
the query, or very few partitioning attributes/keys exist, then the event stream
can not be efficiently parallelized, and data being sent to various processing
nodes becomes very skewed, causing some machines to process much more data
than others, and ultimately leading to unfair distribution of processing load and
overall performance degradation.

Consider the case of two arch rival football teams playing in the world cup
final, where each team is supported by thousands of emotional supporters in
the stadium. To manage any health related emergency each person watching the
game in stadium is made equipped with a sensor that is continuously sending
the vital details about each person's physical conditions as events, and each

© Springer-Verlag Berlin Heidelberg 2015
M. Castellanos et al. (Eds.): BIRTE 2013 and 2014, LNBIP 206, pp. 133–149, 2015.
DOI: 10.1007/978-3-662-46839-5_9

event consists of (heart_rate, breathing_rate, body_temperature). As there is no natural partitioning key or demarcation of events carrying information about heart rate, breathing rate, and body temperature, hence, the best option is to partition them on the basis of time windows. Moreover, if we assume that the numbers of events generated by sensors are associated with every individual's heart rate, then a sudden and dramatic change in the game would greatly affect the number of events generated throughout the game. To handle such situations where the number of generated events change dramatically, and possibly out-perform a single machine, a better option is to process them in a distributed fashion.

Consider another case of event stream partitioning, if there are limited num-ber of partitioning keys in a query, then the resultant stream partitions can be too large to be processed on a single machine, and it would again require further repartitioning. Our proposed scheme does not experience such problem as the volume of data being processed by a machine, and the degree of the paralleliza-tion is subject to the available machines.

Our proposed approach is based on partitioning the incoming data stream on time-windows, it efficiently distributes fast data stream among multiple machines, and detects sequence patterns [3] running queries on machines. The essence of this approach is that, it can be used to parallelize processing of any sort of event stream without need of any partitioning key or attribute in the pattern query. Simultane-ously, while distributing the stream partitions, it ensures a fair and uniform data distribution among multiple machines, avoiding any possible data skew.

The work presented in this paper is summarized as follows.
(i) An event stream partitioning strategy based on time-windows, that does not take into account event stream attributes. *(ii)* A pattern sequence detection strategy that distributes stream partitions across number of machines, and exe-cutes pattern queries over stream partitions. *(iii)* Optimizations are proposed for efficient distribution of overlapping stream partitions across number of machines by removing duplicate events from consecutive partitions. *(iv)* A technique is discussed to prevent data skew while distributing stream partitions to multiple machines. *(v)* A simple cost model is proposed to evaluate the execution cost of pattern queries, based on the structure and complexity of the pattern queries.

The remainder of the text is organized as follows. Section 2 discusses problem description, and provides problem statement, system and cost model. Section 3 provides motivations of the research, challenges and an overview of the exist-ing research work. Section 4 provides some background details. Section 5 briefly explains the algorithms, proposed strategy and optimizations to the approach. Section 6 presents the implementation details, evaluation and outcomes of the experiments. Section 7 concludes the paper and discusses future research avenues.

2   Problem Description

2.1   Definitions and Semantics

Event. A data stream consists of various events, each event can be identified through it's event_id with respect to it's arrival time t and associated values termed as *attr_values* [16,17]. *Time-window*. A time-window can be described as a time-interval/passage of time, between time t_1 and time t_2 such that $t_2 \geq t_1$ [18]. The length of time-window is represented in units of time, as described in WITHIN clause of query-1. *Sequence pattern*. A sequence pattern is a sequence of events occurring in a sequential order. Such as (A; B; Q), a sequence query detects all instances of event B that follows event A, and all instances of event Q that follows B. *Sequence query*. A sequence query Q_s detects all the occurrences of relevant events in a time-window as depicted in Query-1.

Query 1. Pattern Sequence
PATTERN SEQUENCE $(e_3; e_4; e_5)$
WITHIN 5 min

Relevant event. A relevant event e is an event of interest iff e belongs to a sequence pattern S_p. *Stream partition*. A stream partition consists of a finite number of events that arrive in the system between t_1 and t_2. *Query semantics*. A sequence query evaluates all the events one at a time in their arrival order in a partition. Matching of events is non-greedy and contiguous in a stream partition [19], and every event is matched against a sequence pattern from t_1 to t_2 where $t_2 \geq t_1$ in a stream partition as shown in Fig. 1. *Overlapping partitions*. While partitioning the event stream on time-windows it is possible that a stream partition contained sequence of events which are also part of another pattern sequence in successive stream partition as depicted in Fig. 2. In such a case where consecutive stream partitions contain or share some of the events in the identical sequence are termed as overlapping partitions.

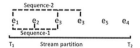

Fig. 1. Query semantics   **Fig. 2.** Overlapping partitions

2.2 Problem Statement and Formulation

The problem is formulated as: *From an incoming event stream S, continuously create stream partitions based on n units of time, send stream partitions to multiple machines over network, and while running sequence queries over stream partitions, detect sequence patterns and simultaneously load balance the entire system.*

While detecting event sequences in distributed fashion, the stream partitions and pattern queries should be distributed among machines in such a way, that none of the machines should be overloaded, the objective function to achieve this goal is described as follows:

$$w_i \leq \frac{\sum_{i=1}^{m} w_i \alpha}{m} \ , \ where \ \alpha \geq 1 \ and \ w_i \alpha \leq T \tag{1}$$

where w_i specifies average workload on a machine, α denotes a slight variation of workload that can be caused by one or many new stream partitions received by a machine, m is the number of available machines and T is a certain threshold based on machine's optimum level of processing that represents maximum load to be allowed on any machine, at any time t. In this equation $\alpha \geq 1$ denotes that average workload on a machine can vary by the processing load of one or many stream partitions. This variation in average workload is caused by the arrival of a single or multiple overlapping partitions.

The objective function is to share the processing load equally among all machines. If on one or more machines $w_i > T$ at some point in time, then the load would be readjusted among available machines. But, in case if average workload on all machines is $w_i > T$ then to avoid any performance degradation a new machine should be added in the system, or T should be adjusted accordingly. The second objective function deals with minimizing communication cost and can be described as follows: Assume that sending an event e_i to a machine on network would cost C_i then the total number of events sent over network would cost:

$$\sum_{i=1}^{n} C_i \qquad (2)$$

While sending stream partitions to machines, events or sequence of events which are part of overlapping stream partitions can be just sent once over the network, without causing common events to be sent in duplicates. This requires careful planning while sending stream partitions to multiple machines. Sending duplicate events can be avoided by considering the similarity of the sequence queries running on a machine. Sending common events just once in the stream partitions can reduce the overall communication cost as described below.

$$C_T = \sum_{i=1}^{n} C_i - \sum_{j=1}^{m} D_j \qquad (3)$$

Here, C_T represents the total cost of sending events without sending duplicate events, C_i represents the total cost of sending events including the cost of sending duplicates, D_j represents the cost of sending duplicate events. While maintaining $w_i \alpha \leq T$ on a machine and removing duplicates from the consecutive event stream partitions, we have certain constraints described as follows. Removing duplicate events from the event stream partitions requires temporary buffering of the events in main memory.

While buffering events we have to be careful about: (i) hardware limits imposed by the unbounded nature of event stream, and (ii) timely response needed by some time critical application. So, the size of the buffer should be carefully chosen to remove maximum duplicates from the stream partitions, without affecting the response required by the time-critical applications. A careful buffering of events would allow us to send events into batches, causing efficient use of network bandwidth, saving CPU cycles, as single interrupt required by a batch vs. multiple interrupts required by events sent individually. But, there are two issues associated with creating batches of events: **(i)** Batching of events would increase the communication latency. **(ii)** After removing duplicates, some of the machines might receive less events to process then some others. If this would continue for sometime, it would cause data skewness, poor workload distribution, and hence overall less efficient resource utilization. Therefore, to keep communication latency at an acceptable level for time critical applications, the following equation is devised.

$$L_B \leq T_L \tag{4}$$

Here, L_B represents increased latency incurred while creating a batch, and T_L is the latency threshold. It means, that while creating a batch of events, the latency must not exceed a certain threshold. The latency threshold is a tunable parameter, tuned as per requirements of the time-critical applications. If latency threshold satisfies the requirement of time critical applications, then it would also satisfy the applications with flexible time constraints.

2.3 System Model

In our model, a machine receives an incoming, unbounded sequence of events, referred to as an event stream. It is assumed that events in stream are externally timestamped, and arriving in strict order. In our model a *partition* of an event stream consists of a finite number of events that arrive in the system between the start and end of a time-window denoted as t_{start} and t_{end}. The length of a time-window is specified in the WITHIN clause of a pattern query as mentioned in Query 1.

Each pattern query before being executed is assigned a weight (see Sect. 2.4). The terms weight, load and cost are used interchangeably in the same context in our text. We assume that all the machines in the network have identical hardware resources. A single machine termed as *Stream Partitioner* in the system handles incoming event stream, partitions it and sends these partitions to other machines termed as *worker* machines over network. Each worker after receiving a stream partition executes a pattern query over the partition, and using NFA (Nondeterministic Finite Automata) evaluates the pattern sequence.

Role of Workers. In our model, at the system startup time, every worker waits in FIFO order for its turn, and receives a stream partition that turns it *busy*. Stream partitions to be sent across workers are scheduled initially on the FCFS basis and later as per current load of the worker. The current load of the workers is maintained in a weight-lookup-table that keeps record of ail the workers participating in the pattern detection process. The load on the workers is determined through the cost (weight) of pattern queries being run and the number of events being processed by the worker. If all workers have identical load then a worker will randomly be selected to receive a new stream partition.

2.4 Cost Model

While maintaining the execution cost (associated wight) of pattern queries in the weight-lookup-table, the following parameters would be considered.

Length of the Time-Window. The size of a time-window determines the size of a stream partition to be sent to a worker represented in units of time. A larger partition usually means there would be more events to process, and more time is required to evaluate a pattern sequence. *Events' arrival rate.* The number of events arrive in a time-window depends on the pace of data stream, a faster data rate means there would be more events to process in a time-window, but in our system we assume that events are arriving in order and in fixed time interval.

Number of Relevant Events Arrived in a Time-Window. The number of events relevant to a sequence query may vary from one time-window to another. Multiple relevant events in a time-window require us to evaluate all the combination of relevant events, increasing the cost of pattern detection. *Number of predicates associated with the events.* A pattern query may have some predicates, that specify rules termed as attributes of the events. Events arrived in a time-window will be evaluated against one or more query predicates. Evaluation of predicates against number of events also affect the query execution time. As all of the above factors play a combined role in the execution time taken by a pattern query, hence, the cost metric can be described as follows.

2.5   Formal Definition of Cost Metric

Given a Query Q, detecting a pattern sequence P, comprised of R events, where $P=(e_1, e_2, e_3...e_n)$, M predicates, within window-size of t time units, the cost of query would be:

$$\left[\sum_{i=1}^{n} \sum_{j=1}^{m} R_i M_j \right] + \left[C \prod_{i=1}^{n} R_i \right] \tag{5}$$

Here, R_i in the left side of the addition denotes the number of relevant events arrived in a time-window, and M_j denotes the number of predicates evaluated against each relevant event. While evaluating a sequence using NFA, from all possible combinations of relevant events denoted as R_i, a fraction of pertinent combinations denoted as C would be considered.

3   Motivation and Challenges

3.1   Motivation

Centralized implementations of CEP systems like Cayuga and SASE+ can handle pattern detection queries running on a single machine [1,13,15]. Single machine CEP implementations are aimed to handle all the queries and event stream in a centralized machine. But, a distributed stream processing approach is more suitable due the reasons as follows.

(i) Processing load can be distributed among multiple machines without putting unnecessary load on a single machine. (ii) Local optimizations can be done on the data available locally. (iii) Unwanted/irrelevant events as well as noise can be filtered out on the server side while partitioning the event stream, and each machine on the network just has to process individual segment of data stream. (iv) High degree of parallelization that can not be achieved on a single machine.

Time-window based partitioning can also be reformed to enforce better security control where each machine over the network would just receive the partition that is relevant to that specific machine.

3.2   Challenges

There are various challenges to efficiently partition and distribute event stream among number of machines. *First*, how to detect patterns involving sequence operators, by partitioning the event stream without considering key attributes, and running pattern queries in parallel on different machines. *Second*, what should be the criteria to partition the event stream. *Third*, how to select a machine that would receive a stream partition. *Fourth*, if there are some inter or intra partition overlapping of pattern sequences then how to handle such situations. *Fifth*, how to load-balance this entire partitioning process to avoid a situation in which a machine receives multiple stream partitions continuously that might overwhelm its processing capacity. The subsequent sections will briefly explain the techniques and strategies to deal with the aforementioned issues.

4   Related Work

Issues related with event stream processing have been studied by many [2–7,14, 15,19–33]. However, the work that is most relevant to ours is done by Balkesen et al. and Hirzel. Balkesen et al. in [14] proposes a run-based intra query parallelism scheme called RIP for scalable pattern matching. The focus of his work is to exploit multi-core architecture of a CPU. In his work an instance of Finite State Machine (FSM) is termed as a *run*. RIP distributes input events that belong to individual run instances of a pattern's FSM to different processing units or cores and each processing unit in a multi-core architecture performs pattern matching on a given sequence of inputs. As this approach is based on multi-core architecture of a single machine so it has some upper bound on the number of queries processed in per unit time. Balkesen et al. termed their RIP based approach skew-tolerant, but as their implementation is based on an isolated pattern matching engine, exploiting the features of a multi-core CPU, hence, their approach can not be compared with the data skew that could be seen across multiple machines processing real distributed pattern matching.

Hirzel proposes in [19], a partitioning scheme and a SPL operator that partitions and parallelizes the event stream [22]. It is based on partitioning the event stream on some stream attributes, referred to as *partitioning key*. The partitioning of event stream takes place using *partitionBy* clause that is identical to SQL's *Group By* clause. The partitionBy clause takes a key (or multiple keys) as its parameter to partition the event stream, and the degree of parallelization is dependent upon the number of distinct keys. If a parameter (partitioning key) is not passed to the partitionBy, or if partitionBy clause is not present in the scheme then the event stream would not be partitioned and sent to a single machine for processing. Hirzel's scheme requires some attributes to partition and parallelize the event stream.

Our work focuses on a different perspective i.e. time-windowing of event stream. The approach we propose is suitable to partition and parallelize any kind of event stream without taking key attributes and using any partitionBy or GroupBy clause.

5   Proposed Method

5.1   Central Theme

Our proposed event stream partitioning method is based on the principle of divide and conquer. A machine after receiving an event stream, partitions it on time-windows, and sends these partitions to individual workers over a network. Each worker after receiving a stream partition, executes a pattern query (or number of queries) over that partition to detect pattern sequences. Assume that Query 1 is registered as a pattern query to detect a pattern sequence over an incoming event stream S, and the pattern sequence specified in the query is comprised of events as shown in Fig. 3 by dotted rectangular. Algorithm 1 illustrates that upon receiving the event stream, the system will first detect event e_3, that is the first event in the required pattern sequence. Detection of e_3 at time t would be marked as start of the time-window or t_{start} and event e_3 and all subsequent relevant events from that point in time would be sent to a worker that would further evaluate the pattern sequence. Figure 3 shows that multiple identical events can arrive at any time, so each e_3 would be considered as a start of a new time-window or t_{start} (depicted by dotted line arrows), and would be sent to a worker that would further detect the pattern sequence. All the events that arrive after the detection of the first event until the end of five minutes time-window would be considered as a partition. After the arrival of the last event in that window that point in time is marked as t_{end} denoting end of time-window, and could be start of a new time-window. As shown in Fig. 3 by solid line arrows that detection of the first event e_3 at t_{start}, and end of a time-window at t_{end} is a logical partition on time.

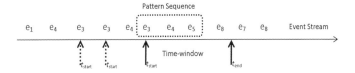

Fig. 3. Detection of an startup event

Algorithm 1. CreatePartition /*Partitioning the event stream */

1: **Input:** S, denotes an event stream, e_i denotes the starting event of a pattern sequence, t_{window}, is size of the partition
2: **Output:** P, denotes a partition
3: **while** e_i is detected in S **do**
4:     Let $t_{start} := e_i.ts$
5:     Let $t_{end} := t_{start} + t_{window}$
6:     Start partition P
7:     Let m:=Getmachine()
8:     Send event e_i in partition P to machine m
9:     **if** $t \geq t_{end}$ **then**
10:        End partition
11:        **break while**
12:     **end if**
13: **end while**

Algorithm 1 deals with creation and termination of a single partition, multiple partitions can be managed by calling the same operation multiple times. Each partition if completes without any overlapped t_{start} would be of identical size (in terms of time) while query 1 is being run, but the number of tuples (or events) in each partition might vary due to some external factors which could affect the occurrence of events. Machines across the network will initially receive partitions in round robin fashion and then as per their respective processing load. For efficient use of network bandwidth, unwanted or irrelevant events which would not be part of any partition, or not be the start of any sequence, would be simply skipped by the machine partitioning the event stream.

5.2   Processing Multiple Distinct Pattern Queries

A pattern detection system detects patterns with varying complexity, and each distinct pattern has a different evaluation cost, as some patterns can be more expensive to evaluate than others. Hence, to handle variety of queries it becomes necessary to carefully distribute the processing workload across multiple machines. Figure 4 depicts multiple varying length pattern sequences, to detect pattern sequence 1, upon detecting the first event i.e. IBM, this point is marked as the start of the window or t_{start}, and the end of the time-window would be marked as the t_{end}. After the start of time-window all the events including the first event would be sent to a worker for further processing. The *start*

Algorithm 2. GetMachine Algorithm

1: **Input:** LM, a priority queue of all machines involved in pattern detection
2: **Output:** m, a worker machine with minimum load
3: LM:=Prioritize(LM)
4: m:=LM.getNext()

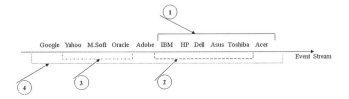

Fig. 4. Processing multiple distinct pattern queries

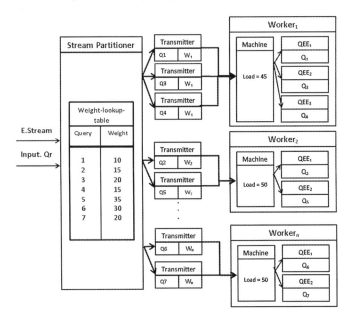

Fig. 5. Distribution of load among multiple machines

time and *end time* of the window sets the boundaries for the stream partition. Refer to Fig. 5, the stream partitioner after detecting the first relevant event of a sequence, partitions the event stream, and the transmitter sends the event stream partition to a worker. The worker after receiving a stream partition executes a pattern query over partition using a Query Execution Engine (QEE). The stream partitioner keeps a weight-lookup-table and ensures before sending a stream partition that the recipient worker should have less load then the other workers. The weight-lookup-table maintains processing load of all the workers in a priority queue, Algorithm 2 takes this priority queue and returns a worker with highest priority (with minimum load) to receive a partition.

5.3   Processing Multiple Overlapping Partitions

During processing of a huge number of complex patterns, it is possible that while partitioning the event stream some of the stream partitions might overlap each other as shown in Fig. 2, in such scenario, a careful decision can increase throughput, and cause efficient use of network bandwidth. While sending overlapping partitions to machines, there are three possible choices: *(i)* To send entire partitions (including common events in each) to different machines, this would lead to transfer duplicate events and cause waste of network bandwidth, specially when large partitions having multiple events in common sent over the network. *(i)* To send entire partitions (including common events in each) to a single machine. As, both partitions (including individual sets of common events) are sent, hence it is also a waste of network bandwidth. *(iii)* To send partitions sharing events with one another to a single machine, without sending common events twice. The third approach is simple, and effective than the first and second to avoid duplicate events to be sent across multiple machines, as it would send common events just once, and save network bandwidth. To efficiently select the most suitable worker machine to process overlapping partitions, we would maintain an in memory list of workers, with respective partition overlaps (if there is any) as depicted in Table 1. Before sending an overlapped partition to any worker, the partitioner checks the list for number of events in overlap, and number of most recent overlapping partitions sent to a worker. The new overlapping partition would be sent to the worker with highest number of overlapping events, Iff there is no other worker who received a non-overlapping partition in its most recent turn.

In Table 1 it is shown that worker 2 is the one with highest partition overlap, but as there is worker 3 whose most recent partition was non-overlapping or zero, hence, the partition would be sent to worker 3 as it must have finished or could be in the middle of processing it's most recent partition. The above solution to send overlapping partition is suitable for most of the cases. To handle a special case where a stream partition has no or zero overlap with respect to the partitions sent to all workers, and all workers have an equal partition count, such situation would be handled using Algorithm 3. This algorithm while sending partitions across workers considers an upper bound of processing capabilities of each worker termed as threshold. The threshold is based on the hardware configurations of the machines. A worker with minimum load is selected through calculating the current load, plus load of the query. Let m_1 denote the most recent machine that has received a partition, and m_2 denotes a machine with minimum processing load; let T be the maximum threshold for machine load, p be the overlapping partition, and Q be a pattern query to detect a pattern over p, then using this algorithm if the current processing load on m_1 plus the new processing load to be assigned to it is less than T then it will receive the next stream partition otherwise a suitable machine will be sought.

Optimization to the approach. As many of the real world applications require a rapid detection of event patterns such as seismographic patterns, there are some applications which do not require a real-time response, and their processing can be delayed up to a certain time interval. Sending individual events to a worker is not an efficient method that leads to poor CPU and bandwidth utilization. Algorithm 4 groups individual events into batches and sends them as a single

Table 1. Worker selection for overlapping partitions

Worker_id	Partition overlap (#of overlap events)	Partition count (# of partitions already received)
1	5	2
2	6	3
3	2	0

batch for further processing. In Algorithm 4, we assume that each pattern query has a priority associated with it, this priority can be assigned to a pattern query as per specific needs of an application. We have set a user defined priority threshold for all the queries in the system. When a pattern query has a priority equal to or higher than the priority threshold it requires that relevant events should be sent without any delay, so, after detection of the very first event such as e_j, it would be checked that is there any existing batch ready to be sent to the worker m, if such a batch exists then e_j would be included in the batch and the batch would be sent without any delay. If there is no existing batch, then e_j (as a start of the new partition) would be sent without any delay to the concerned worker. But, when a query has priority less than the priority threshold, it means that the nature of the application associated with the query can ignore a certain delay and we will start creating a batch of events.

Algorithm 3. Machine selection for sending overlapping partition

1: **if** p is detected **then**
2:    **if** m_1.totalLoad+Q.load<T **then**
3:        send p to m_1;
4:    **else**
5:        send p to m_2
6:    **end if**
7: **end if**

The size of the batches would be based on a user defined threshold set as per time critical needs of the applications. Creating batches of events can be very useful when there is an overlapping between partitions, as certain events in overlapping partitions can be just sent once to a worker, leading to a reduced network traffic. The efficiency of sending events into batches is highly dependent on the batch size, which is further dependent on the priority associated with the query.

6   Experimental Evaluation

Our present work is an evaluation of our proposed method, in future the focus of our work would be to extend our experiments to process real life large data

---

Algorithm 4. BatchOfEvents /* Creating batch of events */

1: **Input:** Q_i is the ith query, e_j is the first event in the relevant partition, p_k is the priority associated with the query, B_T is batch-size threshold
2: **do**
3: **if** $p_k \geq p_t$ */ p_t is some priority threshold */ **then**
4:   **if** Any BoE alreday exists **then**
5:     Attach e_j to BoE
6:   **else**
7:     CreatePartition() /* Call the partition procedure */
8:   **end if**
9: **else**
10:   **if** $p_k < p_t$ */ p_t is some priority threshold */ **then**
11:     Start batching events (BoE)
12:     BoE.end := BoE.currentSize + t_{window}
13:     **while** $BoE.end \leq B_T$ **do**
14:       Add e_j to BoE /* Add every event to the batch of events */
15:     **end while**
16:     Let m := GetMachine() /*Call GetMachine() Procedure */
17:     Send BoE to m /* Send batch of events to machine m */
18:   **end if**
19: **end if**
20: **while(true)**

---

sets increasing queries and machines. In our present study a system based on the strategies and algorithms mentioned in Sect. 5 has been developed, and experiments have been conducted on a cluster of four machines, each running Linux on a dual core 2.6 GHz CPU and 4.8 GB of main memory, 4.6 GB of secondary storage. Our setup was based on a single stream partitioner, and three worker machines, all connected through a local area network. We expect that result would differ on an overlay network due to a higher latency and communication cost.

The experiments have been performed running sequence queries consisting of random sequences of English alphabet with varying size of time-windows, and without predicates. Processing sequence patterns involving predicates would be extended in the future work. Each query detects a pattern similar to the Query 1 discussed in Sect. 2.3. Initially, a synthetic stream of five thousand events was generated, and to perform multiple experiments, the same stream was used to construct ten thousand, fifteen thousand, twenty thousand and twenty five thousand events. In each experiment pattern queries were divided in two categories i.e. high priority queries, and low priority queries. High priority queries were assigned priority than the other half of the queries, to mimic real world scenario where some applications need a time critical response.

6.1   Results and Discussion

While conducting experiments, it was observed that the major factor that affects the hardware resources and processing time is not just the event stream itself,

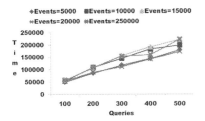

Fig. 6. Processing time of various stream inputs

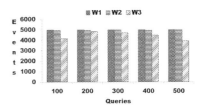

Fig. 7. Distribtion of processing load

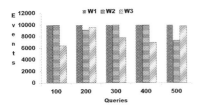

Fig. 8. Distribtion of processing load

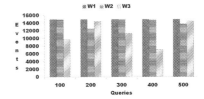

Fig. 9. Distribtion of processing load

but, the complexity of patterns and queries being processed by workers. The complexity and structure of the pattern and the number of predicate decide the evaluation time required by a sequence query. In the first experiment we tested our approach on different sets of input streams, and running one hundred to five hundred queries on each input set. Figure 6 depicts that during all experiments the processing time(ms) shows a linear growth behavior. The reason for this linear growth is that the event streams were distributed fairly well among workers, and there was no worker machine that received huge processing load that would have caused it to spend higher amount of time increasing the overall processing time of the job. To observe the load balancing, possible data skew, and duplicate removals (in overlapping partitions) we conducted many experiments. Figures 7, 8, 9, 10 and 11 depict distribution of processing load among workers, it can be observed that processing load (number of events processed) are distributed fairly well in workers. But, some of the workers have slightly lower processing load, this is due to the reason that overlapping partitions are sent to the workers with maximum partition overlap as described in Sect. 5.3. Sending duplicate events can be avoided while creating partitions by increasing the size of the batches and sending overlapping partitions continuously to some specific worker(s). But, creating larger size batches would effect the time critical nature of some of the applications as well as potentially result in data skew, and load balancing issues. Removing duplicate events to cut down the communication cost is useful in cases where conservation of network bandwidth is of primary concern, but as we have just single stream partitioner with fixed hardware resources, creating larger size of batches can cause a performance bottleneck at the partitioner side. So, the present load distribution among workers

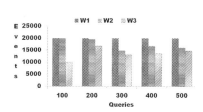

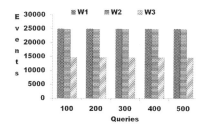

Fig. 10. Distribtion of processing load   **Fig. 11.** Distribtion of processing load

shows a mix of load balancing and duplicate removal. It must be noted that in the figures the number of events processed by each approach are higher than the actual number of events given as input, this is because an event can be associated with multiple sequence patterns, and hence, processed individually for each sequence pattern by respective pattern query.

7   Conclusion and Future Work

Partitioning and distribution of event stream on partitioning keys are potentially prone to data skew, as the parallelization relies on the number of keys. In this paper we propose a stream partitioning scheme that is not dependent on the partitioning attributes, it efficiently partitions and distributes the event stream, and elegantly load balances the entire process of detection of sequence pattern across multiple machines. In future we intend to extend our work to include predicate handling, improved load balancing and want to repeat our experiments on large real life data sets. We also want to introduce multiple stream partitioner to avoid performance bottleneck and any single point of failure.

References

1. Diao, Y., Immerman, N., Gyllstrom, D.: Sase+: An Agile Language for Kleene Closure Over Event Streams. ACM Press, New York (2007)
2. Agrawal, J., Diao, Y., Gyllstrom, D., Immerman, N.: Efficient pattern matching over event streams. In: Proceedings of the 2008 ACM SIGMOD International Conference on Management of Data, pp. 147–160. ACM (2008)
3. Mei, Y., Madden, S.: Zstream: a cost-based query processor for adaptively detecting composite events. In: Proceedings of the 2009 ACM SIGMOD International Conference on Management of Data, pp. 193–206. ACM (2009)
4. Wu, E., Diao, Y., Rizvi, S.: High-performance complex event processing over streams. In: Proceedings of the 2006 ACM SIGMOD International Conference on Management of Data, pp. 407–418. ACM (2006)
5. Liu, M., Ray, M., Rundensteiner, E.A., Dougherty, D.J., Gupta, C., Wang, S., Ari, I., Mehta, A.: Processing nested complex sequence pattern queries over event streams. In: Proceedings of the Seventh International Workshop on Data Management for Sensor Networks, pp. 14–19. ACM (2010)

6. Ramakrishnan, R., Cheng, M., Livny, M., Seshadri, P.: What's next? sequence queries. In: Proceedings of International Conferene Management of Data. Citeseer (1994)
7. Liu, M., Li, M., Golovnya, D., Rundensteiner, E.A., Claypool, K.: Sequence pattern query processing over out-of-order event streams. In: IEEE 25th International Conference on Data Engineering, ICDE 2009, pp. 784–795. IEEE (2009)
8. Law, Y.N., Wang, H., Zaniolo, C.: Query languages and data models for database sequences and data streams. In: Proceedings of the Thirtieth International Conference on Very Large Data Bases, vol. 30, pp. 492–503. VLDB Endowment (2004)
9. Seshadri, P., Livny, M., Ramakrishnan, R.: Sequence query processing. ACM SIGMOD Rec. **23**, 430–441 (1994). ACM
10. Zuo, X., Zhou, Y., Zhao, C.-H.: Elastic non-contiguous sequence pattern detection for data stream monitoring. In: Yin, H., Tino, P., Corchado, E., Byrne, W., Yao, X. (eds.) IDEAL 2007. LNCS, vol. 4881, pp. 599–608. Springer, Heidelberg (2007)
11. Gao, C., Wei, J., Xu, C., Cheung, S.: Sequential event pattern based context-aware adaptation. In: Proceedings of the Second Asia-Pacific Symposium on Internetware, p. 3. ACM (2010)
12. Gyllstrom, D., Agrawal, J., Diao, Y., Immerman, N.: On supporting kleene closure over event streams. In: ICDE, vol. 8, pp. 1391–1393 (2008)
13. Demers, A.J., Gehrke, J., Panda, B., Riedewald, M., Sharma, V., White, W.M., et al.: Cayuga: a general purpose event monitoring system. In: CIDR, vol. 7, pp. 412–422 (2007)
14. Balkesen, C., Dindar, N., Wetter, M., Tatbul, N.: Rip: run-based intra-query parallelism for scalable complex event processing. In: Proceedings of the 7th ACM International Conference on Distributed Event-Based Systems, pp. 3–14. ACM (2013)
15. Brenna, L., Gehrke, J., Hong, M., Johansen, D.: Distributed event stream processing with non-deterministic finite automata. In: Proceedings of the Third ACM International Conference on Distributed Event-Based Systems, p. 3. ACM (2009)
16. Chakravarthy, S., Krishnaprasad, V., Anwar, E., Kim, S.K.: Composite events for active databases: semantics, contexts and detection. VLDB **94**, 606–617 (1994)
17. Peng, S., Li, Z., Li, Q., Chen, Q., Pan, W., Liu, H., Nie, Y.: Event detection over live and archived streams. In: Wang, H., Li, S., Oyama, S., Hu, X., Qian, T. (eds.) WAIM 2011. LNCS, vol. 6897, pp. 566–577. Springer, Heidelberg (2011)
18. Zdonik, S., Sibley, P., Rasin, A., Sweetser, V., Montgomery, P., Turner, J., Wicks, J., Zgolinski, A., Snyder, D., Humphrey, M., Williamson, C.: Streaming for dummies (2004)
19. Hirzel, M.: Partition and compose: parallel complex event processing. In: Proceedings of the 6th ACM International Conference on Distributed Event-Based Systems, pp. 191–200. ACM (2012)
20. Schultz-Møller, N.P., Migliavacca, M., Pietzuch, P.: Distributed complex event processing with query rewriting. In: Proceedings of the Third ACM International Conference on Distributed Event-Based Systems, p. 4. ACM (2009)
21. Sadoghi, M., Singh, H., Jacobsen, H.A.: Towards highly parallel event processing through reconfigurable hardware. In: Proceedings of the Seventh International Workshop on Data Management on New Hardware, pp. 27–32. ACM (2011)
22. Hirzel, M., Andrade, H., Gedik, B., Kumar, V., Losa, G., Nasgaard, M., Soule, R., Wu, K.: Spl stream processing language specification. IBM Research, Yorktown Heights, NY, USA, Technical report RC24 897 (2009)

23. Stonebraker, M., Çetintemel, U., Zdonik, S.: The 8 requirements of real-time stream processing. ACM SIGMOD Rec. **34**(4), 42–47 (2005)
24. Golab, L., Özsu, M.T.: Issues in data stream management. ACM SIGMOD Rec. **32**(2), 5–14 (2003)
25. Wang, Y., Cao, K., Zhang, X.: Complex event processing over distributed probabilistic event streams. Comput. Math. Appl. **66**(10), 1808–1821 (2013)
26. Mani, M.: Efficient event stream processing: handling ambiguous events and patterns with negation. In: Xu, J., Yu, G., Zhou, S., Unland, R. (eds.) DASFAA Workshops 2011. LNCS, vol. 6637, pp. 415–426. Springer, Heidelberg (2011)
27. Kawashima, H., Kitagawa, H., Li, X.: Complex event processing over uncertain data streams. In: 2010 International Conference on P2P, Parallel, Grid, Cloud and Internet Computing (3PGCIC), pp. 521–526. IEEE (2010)
28. Jiang, Q., Chakravarthy, S.: Scheduling strategies for a data stream management system. Computer Science & Engineering, BNCOD, pp. 16–30 (2004)
29. Sharaf, M.A., Labrinidis, A., Chrysanthis, P.K.: Scheduling continuous queries in data stream management systems. Proc. VLDB Endow. **1**(2), 1526–1527 (2008)
30. Wu, J., Tan, K.-L., Zhou, Y.: QoS-oriented multi-query scheduling over data streams. In: Zhou, X., Yokota, H., Deng, K., Liu, Q. (eds.) DASFAA 2009. LNCS, vol. 5463, pp. 215–229. Springer, Heidelberg (2009)
31. Babcock, B., Babu, S., Datar, M., Motwani, R., Widom, J.: Models and issues in data stream systems. In: Proceedings of the Twenty-First ACM SIGMOD-SIGACT-SIGART Symposium on Principles of Database Systems, pp. 1–16. ACM (2002)
32. Babcock, B., Babu, S., Datar, M., Motwani, R., Thomas, D.: Operator scheduling in data stream systems. VLDB J. Int. J. Very Large Data Bases **13**(4), 333–353 (2004)
33. Babcock, B., Babu, S., Motwani, R., Datar, M.: Chain: operator scheduling for memory minimization in data stream systems. In: Proceedings of the 2003 ACM SIGMOD International Conference on Management of Data, pp. 253–264. ACM (2003)

A Multiple Query Optimization Scheme for Change Point Detection on Stream Processing System

[Position Paper]

Masahiro Oke and Hideyuki Kawashima[(✉)]

University of Tsukuba, 1-1-1, Tennodai, Tsukuba, Japan
oke@kde.cs.tsukuba.ac.jp, kawasima@cs.tsukuba.ac.jp

Abstract. To accelerate simultaneous execution of multiple change point detection (CPD) queries, this paper proposes to apply the multiple query optimization scheme which has been studied in DBMS or DSMS. We propose to share a part of steps of CPD procedures, and we propose an algorithm for the sharing. The result of experiments showed that our proposal reduces more than 80 % internal steps and achieved 5 times performance improvement. To the best of our knowledge, this is the first work that applies the multiple query optimization scheme for CPD.

Keywords: Change point detection · Multiple query optimization

1 Introduction

A variety of techniques are used to detect malware. Data stream management systems are effective tools for the problem. For example, TCP syn flood detection is realized group-by-aggregate continuous query as shown in [5]. It should be noted that new types of malware appear every day, and [1] people do not accept to be infected by malware. Therefore new malware detection techniques will be developed continually beyond relational operators. To detect malware, a signature based detection method is used as a basic method. This method does not perform if a signature is not yet created when malware arrives.

Machine learning techniques or data mining techniques are sometimes adopted for such malware. For example, an incident analysis system NICTER [1] uses change point detection technique (CPD) [2] to detect malware in real-time using its dark net traffic generated by more than 160,000 unused IP addresses. CPD is an outlier detection technique for time series data based on autoregressive model with the concept of discounting. CPD requires 6 parameters to be executed. The parameters are deeply related to detection accuracy as other machine learning techniques. Choosing a single parameter set that shows the best accuracy is desirable. Such a choice is impossible without predicting the future. Therefore, multiple parameter sets should be chosen and

© Springer-Verlag Berlin Heidelberg 2015
M. Castellanos et al. (Eds.): BIRTE 2013 and 2014, LNBIP 206, pp. 150–158, 2015.
DOI: 10.1007/978-3-662-46839-5_10

multiple CPD should run simultaneously to improve the accuracy of malware detection. We are developing Falcon, yet another DSMS which provides not only relational operators but also data mining operators including CPD.

On running Falcon, we found a serious performance issue when running N processes. To accelerate simultaneous execution of multiple CPD procedures, this paper proposes a multiple query optimization scheme for CPD. For relational database system, a variety of multiple query optimization (MQO) techniques have been studied such as sharing common sub-expressions [3]. On the other hand, our proposal is dedicated for CPD, and it shares internal steps in CPD, which is different from usual MQO. To the best of our knowledge, this is the first work that describes MQO for CPD.

The rest of this paper is organized as follows. Section 2 describes CPD in detail. Section 3 proposes an efficient computation scheme for multiple CPD operations. Section 4 evaluates our proposal techniques. Finally Sect. 5 concludes this paper.

2   Related Work: Change Point Detection

2.1   CPD (Change Point Detection)

Change point detection is an outlier detection technique for time series data proposed by Takeuchi and Yamanishi [2]. CPD can detect points that change dramatically on time series data. An incident analysis system NICTER [1] uses CPD to detect occurrences of malware over network packets arrived at its dark net consisting of more than 160,000 nodes. CPD uses an auto-regressive (AR) model as a time series model. Roughly saying, CPD is constituted of 4 steps as shown in Fig. 1. They are (step 1 and 3) learning probability density and (step 2 and 4) scoring and moving averages of scores. The learning algorithms used in step 1 and 3 are referred to as sequential discounting AR model learning (SDAR). SDAR can deal with non-stationary time series data. Traditional learning algorithms on AR model are batch processing, while SDAR is an online learning algorithm that executes learning processes with the arrival of new data. Therefore its learning cost is less than batch processing scheme.

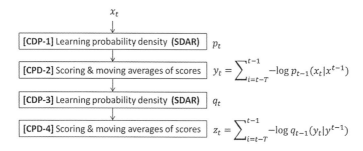

Fig. 1. Steps for CPD

2.2   SDAR (Sequentially Discounting Auto Regressive)

The SDAR algorithm shown in step 1 and 3 in Fig. 1 is a learning algorithm of AR model with discounting and online learning features. The discounting feature decreases the effect of a t-step previous value. The effect is modified to $(1 - R) \times t$, however the range of R is between 0 to 1. Input parameters of SDAR algorithm are R (discounting ratio), $\hat{\mu}$(mean), C_j(auto covariance), $\hat{\omega}_j$ and $\hat{\Sigma}$(covariance). All of the five parameters should be provided by a user before starting the SDAR algorithm. We explain five steps of SDAR shown in Fig. 2.

First, on reading a new data object x_t, SDAR executes the following computations shown as [SDAR-1] and [SDAR-2] in Fig. 2.

$$\hat{\mu} = (1 - R)\hat{\mu} + Rx_t$$

$$C_j = (1 - R)C_j + R(x_t - \hat{\mu})(x_{t-j} - \hat{\mu})^T$$

Then we write a Yule-Walker equation as follows.

$$\sum_{t-1}^{K} \omega_i C_{j-i} = C_j$$

By solving the equation, we obtain $\omega_1 \ldots \omega_K$. This is [SDAR-3] in Fig. 2. Using them, we obtain $\hat{x}_t$ and $\hat{\Sigma}$ as follows. They are [SDAR-4] and [SDAR-5] in Fig. 2.

$$\hat{x}_t = \sum_{i=1}^{K} \hat{\omega}_i (x_{t-i} - \hat{\mu}) + \hat{\mu}$$

$$\hat{\Sigma} = (1 - R)\hat{\Sigma} + R(x_t - \hat{x}_t)(x_t - \hat{x}_t)^T$$

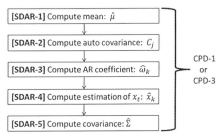

Fig. 2. Steps of SDAR

3   Multiple Query Optimization for CPD

3.1   Problem on CPD: Influence of Parameters to Detection Accuracy

CPD has 3 kinds of parameters for input: discounting parameter R, AR model order K and moving time T. CPD requires 6 parameters: α_R, α_K, α_T, β_R, β_K and β_T, which will be explained in Sect. 3.2. Parameters α_R, α_K and α_T are for 1st stage learning which is shown as CPD-1 and CPD-2 in Fig. 1. On the other hand, β_R, β_K and β_T are for 2nd stage learning which is shown as CPD-3 and CPD-4 in Fig. 2. It should be noted that CPD-1 and CPD-3 are the same, and CPD-2 and CPD-4 are the same, which is the reason why CPD is referred to as 2 step stage learning. Figure 3 shows the effect of parameter sets to detection accuracy for CPD. In Fig. 3, horizontal axis shows time. Left vertical axis shows frequency (the number of accesses) shown by blue graph which locates on the upper side and changes frequently. Right vertical axis shows CPD score shown by brown graph which locates on the lower side and changes infrequently. In the left one, CPD score is responded by outlier accesses. On the other hand, in the right one, CPD score does not show any response with regard to frequency. Left parameter set is appropriate while right parameter set is inappropriate.

If our motivating applications are for stored database, then we can tune parameters and can find out the best parameter set. Streaming applications, however, does not take such a chance. Therefore, to reduce false negatives, multiple parameter sets should be tried simultaneously. Discounting parameter R decreases influence of past data. Therefore if R is small, CPD score is greatly affected by past data. AR model order K expresses the number of data used for learning. If we set K large, an AR model learns from more data. However, it should be noted that larger K does not directly mean better model in the viewpoint of Akaike Information Criterion. Moving time T is used to make outlier scores smoothly and to compute change point score. If T is large, then change detection is for long duration. If T is small, then it is for short duration. Parameters should be set appropriately for each malware. Since malware can be unknown, many types of parameter sets should be carefully tuned.

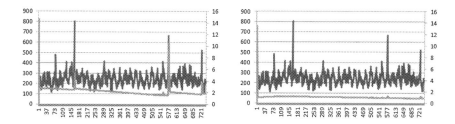

Fig. 3. Appropriate parameter set (left) and inappropriate one (right)

3.2   Coping with Many Runs: Multiple Query Optimization for CPD

As described above, to detect malware appropriately, multiple CPD procedures should be executed simultaneously. Let's think about a situation that we execute many CPD runs each of which has an identical parameter set. Then the amount of computation should be large. It naturally incurs performance degradation such as long latency. Such a long latency is not desired since delay of malware detection may increase damage to internal network by the intrusion.

A simple way is using advanced hardware such as many-core, FPGA or GPGPU that provide massively parallel computations. This is a promising approach. However, it requires additional power and money cost. This paper adopts a different approach. It is multiple query optimization that shares computations.

Moving time T is used for smoothing outlier score and computing change point score. Discounting parameter R and AR order K are used for the computation of SDAR algorithm. Discounting parameter R is only used for computation the mean μ in SDAR algorithm. Obviously, these parameters can be same. The inputs of the second stage learning are generated by the output of the first stage learning, and they are usually different. Therefore, it is difficult to share the computation of the second stage learning.

We denote discounting parameter, AR model order and moving time T of the first stage learning are denoted as α_R, α_K and α_T respectively. Similarity, we denote the inputs of second SDAR as β_R, β_K and β_T.

3.2.1 Sharing Multiple CPDs in Four Patterns

There are six parameters for CPD. Parameter α_R and α_K are used for CPD-1 (SDAR). Parameter α_T is used for CPD-2. Parameter β_R and β_K are used for CPD-3(SDAR). Parameter β_T is used for CPD-4. Depending on situation, we propose to share computations in four patterns as shown in Fig. 4. Assume we have two users, user 1 and user 2 who issue CPD queries. In naïve case, an input (x_t) is routed to inputs of two CPDs, CPD-1s. Even if parameters are the same, four steps (CPD-1, CPD-2, CPD-3, and CPD-4) are executed for each user. It should be noted that shared CPDs should form of tree. It is because all of child nodes must have the same input computation value from a parent. Our proposal reduces the execution cost by sharing computations as follows:

Pattern 1: Sharing CPD-1 if α_R and α_K are the same.
Pattern 2: Sharing CPD-1, 2 if α_R, α_K and α_T are the same.
Pattern 3: Sharing CPD-1, 2, 3 if α_R, α_K, α_T, β_R and β_K are the same.
Pattern 4: Sharing CPD-1, 2, 3, 4 if α_R, α_K, α_T, β_R, β_K and β_T are the same.

3.2.2 Sharing Multiple SDARs

As shown in Fig. 2, SDAR algorithm is constituted of five steps. They are SDAR-1, SDAR-2, SDAR-3, SDAR-4, and SDAR-5. SDAR-1 uses only discounting parameter (α_R for CPD-1 or β_R for CPD-3). The rest of steps use both discounting parameter and AR order (α_K for CPD-1 or β_R for CPD-3). Therefore, if discounting parameter is the same for two queries, then we share the computation to improve performance. We show additional sharing patterns in Fig. 4: pattern-1' and pattern-3'.

Pattern 1': Sharing SDAR-1 in CPD-1 if α_R are the same.
Pattern 3': Sharing CPD-1, 2 and SDAR-1 in CPD-3 if α_R, α_K, α_T, β_R are the same.

3.2.3 Choosing the Sharing Parameters

To improve the performance, the larger sharing is the better. Therefore our policy to choose sharing patterns is as follows.

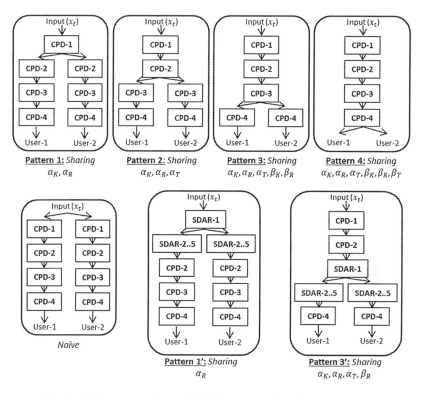

Fig. 4. Naïve computation and sharing computations for multiple runs

Algorithm. 1. Share of Parameters

```
1: BEGIN
2:    Create a cluster in level 0, "cluster-0-1";
3:    Add all of queries to cluster-0-1;
4:    FOREACH αR, αK, αT, βR, βK and βT
5:        Divide queries to multiple clusters so that all the
          queries in a cluster have the same parameter, and all
          the queries have the same parent;
6:    ENDFOR
7: END
```

Step 5 of algorithm 1 is important. When we have N queries, step 5 executes scan operation over K queries to find the same values in a cluster. Therefore its time complexity is O(N) for N queries (where N is the sum of queries in all of clusters) in a step. Since we have six parameters, total scan cost becomes 6 N.

4   Evaluation

Our experimental environment is as follows. OS: Ubuntu 10.04 LTS, CPU: Intel(R) Xeon(R) CPU E5640, 2.60 GHz, 4 cores, RAM 16 GB.

4.1   Performance Improvement by Number of Operators

We first investigated how much of micro operators can be reduced by using our proposal. Micro operator means a part of CPD or SDAR denoted as CPD-x or SDAR-x in the above. We tried three kinds of parameter sets. In the first parameter set, each parameter can be shared by all the queries. In the second parameter set, parameter values are provided randomly. In the third parameter set, parameter values are provided in the grid style, which requires additional explanation. Let's assume we have integer parameter x and y. Since both parameters can take infinite types, we should pick up some representative parameter sets. If we sample two points for each parameter, the number of parameter sets becomes 4 (= 2 × 2). Figure 5 shows x and y take 1 and 2 respectively, and parameter sets become {1,1}, {1,2}, {2,1}, and {2.2}. Grid style sampling is often used as a parameter set selection policy. The result of multiple runs are summarized using aggregation technique such as majority voting.

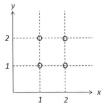

Fig. 5. Parameter sampling in grid style ({1,1}, {1,2}, {2,1}, and {2.2})

We show the result of experiments in Table 1. Parameter pattern used for the experiment was uniform, 3 random pattern sets, and 3 grid style sets. Applying multiple runs with different parameter sets and aggregating result is common in data mining [4]. However, to the best of our knowledge, appropriate tuning method for parameter sets is not yet matured. Obviously uniform dataset provides dramatic performance though such a case does not happen in the real. In random cases, performance gain is deeply related to types of random values. As types increase, performance gain reduces. In grid style cases, performance gain is also related to N (number of sampling values). As N increases, performance gain increases. Our proposal is especially effective for grid style policies.

Table 1. Reduction of operators by sharing techniques

Parameter pattern	# Queries	Naïve (# operators)	Sharing (# operators)	Performance gain (reduction ratio)
Uniform	64	384	6	98.4 %
Random (2 values)	64	384	101	73.7 %
Random (10 values)	64	384	315	18.0 %
Random (100 values)	64	384	366	4.7 %
Grid style (N = 2)	64	384	126	67.2 %
Grid style (N = 4)	4096	24576	5460	77.7 %
Grid style (N = 8)	262144	1572864	299592	80.1 %

It should be noted that that "performance gain" does not mean execution time. It means the number of reduced micro operators.

4.2   Performance Improvement in Execution Time

To measure the performance in execution time, we prepared a dataset. It is a data sequence generated by the following AR model.

$$x_t = 0.6x_{t-1} - 0.5x_{t-2} + \varepsilon_t \tag{1}$$

In the equation, ε_t is a Gaussian random variable with mean 0 and variance 1. This dataset consists of 10000 records. Change points occur at times $1000 \times k + 1(k = 1, \ldots, 9)$.

We consider a situation that we apply 100 CPDs simultaneously to the dataset. We measure execution time for both our proposal and naïve policy. Here we explain the meaning of symbols in Table 2. α_K and β_K expresses AR order. α_T and β_T express averaging time. α_R and β_R express discounting parameters.

4.3   Result

Table 2 shows the result of experiments. "Shared CPD-1" denotes a case that shares multiple CPDs when $\alpha_R, \alpha_K, \alpha_T$ are the same can be shared. "Shared SDAR-1" denotes a case when only α_R can be shared. We chose 10 patterns of parameter sets as shown in the Table 2.

Table 2. Execution time of naive, shared CPD-1 and shared SDAR-1.

ID	Parameters						Execution time (s)			Performance gain (times)	
	α_R	α_K	α_T	β_R	β_K	β_T	Naive	Shared CPD-1	Shared SDAR-1	Shared CPD-1	Shared SDAR-1
1	.02	2	5	.02	3	5	2.92	1.77	2.84	1.65	1.03
2	.02	4	5	.02	3	5	3.65	1.77	3.58	2.06	1.01
3	.02	2	5	.02	4	5	3.29	2.17	3.22	1.52	1.02
4	.005	2	5	.02	4	5	2.91	1.76	2.82	1.65	1.03
5	.02	2	5	.005	3	5	2.89	1.77	2.82	1.64	1.03
6	.02	2	7	.02	7	5	3.00	1.87	2.88	1.60	1.03
7	.02	1	5	.02	1	5	1.96	1.11	1.88	1.78	**1.04**
8	.02	**10**	10	.02	10	10	11.2	5.84	11.1	**1.92**	1.01
9	.02	1	10	.02	10	10	6.66	5.80	6.61	1.15	1.01
10	.02	**10**	10	.02	1	10	6.68	1.34	6.57	**5.00**	1.02

We found that AR order is an important factor for performance. Experiment 10 shows that "shared CPD-1" is 5 times faster than "naïve", which is the best performance improvement. In this case, AR-order α_K is set to 10, which is the highest in parameter sets. An interesting case is experiment 8 which achieves at most 1.92 times improvement though AR-order α_K is 10. The reason may be because of latter part. Since second AR-order β_K is also set to 10 in experiment 8. Our experimental condition does not execute sharing in the latter part, and therefore larger β_K incurs performance degradation indicated as the worst execution times which are 11.2 s for Naïve, 5.84 s for shared-CPD1, and 11.1 sec for shared-SDAR-1 respectively.

Another observation is small improvement gained by sharing SDAR-1. Performance improvement by SDAR-1 is at most 4 %, which is negligible when comparing with CPD-1.

5   Conclusions and Future Work

This paper proposed to incorporate a multiple query optimization scheme for change point detection. We found 6 sharing patterns for CPD. The result of experiments showed that our scheme reduces 80.1 % of operators when parameter setting policy is grid style (N = 8), and achieves 5 times performance improvement compared with naïve approach. This paper concludes that our scheme for CPD is effective for at least synthetic datasets.

There are some future works. First future work is investigating the degree of effectiveness using real datasets including packet streams including malware. Second future work is reducing the cost to decide whether sharing or not. Our current algorithm shown in Algorithm 1 takes O(N), which is too large then N is enormous.

Acknowledgement.   This work is supported by KAKENHI(#24500106).

References

1. I, D., Yoshioka, K., Eto, M., Yamagata, M., Nishino, E., Takeuchi, J., Ohkouchi, K., Nakao, K.: An incident analysis system NICTER and its analysis engines based on data mining techniques. In: Köppen, M., Kasabov, N., Coghill, G. (eds.) ICONIP 2008, Part I. LNCS, vol. 5506, pp. 579–586. Springer, Heidelberg (2009)
2. Takeuchi, J., Yamanishi, K.: A unifying framework for detecting outliers and change points from time series. IEEE Trans. Know. Data Eng. 18(4), 482–492 (2006)
3. Madden, S., Shah, M., Hellerstein, J.M., Raman, V.: Continuously adaptive continuous queries over streams. In: Proceedings of ACM SIGMOD, pp. 49–60 (2002)
4. Li, H., Sun, J.: Majority voting combination of multiple case-based reasoning for financial distress prediction. Expert Syst. Appl. 36(3), 4363–4373 (2009)
5. Srivastava, D., Golab, L., Greer, R., Johnson, T., Seidel, J., Shkapenyuk, V., Spatscheck, O., Yates, J.: Enabling real time data analysis. Keynote Proc. VLDB Endowment (PVLDB) 3(1), 1–2 (2010)

SynopSys: Foundations for Multidimensional Graph Analytics

Michael Rudolf[1]([⊠]), Hannes Voigt[1], Christof Bornhövd[2],
and Wolfgang Lehner[1]

[1] Database Technology Group, TU Dresden, Dresden, Germany
`michael.rudolf01@sap.com`, {`hannes.voigt,wolfgang.lehner`}`@tu-dresden.de`
[2] SAP Labs LLC, Palo Alto, CA 94304, USA
`christof.bornhoevd@sap.com`

Abstract. The past few years have seen a tremendous increase in often irregularly structured data that can be represented most naturally and efficiently in the form of graphs. Making sense of incessantly growing graphs is not only a key requirement in applications like social media analysis or fraud detection but also a necessity in many traditional enterprise scenarios. Thus, a flexible approach for multidimensional analysis of graph data is needed. Whereas many existing technologies require up-front modelling of analytical scenarios and are difficult to adapt to changes, our approach allows for ad-hoc analytical queries of graph data. Extending our previous work on graph summarization, in this position paper we lay the foundation for large graph analytics to enable business intelligence on graph-structured data.

Keywords: Graph databases · Graph analytics · Graph OLAP

1 Introduction

In the past decade graph data has become abundant. In the form of social networks and road networks it pervades everyday life, but the capability of storing and processing graph-structured data has also become crucial in enterprise tasks, such as supply chain management and product batch traceability. As the amount of graph data grows at an ever-increasing pace, the need for flexible graph analysis technology becomes more and more important. Whereas data warehousing tools and online analytical processing (OLAP) solutions for relational data are well-understood and mature, approaches for multidimensional analysis of graph data are still in their infancy (cf. Sect. 2). In the context of our research project SynopSys we aim at closing this gap.

There is a plethora of graph models used in research, each tailored to the specific problem at hand. In its most basic definition a graph $G := (V, E)$ is a tuple consisting of a set of vertices V and a relation $E \subseteq V \times V$ denoting the edges between them. For the remainder of this paper we employ the property graph model [1] where vertices and edges can have attributes and edges are

© Springer-Verlag Berlin Heidelberg 2015
M. Castellanos et al. (Eds.): BIRTE 2013 and 2014, LNBIP 206, pp. 159–166, 2015.
DOI: 10.1007/978-3-662-46839-5_11

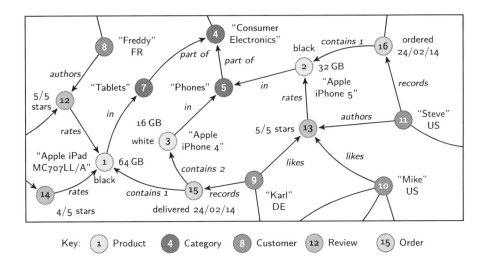

Fig. 1. Property graph illustrating a typical business scenario.

directed links between pairs of vertices. Its generality allows other graph models to be mapped to it easily while being flexible enough to support a broad variety of use cases. Figure 1 shows an excerpt of a property graph capturing a typical business scenario consisting of products, categories, customers, orders, and customer reviews. Note that vertices and edges of the same "type" can differ with regards to the attributes they expose. This scenario will serve as a running example throughout the following sections.

In our previous work [2] we have already outlined the use of graph pattern matching and transformation for deriving graph summaries. By means of summarization rules instantiated from an assorted set of templates, graph data can be grouped and aggregated numbers computed.

In this paper we extend our approach for graph analytics with the well-known concepts from multidimensional analytics [3]. We introduce a formal description of a general-purpose data model linking the concepts *fact*, *dimension*, and *measure* to the property graph model (cf. Sect. 3). Also, we present the semantics of operations for creating graph summaries along dimensions (cf. Sect. 4). Finally, we outline our plans for future research (cf. Sect. 5).

2   Related Work

The multidimensional model [3] is well-established as the theoretical foundation of the vast majority of online analytical processing (OLAP) tools. Data warehouses are usually created by designing a schema containing facts and dimensions. In an analytical session a set of measures has to be defined, and a (hyper-)cube is then constructed to capture both measures and dimensions. Unfortunately this intensional approach of up-front modelling is unable to meet the requirements of today's ever-changing IT and business landscapes with the dramatic increase of data volumes to process and number of sources to integrate.

For a specific analytical session users should be able to specify in an ad-hoc manner what the facts and dimensions of interest are.

In 2008 Chen et al. presented their approach for extending OLAP to graphs [4]. They introduce two kinds of dimensions and map the well-known OLAP operations roll-up, drill-down, and slice/dice to them. *Informational dimensions* are derived from the attributes associated with snapshots of an evolving graph, whereas *topological dimensions* stem from the attributes of vertices and edges in each such snapshot. Building on that, they describe a theoretical foundation for aggregated graphs, which form the measures in OLAP terminology, and propose the use of partial materialization techniques for reducing memory consumption. However, their approach is not accompanied by any processing or evaluation specification, concepts, or architecture. Also, singularizing the temporal dimension of system time does not seem to be sufficient, because application time is often more relevant in practice, and it unnecessarily complicates the formal framework.

In the same year Tian et al. proposed an operator for summarization by grouping nodes on attributes and pairwise relationships (SNAP) [5]. Whenever a vertex of one group is connected to any vertex of the other, the two vertex groups will also be connected. In practice this behavior turns out to be quite limiting, because it can result in a large number of groups. Therefore, they propose the *k-SNAP* operation as an extension, where the homogeneity constraint for group relationships is relaxed and the user can specify the number of groups in the graph summaries. By changing the parameter k, the user can emulate the OLAP operations drill-down and roll-up. The authors prove that the computation of the *k-SNAP* operation is NP-complete and propose heuristics to approximate it. Although the two proposed operations are designed to work with different edge types, additional edge attributes are not supported. Furthermore, there is no support for an independent filtering of the input graph (similar to slicing or dicing in OLAP terms).

In a follow-up paper from 2010 Zhang et al. [6] improve the previous approach in two ways: first, they provide an automatic means of discretizing numerical attributes based on the user-specified number of partitions and the graph topology. Second, based on what they call the diversity, coverage, and conciseness, the authors define an *interestingness* measure for graph summaries. This is then used for helping users to specify a sensible number of groups for the *k-SNAP* operation. The paper improves the practical usability of the overall approach, but does not address the limitations discussed above.

In 2011 Zhao et al. introduced a novel data warehousing model called Graph Cube [7]. Their notion of a multidimensional network is based on a restricted graph model (e.g., no attributes on edges) with the dimensions being the vertex attributes. An aggregate network (called *cuboid*) is then formed by computing equivalence classes for vertices according to the chosen dimensions and by constructing a weighted graph. All possible aggregations of the original network then form a *graph cube*. The authors propose two kinds of OLAP operations: cuboid and crossboid queries. The former simply returns the aggregate network of the desired cuboid from the graph cube, while the latter is somewhat similar to a join operation between multiple different cuboids. As for the specification and evaluation of such queries, the authors do not propose any mechanism but focus on partial materialization techniques instead.

There are various other approaches to summarizing graphs, but most of them are statistical in nature—computing a number of figures (e.g., degree distributions, hop-plots, and clustering coefficients), which describe some characteristics of the graph. The approaches presented above are different in that they can produce aggregated views on the graph data in various, user-controlled resolutions by means of OLAP-like operations. Although much more flexible, in our opinion these approaches are still too rigid, because they fix facts and dimensions up-front.

3   Data Model

In this section we introduce the various elements of the data model underlying our approach for graph analytics. It is heavily inspired by the well-known multidimensional model for analytics in data warehouses [3] but is crafted as a separate layer on top of the property graph model [1].

3.1   Facts

The most fine-grained elements of interest are called *(base) facts*. In the context of graph data, a fact can be an attribute of a vertex or an edge or the presence of an edge itself. For example, interesting facts from our running example can be the price of products, the amount of products in an order, or the existence of an edge between products and reviews.

We propose to specify facts using *summarization rules*, i.e. additive graph transformations rules consisting of a graph pattern and an action for creating a representative. Figure 2 depicts such a summarization rule for selecting customers and the reviews they have authored as facts. Each pattern element is assigned an alias (e.g., "$c" for customer vertices), which can be used for specifying dimensions and measures. The action part of the transformation is colored green and annotated with "++" to indicate the addition of a so-called *representative vertex*. Note that these vertices need not necessarily be materialized; their primary purpose is to provide references to all facts that are relevant for

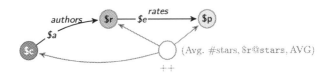

Fig. 2. Summarization rule for selecting customers and their review as facts and for computing a measure for the average number of stars of customer reviews.

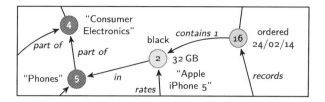

Fig. 3. Explicit and implicit dimensions in a property graph.

the analytical scenario at hand. The use of graph transformations enables the specification of complex patterns consisting of both informational and topological predicates in a graphical form, and it does not require the user to learn a dedicated domain-specific language.

3.2   Dimensions

As the name suggests, the principal element of multidimensional analysis is the concept of a *dimension*. First and foremost a dimension is an aspect of some or most of the facts, and as such a set of values.

Additionally, dimensions can be structured. If the structure neither is embodied in the graph data itself nor can be derived from it but has to be provided from external sources instead (e.g., by joining it to the GeoNames dataset to obtain the relationship between cities, countries and continents), it is said to be *extrinsic*, otherwise the structure is *intrinsic* in the graph data. Regarding intrinsic dimensional structure we can further differentiate between *explicit*, if it is present in the form of connected vertices (e.g., a product category hierarchy), and *implicit*, if it can be derived from attribute values (e.g., extracting the day, month, and year components from an order date). Figure 3 shows examples for both explicit and implicit dimensional structure.

Dimensions are usually structured into levels; often more than one structure can be distinguished in a single dimension (e.g., a temporal dimension can be structured into days, months, and years as well as into days, months, and fiscal years). Each level can be identified by a unique name and described by a function mapping an aspect of facts to arbitrary values (e.g. vertices of type `order` to the month component of their delivery date attribute).

Definition 1 (Level). *A level $l := (\text{Name}, \varphi)$ is a tuple, where $\varphi : \mathcal{G} \to X$ is a unary function mapping a match of the corresponding dimension's seed pattern to an arbitrary value.*

Since the topmost level of a dimension has to produce a single element, we add an artificial root to the hierarchy. This is beneficial if all elements of a dimension should be placed in a single group.

Corollary 1 (Artificial Root). *The artificial root level $\top = (\text{Top}, \varphi_\top)$ yields a single root value $\forall G \in \mathcal{G}.\varphi_\top(G) = \top$ and is the topmost level, i.e. $\forall l \in L.l \leq \top$.*

Table 1. Two dimensions applicable to the previously selected facts.

Name	Seed Pattern	Levels
Nationality	(image)	`$c@nationality`
Category	(image)	1. Subcategory: `$p-[@type='in']->` 2. Category: `$p-[@type='in']->-[@type='part-of']->` 3. Super category: `$p-[@type='in']->-[@type='part-of']->(2)`

In addition to the totally ordered set of levels, a dimension specification (also uniquely identified by a name) consists of a seed pattern, which is applied to the facts. Table 1 illustrates these components for two dimensions that are applicable to the pairs of customer and review that were previously selected as facts. The syntax *alias@attribute* encodes the access to an attribute of the aliased vertex or edge, while –[*predicate*]–>(*length*) denotes paths of a given length satisfying a given predicate.

Definition 2 (Dimension Specification). *A dimension specification* $d :=$ (Name, $S, L \cup \{\top\}, \leq$) *is a tuple, where* $S : \mathcal{G} \rightarrow \mathcal{P}(\mathcal{G})$ *is the seed pattern,* $L \neq \emptyset$ *is a non-empty set of levels, and* $\leq \subseteq L \times L$ *is a total ordering of the levels. Level names are unique, i.e.* $\forall l \in L.(\exists m \in L : \text{Name}_m = \text{Name}_l) \iff m = l$.

Without loss of generality, the total ordering of the levels can be chosen such that the number of items per level decreases monotonically as the level increases. For example, while a (non-leap) year has 365 days, it has only 52 weeks and just 12 months.

Corollary 2 (Monotony). *Given two levels* $l, m \in L, l \neq m$, *it holds that* $l \leq m \implies |\varphi_m(\mathcal{G})| \leq |\varphi_l(\mathcal{G})|$.

The levels in a structured dimension often form hierarchies, meaning that seed pattern matches mapped to the same value in a lower level will also be mapped to the same value at a higher level. For example, all purchase orders recorded in January 2014 will be mapped both to January and to 2014.

Corollary 3 (Hierarchy). *Given two levels* $l, m \in L, l \neq m$, *and two matches of the seed pattern* $G, F \in \mathcal{G}, G \neq F$, *it holds that* $l \leq m \iff (\varphi_l(G) = \varphi_l(F) \implies \varphi_m(G) = \varphi_m(F))$.

3.3   Measures

A *measure* is derived from facts using arithmetic operations.

Definition 3 (Measure). *A measure* $m := (\text{Name}, f, \sigma)$ *is a tuple, where* $f : \mathcal{G} \rightarrow \mathbb{R}$ *is a function computing a numerical value for a fact and* $\sigma \in$ {SUM, AVG, MIN, MAX, ...} *is an aggregation function for combining numerical values when grouping facts.*

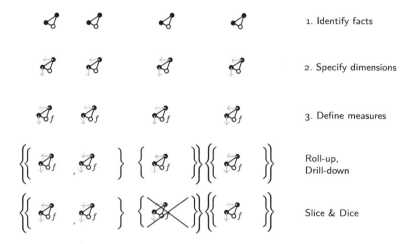

Fig. 4. Workflow for multidimensional graph analysis.

Measures are specified as part of the fact definition as an attribute of the newly introduced representative vertex. For example, in Fig. 2 a measure for the average number of stars of a customer review is given as (Avg. #stars, $r@stars, AVG), where the syntax for the specification of f means: starting from the vertex with the alias "$r", obtain the value of the attribute "stars".

4   Workflow

Building on the concepts defined in the previous section, we now introduce a workflow for performing multidimensional analytics on graph-structured data (cf. Fig. 4). First, a *graph cube* has to be defined using the following steps:

1. **Identify facts.** By means of a graph pattern the user has to select the subgraphs of interest. For each fact a representative vertex that serves as a handle is created.
2. **Specify dimensions.** A dimension consists of at least one level. A level is a function that maps a subgraph to an arbitrary value. The connection between facts and mapping functions is achieved with the help of a seed pattern.
3. **Define measures.** By annotating the summarization rule used in the first step with a computation function and an aggregation function, a measure can be defined.

Definition 4 (Graph Cube). *A graph cube $c := (F, D, M)$ is an analytical scenario, where $F : \mathcal{G} \to \mathcal{P}(\mathcal{G})$ is the fact summarization rule, D is a set of dimension specifications, and M is a set of measures. Its granularity $\gamma : D \to L$ is initially set to the lowest level of each dimension: $\forall d \in D.\gamma(d) = \min(L_d)$.*

The dimensional structure can then be exploited to compute different groupings of facts and thereby transform the graph cube (or more specifically the measures associated with it).

Definition 5 (Roll-up/Drill-down). *The roll-up operation* $\uparrow: \Gamma \times D \to \Gamma$ *decreases the granularity for the specified dimension* $d \in D$ *by grouping facts according to the next higher level (where* $L_d = \{l_0, l_1, \dots, l_n\}$ *and* $\gamma(d) = l_i$*). The drill-down operation* $\downarrow: \Gamma \times D \to \Gamma$ *increases the granularity by switching to the next lower level of the dimension. Derived granularities are defined as follows:*

$$\gamma_d^\uparrow(x) := \begin{cases} l_{i+1} & \text{if } x = d \\ \gamma(x) & \text{otherwise} \end{cases} \qquad \gamma_d^\downarrow(x) := \begin{cases} l_{i-1} & \text{if } x = d \\ \gamma(x) & \text{otherwise} \end{cases}$$

Definition 6 (Slice and Dice). *Given a set of level-predicate pairs, the function* filter $: C \times \mathcal{P}(L \times P) \to C$ *filters the fact base of a graph cube:*
filter$((F, D, M), p) := (F', D, M)$*, where* $F' = \{f | f \in F \wedge \forall (l, \lambda) \in p.\varphi_l(f) \models \lambda\}$*.*

If $|p| = 1$ a single predicate is applied to only one dimension and the operation is called *slice*, otherwise it is called *dice*. For example, to slice product reviews by German customers from the cube c, use filter$(c, \{(\text{Nationality}, \lambda = \text{``DE''})\})$. Now we have the basic concepts for multidimensional graph analytics in place.

5   Conclusions and Future Work

In this paper we presented a formal framework for graph analytics by mapping the well-known concepts *fact*, *dimension*, and *measure* from the multidimensional model to the property graph model. By relying on additive graph transformation rules as the means for selecting facts, we overcome the limitations of existing approaches: first, we can offer the user a graphical specification paradigm and avoid the introduction of a domain-specific language. Second, we can leverage the extensive research on efficient graph transformations from the past decades.

In the context of our research project SynopSys we will investigate the support of cross-cube measures for gaining insights into more complex topological aspects and anticipate additional OLAP operations based on our data model.

References

1. Rodriguez, M.A., Neubauer, P.: Constructions from dots and lines. Bull. Am. Soc. Inf. Sci. Technol. **36**(6), 35–41 (2010)
2. Rudolf, M., Paradies, M., Bornhövd, C., Lehner, W.: SynopSys: large graph analytics in the SAP HANA database through summarization. In: Proceedings of GRADES 2013, pp. 16:1–16:6. ACM (2013)
3. Kimball, R., Ross, M.: The Data Warehouse Toolkit: The Definitive Guide to Dimensional Modeling, 3rd edn. Wiley, New York (2013)
4. Chen, C., Yan, X., Zhu, F., Han, J., Yu, P.S.: Graph OLAP: towards online analytical processing on graphs. In: Proceedings of 8th ICDM, pp. 103–112. IEEE (2008)
5. Tian, Y., Hankins, R.A., Patel, J.M.: Efficient aggregation for graph summarization. In: Proceedings of SIGMOD 2008, pp. 567–580. ACM (2008)
6. Zhang, N., Tian, Y., Patel, J.M.: Discovery-driven graph summarization. In: Proceedings of 26th ICDE, pp. 880–891. IEEE (2010)
7. Zhao, P., Li, X., Xin, D., Han, J.: Graph cube: on warehousing and OLAP multidimensional networks. In: Proceedings of SIGMOD, pp. 853–864. ACM (2011)

Big Scale Text Analytics and Smart Content Navigation

Karsten Schmidt[1]([✉]), Sebastian Bächle[1], Philipp Scholl[1], and Georg Nold[2]

[1] SAP AG, Walldorf, Germany
{karsten.schmidt01,sebastian.baechle,p.scholl}@sap.com
http://www.sap.com
[2] Springer Science+Business Media, Berlin, Germany
http://www.springer.com

Abstract. Identifying and exploring relevant content in growing document collections is a challenge for researchers, users, and system providers alike. Supporting this is crucial for companies offering knowledge in the form of documents as their core product. Our demo shows an intelligent way of doing guided research in big text collections, using the collection of the major scientific publisher Springer SBM as an example data set. We use the SAP HANA platform for flexible text analysis, ad-hoc calculations and data linkage, in order to enhance the experience of users navigating and exploring publications. We integrate unstructured data (textual documents) and structured data (document metadata and web server logs), and provide interactive filters in order to enable a responsive user experience while searching for relevant content. With HANA, we are able to implement this functionality over big data on a single machine by making use of HANA's SQL data store and the built-in application server.

Keywords: SAP HANA · Analytics · Information retrieval

1 Context-Sensitive Information Retrieval

Helping users to locate relevant information in large text collections requires sophisticated search functionality with meaningful result ranking. The actual information need is often fuzzy and hard to determine in advance. Typically, a research session starts with a simple keyword search, which is incrementally refined and adjusted according to the results delivered. In this demo, we demonstrate an application for exploring a large repository of unstructured content through an advanced integration of full-text search and text analytics. In addition to fast live search with as-you-type results, the application provides user guidance through domain-specific search, context-sensitive linking and content-based recommendations. Beyond the scope of a conventional text retrieval system, our application integrates further data sources, e.g., to improve the quality of search results and recommendations. Furthermore, we include structured web server logs for popularity analytics, a custom vocabulary for searching medical content, and context-specific embedding of third-party content.

© Springer-Verlag Berlin Heidelberg 2015
M. Castellanos et al. (Eds.): BIRTE 2013 and 2014, LNBIP 206, pp. 167–170, 2015.
DOI: 10.1007/978-3-662-46839-5_12

Single-Box Architecture. Big-scale content retrieval typically requires a multitude of dedicated systems for storage, text processing, and analytics, as well as an application server and a web server. In such a setting, data is stored across multiple machines (see Fig. 1) and costly joins are always unavoidable. Furthermore, different access languages and layers increase latency due to data transformations and translations. Pre-calculated aggregates mitigate these issues, but increase the data volume significantly and cause additional update and maintenance overhead.

Using the HANA platform, all functionality can be consolidated in a single box (see Fig. 2). HANA features a powerful column store, an integrated text analytics engine and a built-in application server, with all data being accessible via SQL. This turns HANA into a convenient, lightweight, and scalable platform for managing structured *and* unstructured content.

Our demo application runs on a HANA server with 80 cores (8 CPUs à 10 cores at 2.5 GHz) and 1 TB main memory. On this machine, response times are between 40 ms for simple search requests and 500 ms for complex recommendations. Due to the tight integration of the built-in application layer, the response times are close to those of plain SQL.

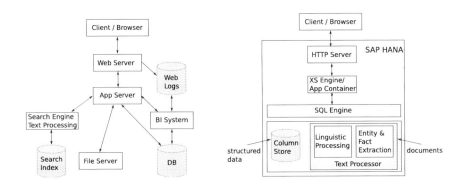

Fig. 1. State-of-the-art architecture   **Fig. 2.** Single box HANA architecture

The Big Data Challenge. Our database consists of 3.7 million scientific articles and book chapters[1], all in PDF format, with a raw data volume of 3.6 TB. Extracting valuable pieces of information from such a large amount of unstructured text data is a challenge in many ways. Aside from standard full-text search, complex text analysis is required to identify relevant terms and topics for similarity search, recommendations, and relevance rankings. Creating, materializing, and maintaining search indexes and pre-computing similarity measures is expensive, and should be avoided for quickly growing document bases. Hence, we avoid materialized redundant data wherever possible. Our queries operate directly on a few basic data structures and exploit the parallel hardware to compute document statistics and similarities on the fly.

---

[1]   Published by Springer Science+Business Media [2].

Fig. 3. Search features and response times for demo application.

We create a full-text index and extract more than 2.8 billion text entities from all documents and store them in a plain relational table. As the automatic indexing and entity extraction runs incrementally, new documents can be added without re-indexing and re-extracting. SAP HANA's built-in text analytics extract additional information to cluster and qualify entities.

Computing ad-hoc similarity over the whole collection for giving recommendations is an extremely expensive task and heavily depends on the similarity measure. To solve this issue, entity statistics per document form our baseline. This small metadata is retrieved during entity extraction and needs no further maintenance when new documents are added to the collection.

Along with the documents, we stored 1 GB of structured metadata with information about authors, publishers, etc. Additionally, we have loaded 14 months (1.3 billion rows) of web server log data into the same database instance. This corresponds to 392 GB of raw log data and 43 GB in the in-memory format.

2   Demo Content

The demo comprises an appealing web application presenting four key aspects:

Search. Searching and filtering of *unstructured* text, which is enhanced by *structured* metadata and a domain-specific vocabulary for medical terms (Fig. 3).

Browsing. An embedded document viewer provides highlighting of extracted entities, links for inter-document navigation, and ad-hoc analysis and recommendations for freely selectable text fragments (see Fig. 4). The linkage to third-party content is exemplified by integrating the Wikipedia API [3].

Analytics. Analytics for *unstructured* data is shown with a live-updating tag cloud and content-based recommendations. Analytics for *structured* data is exemplified by live popularity analysis over the web log data.

Internals. The SQL-based backend of the application is exposed using our developer workbench (see Fig. 5). The audience gets direct insight into the base tables, extracted entities, and can issue SQL statements.

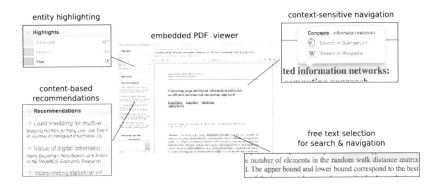

Fig. 4. Selected features for content navigation.

Visitors can freely play with the web application to experience the performance and responsiveness of the system. The application connects via HTTP to a HANA server hosted by SAP.

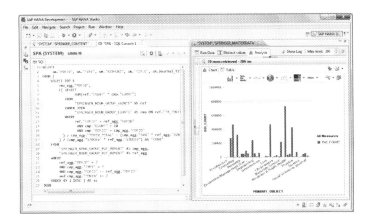

Fig. 5. SAP HANA Studio

Acknowledgements. The authors would like to thank the whole Strategic Projects Team SAP/Walldorf, especially Spyridon Antonopoulos, Jens Böning, Fredrick Chew, Enno Folkerts, Christian Heller, Nick Lanham, Andrew McCormick-Smith, Martin Sommer, Frederik Transier, and Patrick Zamzow. Furthermore, we thank Springer for their support.

References

1. Plattner, H., Zeier, A.: In-Memory Data Management: An Inflection Point for Enterprise Applications. Springer, Berlin (2011)
2. SpringerLink Corpus (2013). http://link.springer.com
3. Wikipedia Encyclopedia API (2013). https://www.mediawiki.org/wiki/API

Demo: Dynamic Generation of Adaptive Real-Time Dashboards for Continuous Data Stream Processing

Timo Michelsen$^{(\boxtimes)}$, Marco Grawunder, Dennis Geesen,
and H.-Jürgen Appelrath

University of Oldenburg, Oldenburg, Germany
{timo.michelsen,marco.grawunder,dennis.geesen,appelrath}@uni-ol.de

Abstract. Conventional database management systems are usually not capable to deal with continuous processing of potentially infinite data streams. Therefore, special data stream management systems and frameworks are developed. They use continuous queries which produce also streams as results, so that static visualization is not feasible, since the results are changing constantly. To handle this, we developed a dashboard concept, which we want to propose in this demonstration. A dashboard can be considered as an control or monitoring panel for real time data stream results. The user is free to define and configure individual dashboard parts. Each part is connected to a (user defined) continuous query, whose results are received and visualized in real-time. In this demonstration, we provide different data stream sources, continuous queries and dashboard parts. With them, the user can compose his own individual presentation of his processing results.

Keywords: Data stream · Continuous visualization · Continuous queries · Framework · Odysseus

1 Introduction

Active data sources like sensors continuously produce data and send them to processing systems. The resulting data streams are potentially infinite and cannot be persistently stored at once. Conventional database management systems (DBMS) are not capable to deal with these type of sources. It is inevitable that each incoming data element has to be processed immediately. For this purpose, data stream management systems (DSMS) are developed. Instead of queries, which are executed once at a given time, DSMS use continuous queries. Continuous queries are installed into the DSMS and are running infinitely, producing streams of results [4].

Many DSMS are hard-coded, specified for one given task. Others provide entire frameworks with basic components to develop application-specific DSMS at a higher level. Odysseus[1] is such a framework. It uses the OSGi Service Platform to provide basic components, which can be easily replaced or extended

---

[1] odysseus.informatik.uni-oldenburg.de.

© Springer-Verlag Berlin Heidelberg 2015
M. Castellanos et al. (Eds.): BIRTE 2013 and 2014, LNBIP 206, pp. 171–174, 2015.
DOI: 10.1007/978-3-662-46839-5_13

to meet specific requirements. For instance, Odysseus provides CQL, a SQL-like query language, other specific languages can be implemented. The graphical front-end of Odysseus uses the Eclipse Rich Client Platform (RCP). RCP is build on top of OSGi, providing the same extensibility as Odysseus itself [2].

2 Dashboards

The continuous processing of data streams prohibits a static visualization of query results. The results have to be presented in real-time. So the visualization component of a data stream management system has to update its visualization each time a new result is calculated. Additionally, the system has to deliver the user the tools to individualize the visualizations. For instance, if data streams come from special sources or the results of multiple queries should be shown in one picture. The most suitable solution allows changes even during the continuous data stream processing.

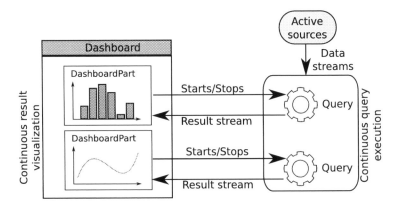

Fig. 1. Correlation between dashboards and continuous query execution in Odysseus.

To meet these challenges, we developed a framework for visualizing multiple results in one huge visual surface and implemented it in Odysseus (see Fig. 1). Therefore, we split the visualization into smaller parts which can be handled easier. If a user defines a continuous query, he can connect its (future) results to so-called *dashboard parts*. Dashboard parts are responsible for the execution of the queries: if one part is shown on screen, the underlying query will be installed, immediately started and the results are send to the presenting part. Since the queries are defined independently from the dashboard parts, the queries can be as complex as needed (with complex results to visualize). Additionally, the dashboard part is highly configurable: First, the user can decide which type of part he wants to show (e.g. classical line diagrams or scatter plots). A developer can easily add additional (application specific) types, if needed. Second, each part can be individually configured in more detail (e.g. which exact attributes of one data stream should be visualized).

With the underlying RCP-Framework it is possible to save dashboard parts persistently and send them to other users who want to work with them. Next, a set of dashboard parts is composed to one complete visualization. In our concept, we call them *dashboards*, which usually occupy the whole screen. A dashboard is a central control and monitoring panel, which enables the user to see the processing data (and its results) graphically pleasant in real-time. A dashboard is responsible for the positions and sizes of the containing dashboard parts. Beginning with an empty dashboard, the user can include his predefined parts to it (e.g. by drag-and-drop), and move or resize each part inside the dashboard. At the same time, the results of the underlying continuous queries are already shown in real-time. Most likely, all parts are placed in a way, that each part is shown completely. In many situations, the user is only interested in showing his dashboard parts (and does not care about the exact positions and sizes). Therefore, we provide a function to layout all parts automatically (so-called *layouter*). In its simplest form, it positions all parts side-by-side in a grid-pattern. A developer can implement additional layouter for special requirements.

3 Related Work

Visualizing continuous data streams and results are not new. Many commercial and research DSMS provide visualization of continuous query results. For instance, the commercial DSMS StreamBase [5] provides a similar environment (so-called *LiveView*) showing materialized views, aggregations and notifications of data streams. We think, that their solution aims at end-users: their feature-rich graphical environment provides fast access to visualize streaming results. Our solution focuses on the extensibility of visualizations as a framework to meet the existing extensibility of Odysseus: this allows users and developers (1) to have complete control of their queries, data sources and results, (2) extending and modifying the visualization to meet special requirements and (3) combining parts of different visualizations to form a new dashboard.

4 Demonstration Contents

In this demonstration, we want to show our concept of the dashboards: the dynamic generation and real-time presentation of continuous data streams. Some predefined active data sources continuously send data stream elements to Odysseus. We propose a number of predefined queries which are running in the background. Of course the user can define his own continuous queries if he wants to. For generic data streams, we provide the classical set of diagrams as dashboard parts: line graphs, scatter plots, pie charts, etc. These are suitable for fast and easy visualizations. We also provide some specialized dashboard parts, which are implemented for one specific data stream and their corresponding queries. This shows the high adaptability of our concept. In this demo, we provide two data sources. First, the NREL dataset, containing data from about 32,000 wind power stations. Each station sends a data element each ten minutes which describes the actual amount of generated power, the speed of the wind and several other attributes [3]. Specialized dashboard parts (and dashboards) visualize these data in real-time to give an overview of the current status of the wind power stations. The second data source is a data set provided by the DEBS Grand Challenge 2013, containing position coordinates and moving data from a recorded soccer game [1].

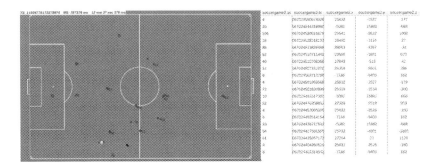

Fig. 2. Screenshot of a dashboard containing two dashboard parts for a soccer game.

Finally, the user can create an empty dashboard and drag some of our dashboard parts into it. During this process, the continuous queries connected in the background are installed and executed. The user can actually see the results in real-time. If the user removes one part, the corresponding query will be stopped and removed from Odysseus. Figure 2 shows a exemplary picture of a dashboard. It contains two different visualizations/dashboard parts: A specialized part, showing the current position of each player, and a classical table, showing the raw data (e.g. useful for debugging purposes). These parts are rendered during the data stream processing in real-time, which is indicated in a static picture here. It shows, how our concept can be used to build a dynamic, component based real-time visualization of streaming data.

References

1. Debs grand challenge (2013). http://www.orgs.ttu.edu/debs2013/index.php? goto=cfchallengedetails. Accessed 6 Dec 2013
2. Appelrath, H.-J., Geesen, D., Grawunder, M., Michelsen, T., Nicklas, D.: Odysseus: a highly customizable framework for creating efficient event stream management systems. In: DEBS 2012, pp. 367–368. ACM, New York (2012)
3. Hammond, S.: Challenges and opportunities in renewable energy and energy efficiency. In: ICS 2011, pp. 151–151. ACM, New York (2011)
4. Krämer, J.: Continuous queries over data streams - semantics and implementation. Ph.D. thesis, University of Marburg (2007)
5. Tibbetts, R., Yang, S., MaxNeill, R., Rydzewski, D.: Streambase liveview: push-based real-time analytics. StreamBase (2011)

Author Index

Printed in the United States
By Bookmasters